MENU PLANNING FOR EVERY OCCASION

Menu Planning

for

Every Occasion

Robert S. Pile

Illustrated with color photographs

Doubleday & Company, Inc.
Garden City, New York
1968

Library of Congress Catalog Card Number 68–11799
Copyright © 1968 by Robert S. Pile
All Rights Reserved
Printed in the United States of America

CONTENTS

PART TWO: ENTERTAINING AT HOME AROUND THE CLOCK

PART THREE: THE FOUR SEASONS

COLOR PHOTOGRAPHS

INTRODUCTION

I have one of the most fascinating jobs in the world. Day after day I talk with a great many women, and some men, about food, and especially about planning menus that will be practical and varied.

My job began a very long way from Cleveland, Ohio, where I live and work. It started on Plum Tree Plantation, looking out over the north coast of the tiny windswept island of Barbados, in the West Indies. There my father, Lionel Archibald Pile, was born and grew up before he came to America and eventually founded Hough Bakeries, Inc., the family business of whose catering division I am now president.

Like other plantation households of the eighties, Plum Tree was well stocked with children and servants. The main house had a variety of spacious, airy rooms, but most important was the large dining room, with its cream-colored, painted walls and solid mahogany dining table, eighteen feet long. Eating was a serious business in the nineteenth century.

My grandmother, Margaret Elizabeth Lewis Pile, presided at this table with dignity and authority, and always with the most gracious hospitality. Even the piano tuner, Mr. Teodorini, was invited to stay for the noonday dinner on his biannual appearances to give the instrument a thorough checkup. Mr. Teodorini was a small, stocky gentleman, who always gave the same performance at mealtime, to the delight of the children. He would look over the meat platter and remark, in his most polite voice, "Let's see now, I really don't want a very big piece." Then, while the young fry tried to hide their grins and titters, he always contrived to pick out the largest slice of meat on the platter.

There were plenty of starches served at those West Indian meals, and the custom remains unchanged even today. It is still usual to have rice, English potatoes, sweet potatoes, yams, eddoes, and fried plantain at the main meal. The "Bajans" of Barbados also love delicious brown onion pan gravy, with plenty of onion; a fair amount of spices, especially curry; and sometimes stewed okra. Dessert isn't so important to them after the big meal. Often it's no more than cut-up fruit. But at five o'clock high tea, there may be four or five lovely things, such as fresh coconut layer cake, sand tarts, shortbread, and cookies.

From this background of comfortable living and good food, my father, who was called Archie, came to Brooklyn in 1900 and worked there for a year in a grocery store before he came to live with relatives in Cleveland. He found a new job in the Homier Grocery store on Hough Avenue, which was then the main street of a pleasant residential district.

Within two years, Archie had saved up fifty-seven dollars, enough to buy a small and struggling bakery at 8708 Hough Avenue. Along with it went a thousand dollars in debts. From this unpromising beginning, and after long years of extremely hard work, he built one of the largest multiple-unit retail bakeries in America. The young red-haired baker delivered his own bread in a horse-drawn wagon, and soon one of his favorite stops became the Edward G. Buckwell house, where the chief attraction for him was the family's maid and governess, Katherine Rose Welker, a petite girl with a soft pink complexion, chestnut hair, and a charming smile. Archie married her after a courtship of six months, and in time they were the parents of six children: Arthur, Alice, Lawrence, Kenneth, Helen, and, of course, me.

As far back as my memory goes, our household always had company and plenty of it—family reunions, relatives from Toledo and New York, and career girls who were then known as old maids. We didn't have a solid mahogany table like the one in Barbados, but it was substantial enough, of solid oak, covered with damask linen and Haviland china. When it failed to stretch out far enough to accommodate the guests, the children were privileged to eat separately in the kitchen. Since Mother's background was German, we often had the sweet-sour dishes that give real variety to a meal —German sour beans, wilted lettuce with bacon, and cucumbers with vinegar and cream. We loved them all, except one that none of us would touch: "cidderly," jellied pig's feet.

One important visitor we always welcomed was our maiden aunt Till, who came frequently to see us on her afternoon off, almost always dressed in well-tailored brown clothes, with stout, low-heeled brown shoes, and an expensive brown purse. Once she overheard me announce her arrival: "Here comes our aunt Till— she bosses our whole family." I think she took it good-naturedly, and in a way it was true. Her influence on us was profound. We loved to hear her describe, in her well-modulated voice, the wonderful meals she served for her employers, the George Gardner family, who lived on North Park Boulevard. Unconsciously, under Aunt Till's spell, we came to admire and respect the serving of food, and thought of it as a truly interesting and important profession.

Our neighbors also contributed to our interest in food, and in flowers as well. When Dad built a new house on Eddy Road, we had a Bohemian neighbor, Mrs. Coke, who filled her back yard with pansy beds and made a small fortune selling them and other products of her garden. Her rhubarb meringue pies linger lovingly in my memory. Next door to her lived a Mrs. Whitehouse, who concocted one of the most magical household remedies for stiff necks, sore knees, and bronchial colds I've ever known. We called it Whitehouse Grease, and it is so good that I've included the recipe:

Whitehouse Grease

4 ounces spirits of turpentine
4 ounces cider vinegar
4 ounces water
1 egg

Spirits of turpentine can be purchased at a drugstore. Put all ingredients into 16-ounce bottle in order listed. Shake well.

Rub well into chest or on any part of the body that aches. If used on neck, do not tie up the neck. Use every two hours until pain is relieved, then two or three times a day.

The mixture will keep for several years.

Later we moved into an old neighborhood on East Eighty-fifth Street, next door to a "family" of single people, consisting of (as we called them) Buddy Gus, Buddy Frank, and Buddy Amelia, and their two frequent visitors, Miss Buddy Howell and Buddy Fisher. Buddy 'Melia was a tiny German woman who presided over this singular homestead, and I was the volunteer houseboy, doing the chores. I discovered that their pantry had a certain aroma that was not present in our kitchen. It was Liederkranz cheese, I learned.

Often as Miss 'Melia sat on her front porch swing, admiring her beautiful hanging flower baskets, she would inquire, "Robbie, what are you having for supper tonight?" Then we would have long discussions about food. That, too, I believe, was a real influence in shaping my almost lifelong interest in menu planning.

Meanwhile, the little store on Hough Avenue was growing into a large and thriving bakery business, which soon involved all the male members of our family. Arthur joined Father in 1927; Lawrence and Kenneth came between 1931 and 1933; and I followed in 1935, after college and two years at Fisher Brothers, a Cleveland chain of supermarkets.

Two years later, at a time when the business had already grown to nearly a dozen stores, we suddenly found ourselves in the catering business, as a result of my brother Arthur's decision to experiment with the making of canapés. It was fun to work with so many varieties of spreads, and the results were rewarding. Since we already baked wedding cakes, we were soon in a position to suggest that customers order canapés or tea sandwiches as well. The orders were small at first, 100 or 200, but it wasn't long before we had an order for 1,000, to be served at a large reception. Today, during the holiday season, we may make as many as 80,000 canapés in a day.

So Hough Caterers grew. A customer asked if she could rent a punch bowl and glasses for a reception. That seemed a profit-making possibility, so we began to develop it with a few punch bowls, ladles, and punch glasses. Today we can set table for 4,000 people or handle as many as 100 dish orders in a weekend.

The next inquiry, naturally, was, "Do you have any waitresses to serve?" We didn't, but we found them—efficient women who in earlier years had worked in private homes or had been waitresses before they married. They welcomed the chance to leave their own households two or three days or nights a week to earn extra income in a pleasant way. It is an expanding staff, and still growing. We think the friendly and gracious service these ladies give has been a major factor in creating our business reputation.

In the kitchen, most of our cooks are Swedish, Hungarian, German and Italian, among other nationalities, because we insist on the "home" touch, with subtle seasonings and generous portions.

An important part of our party catering is the availability of custom-designed cakes, and individual cakes turned out by our large staff of twenty-eight decorators. Their workmanship and versatility are superb. We ship their products everywhere in the United States, and occasionally abroad. Even tiered wedding cakes can be shipped anywhere, by rail in "dog house" crates, which are returned, or by air in a carton with a window.

This book is the product of all we have learned in my more than thirty years with Hough Bakeries and Hough Caterers—about wedding cakes and a great many other things. It is intended to help women who are so busy with a thousand other matters that it's very often hard for them to plan interesting menus. It's designed for that moment when a woman just can't think of "what to have," and wishes there were a book written to inspire her. She has a whole shelfful of cookbooks at her disposal, I'm assuming, and so not many recipes will be given here. What I plan to do in the pages that follow is to give *you* the ideas and trust you to put them to work. They're not difficult. Any good or even mediocre cook can make them. However, I haven't been able to resist including a few of our special favorite recipes at the end of the book. Items starred with an asterisk (*) may be found by consulting the Index.

To properly use what is in this vloume, you should have (and know how to use) three or four of the good basic cookbooks, so that you can do such things as make a standard cream sauce—a "white sauce," as most people say. With the basics available elsewhere, my approach is to give you ideas and combinations to help you plan meals from early morning until late at night—menus for any occasion, for any season of the year. In the process, I'll describe some of the thousands of parties we have catered, in the hope that these, too, will be a spur to your own imagination and initiative.

My father used to say there were no secrets in the bakery business —anyone could succeed if he employed quality ingredients, used plenty of butter, and didn't mind lots of hard work. The same thing can be said of catering; anyone can copy what he sees and hears. Consequently I won't hold back any of the ideas that have made my own company famous.

It is also said that all good food is fattening, and that's true to a great extent. It would be silly to pretend that when people entertain or are entertained they will always be able to follow a low-calorie diet. Nevertheless, in recognition of the fact that heart disease is something of which many people are conscious, if it is requested we use the new corn oil margarines instead of butter, we do so, and you may want to substitute them, too, wherever butter is mentioned. It is well known, too, that many good cooks use sour cream freely, but for the same reason I urge its use sparingly because of its high animal fat content and its tendency to increase cholesterol. As for those whipped cream desserts, just remember to keep the servings proportionately small if you can't resist them. In any case, rich foods should be eaten in moderation.

In most instances, I have omitted beverages from this book, since that is another subject in itself. Usually you will want to serve tea, coffee, or both, or perhaps decaffeinated coffee.

I hope this book will be primarily a reference work you can use when you have a party, whether it's a big affair or two other people in for dinner. Use it for inspiration, as an idea book. Be sure to read the suggestions following each menu, so that you will have all the necessary ingredients at hand. Obviously, some of the things I suggest may have to be done by your caterer, or else adapted to your needs. But in working with her for so many years, I have come to have a great respect for the ingenuity and adaptability of the American woman, especially when she's planning a party. For that woman, this book offers an endless source of ideas for happy entertaining.

Robbie Pile

Part One

From the Cradle to the Grave

CHAPTER 1

THE STORK SHOWER

If we could only remember our first party, it would probably be the stork shower. True, we couldn't enjoy the food but those who came to honor the expectant mother had to be served after the gifts were given. This first section, then, is for the woman who doesn't know what to have on that occasion, when the coming baby may seem far more important than the food.

A good place to begin with a stork shower is to choose a color scheme. Pink and blue are most popular, of course, but variety can be achieved now and then with pastel yellow or mint green. Often this is an evening affair when the young marrieds who attend have put their children to bed, so a centerpiece cake will be very practical and popular. A sheet cake is easy to cut up and serve after presents are spread. Usually a 12-by-16-inch cake (half a baker's cake pan) will be large enough. It serves 30 to 48 people.

For a design on the cake, you might have old Dr. Stork himself holding a diaper cradle in his mouth, with the baby (possibly twins) inside the diaper. The twin idea could be carried out with "We hope it's twins!" in icing at the top.

Look for clever party napkins in the gift shop, stationery, or department store. Then a good cake artist can duplicate this design for you on your cake. A bassinet or cradle cake is also effective. For small showers, individual petits fours may be more practical. They can be decorated with rattles, booties, baby buggies, and miniature storks. Serve them in a small doll bed or doll buggy decorated with fresh flowers. If it's summer, you might use ruffled pink petunias.

Sometimes, instead of cake, we serve a half sheet of French pastry Napoleons. The top of the pastry is frosted with a smooth butter cream blended with whipped cream or egg custard. Use half and half; it's less sweet. If Napoleons are served with coffee, little else is needed except perhaps salted nuts.

Here are some of my favorite baby shower menus:

MENU NO. 1

Finger Sandwiches
Decorated Sheet Cake
*Cranberry Raspberry Hallon Punch**
Pink and Baby Blue Mints

Arrange the finger sandwiches on leaf lettuce in doll beds or in a toy cradle instead of on trays. This will be quite impressive. You can also decorate the wafer mints, for an extra touch.

MENU NO. 2

Individual Ribbon Sandwich Loaves
Unblanched Salted Almonds
Pink and Baby Blue Mints

Fill the sandwiches with any combination of the following: chicken salad, ham salad, egg salad, crab or tuna salad, olive cream cheese. Coat the loaves very thinly with cream cheese and decorate the sides with chopped hard-cooked egg white. Enhance with a suitable design. You must provide forks with this dish.

Dip the ends of the pink and baby blue mints in chocolate.

MENU NO. 3

Cradle or Doll Crib Filled with Fruit
Small Cradle Filled with Relishes
Small Cradle Filled with Cream Cheese Teddy Bear and Crackers
Toasted Parsley-buttered English Muffins
Blanched Almonds
Mint Marshmallows

Fill the cradle or crib with cut-up fresh fruits of the season. The Teddy Bear is made with seasoned onion cream cheese, molded with the hands, decorated with raisins for the eyes and nose and pimiento for the mouth (PLATE III).

Dip the ends of the blanched almonds in melted pastel pink chocolate.

Mint Marshmallows are regular commercial marshmallows dipped in very pastel pink or ice-blue minted fondant. On each one you can place a fresh mint leaf, or perhaps fashion a baby face.

MENU NO. 4

French Pastry Napoleons
Salted Pecans
Fresh Strawberries or Bing Cherries

The filling in the Napoleons is egg custard with crushed pineapple added. Top with whipped cream or this Three-way Icing: ⅓ butter cream, ⅓ boiled icing, and ⅓ white divinity fudge. This is the kind of pastry you can decorate appropriately with a replica of the design on your party napkins.

Leave the stems on the fresh strawberries or cherries. You can dip these in melted pastel chocolate. "White" chocolate can be tinted with vegetable coloring for this purpose. In hot weather, chocolate holds up better than fondant, which disintegrates quickly if the weather is muggy. Or let the guests dip their strawberries in powdered sugar.

MENU NO. 5

Pastel Pink Meringue

No, it's not *that* simple. Fill meringue shells with strawberry ice cream, marbleized with pineapple or strawberry sherbet. On each mound of ice cream, place a plastic or celluloid stork. Or a baby, or babies, a tiny rattle, or booties.

MENU NO. 6

Chicken or Crab Meat Salad
Hot Rolls
Sherbet
Cake or Petits Fours
Nuts

Go to the dime store and get a plastic toy baby set—scales, tubs, bassinets, etc.—for each guest. Fill the largest container with the salad, to which have been added white grapes. Take a medium one for sherbet. Use one of the smaller items for a nut cup.

Serve hot rolls and the cake or petits fours as accompaniments.

All this can be arranged on lap trays in the kitchen, so you won't need a buffet table.

CHAPTER 2

THE CHRISTENING

A christening is a short ceremony, and this is a chapter to match.

Usually it's a small group, only the family and a few intimate friends, to be served at a christening party. Probably the most popular time is immediately after the ceremony, customarily be-between 1 P.M. and 3:30 P.M., on a Sunday afternoon. Here is what you might have.

Shaved Ham Sandwiches
Breast of Turkey Sandwiches
Chicken Salad Envelope Sandwiches
Zippy Watercress Rolls
Decorated Sheet Cake
Wafer Mints

Usually the ham sandwiches should be made with rye bread.

Place layered thin slices of the turkey breast on white and whole wheat bread.

To make Envelope Sandwiches, take a piece of thinly sliced bread about 2¼ inches square. Butter lightly the tips of the four corners. Put the filling in the center and fold over the corners of the bread to meet in the center. (Illustration on next page.)

One suggestion for decorating the sheet cake is a picture of a baby on a blanket or in a bassinet, with the child's full name written out. Pink decorations for a girl, of course, blue for a boy.

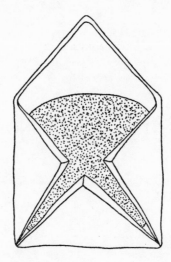

The wafer mints should be in the same color as the cake, and they too may be decorated with the baby's name. Use a nickname or short name to save space, especially if the parents are planning to call the child by any other than the formal name, such as "Bob" or "Bobby" for Robert.

If you have any help in the kitchen, toasted hot canapés or closed sandwiches may be passed. You might also add a few relishes. But the rule is to keep the menu simple. Play it all down, and encourage the guests not to linger, because often the mother of the child hasn't fully regained her strength.

CHAPTER 3

BIRTHDAYS

A child's first birthday is very important to family and close friends, even if the honored guest hasn't the slightest idea what the excitement is all about.

The cake, of course, is the center of attention. You can make it unusual by ordering a teddy bear cake, or a cake made to look like a big block, with ABC and 1 2 3 on the sides. An extra-large candle underlines the importance of the first milestone. On the top of the block, have the decorator write "Johnny Is 1," or "Happy 1st Birthday to Our Johnny."

Families observe the event in various ways. Some do it as simply as possible, serving ice cream and the birthday cake. Others want a real dinner or a buffet supper.

A year-old child usually isn't up to blowing out a candle, but subsequent parties will require plenty of candles on hand, since most children get so much fun from blowing out the flames with a big puff. At each succeeding party, it's nice to have the boy's or girl's name and his age written on the cake. Occasionally a baker can make a numeral cake, in the shape of a 4 or 5 or 7, which emphasizes the age.

Another idea is to have sketched on the cake an icing picture, depicting one of the child's favorite story characters—Cinderella, Little Red Riding Hood, Peter Rabbit. This can be complicated, however, at an early age, when the favorite may be a television character or a baseball player.

Older boys will be better pleased with a chocolate cake carved to represent a baseball glove, with a real ball in the "mitt."

One of the easiest ways to have a birthday party for youngsters eight to ten years old is to pack lunch boxes or baskets, or have a hobo party, with lunches tied up in large bandanna handkerchiefs on sticks. The menu might include:

Peanut Butter and Jelly or Honey Sandwiches
Ground Ham and Sweet Pickle Sandwiches
Raisin Bread and Butter Sandwiches
Celery and Carrot Sticks
An Apple or Pickles and Olives
Potato Chips
Individual Cupcakes

The sandwiches might be cut in the shape of animals, using cookie cutters. The ground ham and sweet pickle sandwiches should be on white bread. (Minced chicken might be substituted for the ham and pickle sandwiches.)

If you are serving at a table, each cupcake could have the child's name on it, with a lighted candle.

Youngsters this age are not enthusiastic about anything too fancy. They'd rather find a baked cold chicken drumstick in the package, and we occasionally put one in.

If you *must* be fancy, there are ways to do it. Some people select a paper napkin with a design of cowboys, Indians, or firemen and then have the baker duplicate it on the cake. I knew a fond grandmother who ordered an old-fashioned organ grinder with his monkey to come to the house and put on a performance. Naturally, roasted peanuts in the shell were on the menu that day.

Girls love "sweet sixteen" parties, and they can be extremely pretty affairs. Often the color scheme is pink, and if the birthday happens to fall in the summer, you can use loads of pink roses very effectively. The birthday cake should be frosted in light pink and have 16 big pink buttercream roses around the border, with large 4-inch pink candles.

An old wheelbarrow could be painted pink, the handles wrapped in pink ribbon with satin bows. Fill the barrow with ice snow (pulverized ice) and pile it up with Cokes, Pepsi, or 7-Up—maybe all three.

If the cake is large, it will be enough to serve in addition only small ham and chicken sandwiches, an onion soup dip with beet juice added to make it pink, plenty of potato chips, and Fritos. If it's summer, you may want to serve pink lemonade.

A dinner party for Miss Sweet Sixteen should be kept small. Here's an easy menu:

Creamed Chicken in Pastry Shells
Green Peas with Melted Butter
Individual Jellied Fruit Salads
Hot Rolls
Strawberry Sundaes
Birthday Cake

As a child grows up, he'll appreciate hobby trimmings on his birthday cake—a boy wrestling, or skiing, or playing ball, or snapping a photograph. If you're still giving parties for him on his twenty-first birthday, he might be depicted on the cake as marching into a voting booth under the slogan, "Today you are a man!" A girl and her friends will enjoy seeing her depicted talking on the phone or learning to drive a car.

Birthdays for those over twenty-one are another matter. I'll talk about them later on in the book.

CHAPTER 4

CONFIRMATIONS AND
SIMILAR RELIGIOUS OCCASIONS

When a child is about twelve to fourteen years old he loves to see his name in print. Personalized napkins, individual iced cakes, and mints served at parties for this age group should carry first names or nicknames. On religious occasions, most boys and girls enjoy seeing the cake made in the shape of an open book, a Torah or scroll, to remind the guests of the occasion.

Select a color scheme that is becoming to the decor of your home. For a boy's Bar Mitzvah, blue and white is the traditional choice. For other events, we try to avoid pinks for the boy. Almost any color, or any two colors, may be used for the girl.

Finger foods are the most practical, since the home is usually crowded with relatives and friends. In hot weather, don't use chafing dishes unless they can be outdoors or in the basement. If you employ a caterer, having hot canapés passed will enhance any selection of food. They're always popular.

SAMPLE KOSHER MENU FOR A BAR MITZVAH

Cucumber Sandwiches
Avocado Pinovers*

Hot Canapés (select 5 or 6):

Swiss Cheese Onion Tarts
Cheese Soufflé Dreams* Sprinkled with
Caraway Seeds

Ivy League Triangles*
Hot Toasted Mushroom Sandwiches*
Cheddar Cheese Rolls with Sesame Seeds
Open Sardine Sandwiches with Grated
      Orange Rind and Caraway Seeds on
      Toast

Cold Canapés (select 6 or 8):

Open Smoked Salmon and Green Pepper
      Canapés on Pumpernickel Bread
Egg Slice Canapés with Button Anchovies
Caviar Canapés
Tuna Fish Salad Canapés
Egg Salad Canapés
Mexican Cheese Canapés
Mandarin Oranges and Walnuts on
      Pineapple Cheese Canapés
Cucumber on Chive Cheese Canapés
Sliced Tomato on Anchovy Paste Cream
      Cheese Canapés
Ripe Olive Cheese with Toasted Sesame
      Seed Canapés
Pimiento Pistachio Nut Cream Cheese
      Canapés

Assorted Sweets:

Finger Pastries
Delco Cream Cheese Puff Pastries
      with Fruit Fillings
Tiny Pecan Rolls

Punch   Coffee
Mints   Nuts

As an alternative to the Hot Toasted Mushroom Sandwiches*
you might try broiled mushrooms stuffed with bread and onion,
or with hamburger, or a mixture of the two.

Delco Cream Cheese Puff Pastries are made of very rich cream
cheese pastry dough, usually filled with an apricot, prune, honey-
nut or cream cheese mixture before baking.

If dietary laws are not observed, you may want to add shellfish (shrimp, crab and lobster), as well as turkey, chicken sandwiches and water chestnuts wrapped in pastrami.

CONFIRMATION LUNCHEON

Whole Poached Salmon
Dill Watercress Remoulade Dressing* or
Cucumber Sour Cream Sauce with Capers
Cheese Blintzes*
Fresh Fruit Salad Platter
Poppy Seed Dressing*
Hot Rolls
Caramelized Cornflake Ring* with Assorted Ice Cream Balls
Mr. Arthur's Butterscotch Sauce*

BUFFET SUPPER—MENU NO. 1

Cold Meat Platter
Swiss Cheese
Potato Salad
Thinly Sliced Rye and White Bread
Brown Mustard
Celery Seed Mayonnaise
Relish Tray
Decorated Sheet Cake

Arrange sliced kosher corned beef, turkey, and rare and medium roast beef on a large platter. Garnish the potato salad with deviled egg halves.

Butter the rye and white bread ahead of time.

Baked beans may be added to this supper menu if desired.

BUFFET SUPPER—MENU NO. 2

Chicken Pie or Chicken à la King in Deep Tart Shells
Molded Fruit Salad or Fresh Fruit Platter
Porcupine Celery   Carrot Sticks
Decorated Sheet Cake
Ice Cream or Sherbet

To make the shells for the chicken pie or chicken à la king, bake the pastry over the *backs* of cupcake tins.

To make Porcupine Celery, feather the edges of celery stalks early in the day and put in ice water.

CHAPTER 5

SCHOOL GRADUATIONS

Graduations and the parties which accompany them require not so much menus as common sense and, in some cases, large-scale planning rather than fussy specific details.

High school proms, usually held about graduation time, are always party times and provide young people with a chance to plan refreshments for themselves. If there isn't much money in their budgets, they won't be able to do any more than serve punch or soft drinks and cookies. Nevertheless, a few touches will enliven the occasion.

When we cater these affairs, most often in a local gymnasium, we try to use school colors, such as blue and gold, in our table-cloths. Most schools do not permit candelabra, because of the fire laws, but may let you use tall hurricane globes with single candles, again in blue or gold. We try to use gold or yellow napkins with "Class of '70" or the school name printed in royal blue.

When planning quantities for punch, try to estimate how many hours the bulk of the crowd will be there. For two or three hours, you should allow three to four glasses of punch per person. As a safety valve, be sure to have extra ginger ale and soda to stretch out the punch, particularly if it happens to be a hot night. In a real pinch, you could even use the water tap. The important thing, however, no matter what happens, is to keep the punch *always* ice cold. At many parties I've found that the block of ice for the punch bowl is allowed to melt down without being replenished. Any punch is more palatable—and seems to be less sweet—if it's served at an icy temperature.

Never use ice cubes in punch unless block ice is nowhere to be found. Cubes melt too quickly, with a consequent diluting of the punch. The wise hostess plans ahead of time for this seemingly small but so important detail. Sometimes gas stations have ice machines, or there may be automatic dispensers somewhere in your neighborhood. It's a nuisance, true, but it's possible to freeze your own blocks in kettles in your own freezer.

And don't forget the ice pick! Many a well-equipped home has everything under the sun but an ice pick. Yet they're cheap enough to buy, and you can get one at any hardware store.

Usually a gallon of punch base, plus one pint of pineapple or lemon sherbet, plus two bottles of ginger ale, yields 60 glasses of punch. I like a little sherbet in fruit punch, as long as it's kept to a minimum and doesn't make the whole thing too frothy. For that reason I don't like punch made entirely of sherbet and ginger ale. You'll have no problem, of course, if you happen to live in a town where you can buy the *ice* sherbets that don't have egg white in them. But if using all sherbet and ginger ale is unavoidable, the proportion is 1 pint of sherbet to 1½ or 2 bottles of ice-cold ginger ale, and it's better to blend two or three flavors.

Figuring 3 4-ounce cups of punch for each guest, a party for 200 guests would require 600 cups of punch, or approximately 10 gallons of punch base. Here is a quick calculation for a short reception held in hot weather:

> For 100 guests: 4 gallons of punch
> 4 pints of sherbet
> 8 to 10 quarts of ginger ale

And here's another for a long evening at a prom:

> For 100 guests: 5 gallons of punch
> 5 pints of sherbet
> 10 to 12 quarts of ginger ale

This is a generous recipe. If it happens to be a cool night and the punch isn't being consumed, hold back on the ginger ale and sherbet; it can be salvaged. Most good punches don't keep too long, however, because the fresh fruit juices ferment.

As for cookies as an accompaniment to punch, I usually figure 3½ to 4 cookies per guest. Some girls don't eat any—their *figures!* —so allowing for that, 200 people will use about 15 pounds of cookies. Most small cookies weigh about 50 to the pound.

It doesn't cost much to add mint wafers to the "sweet table" reception. Most candy makers will tint the wafers in the school colors. Two pounds of mint wafers per 100 guests is the usual portion, since there are 60 to 75 mint wafers to the pound.

If mixed nuts are used, figure 40 to 50 people per pound at a big reception, which means 4 to 5 pounds of nuts for 200 people. I find that people seldom use them, however, because of the expense.

High school graduates today sometimes have a family gathering after the ceremonies (or the next night), or it may be a party for fifty. We've found that the sheet cake is by far the most popular thing to have at such affairs, since it cuts easily and makes an impressive showy centerpiece for the table. Again, school colors will personalize the cake, and we recommend them in most cases unless the colors happen to be red and black, in which case you may not relish black icing trim on your cake. If it's requested, we do use it in thin piping. The inscriptions can be formal—"Congratulations, Janice, Class of 1968"—with a mortarboard, diploma, and sometimes a school pennant. Occasionally we get a request for a picture of a boy or girl in cap and gown, or sometimes a doll ornament, which can be kept as a souvenir. You may want an informal inscription, and in that case it could be something like, "Whew! You really made it! Congratulations, Pete!" with an Oscar or some such symbol of victory.

What to serve? Cake and ice cream may be enough. If this is done, the most important thing is to remember what the graduate's favorite flavor may be. Keep in mind, too, that many teen-agers give up chocolate cake, chocolate icing, and ice cream for several years for the sake of their complexions, if they're having any adolescent skin troubles.

It's always nice to celebrate with open-faced canapés or little finger sandwiches—something all ready to whisk out of the refrigerator as guests come in.

When the group is small, a cold meat platter, relishes, and potato salad are still popular for hearty eaters, although they're a little expensive for large groups. Mints and nuts will make your table "partyish," and can be arranged ahead of time.

College graduation parties are not a great deal different, although naturally they are usually done with more sophistication. Those who have earned a graduate degree after years of struggle especially deserve a party.

For such an occasion, it's often possible to use symbols of the earned degree—the entwined serpents for the new doctor, the scales of justice for the fledgling lawyer, and so on. Our pastry artists sometimes depict a doctor with a stethoscope listening to a patient's heart, or a cartoon sketch that conveys the message, "There's a doctor in the house!" The sentence itself can be written across the top of the cake.

By all means, serve canapés and sandwiches for the college graduate's open house. A buffet supper may seem called for. I have a chapter on them later in this book.

CHAPTER 6

DEBUTANTE PARTIES

Not every girl has a "coming out" party, but there seems to have been a resurgence of this kind of affair in the past four or five years. Often several young debs make their bow together at a cotillion ball, usually held at a country club, but for some girls that kind of group affair isn't personal enough. Sometimes grandmothers enjoy entertaining to honor their granddaughters, and I note that these parties are generally done on a little grander scale than when the parents give the party. Occasionally two nieces or granddaughters are honored together. June and August are the most popular months. This includes Labor Day weekend.

These parties are often planned in two or three parts. First there is an afternoon high tea, mainly for ladies, although sometimes gentlemen are included. The tea is from four to seven or five to seven, in the afternoon. This is followed by a dinner for 50, 60, or 80 close friends of the deb, at 8 or 8:30 P.M. Perhaps five or six older couples will also be invited. At ten o'clock an additional 50 to 100 young people are invited for the dance.

In some cases, professional decorators take over the affair. They erect a tent and dance floor and provide the decorations. Sometimes they use a theme, and always there is a definite color scheme. Color, in fact, always seems to be very important and the debutante's personal taste has to be considered. If a girl hates pink, for instance, her party should be in blue, apricot, gold, or green— or perhaps two colors, such as aqua and green, or blue and lilac.

But let's begin with the tea. The dining room is very often the center of this affair, because the older guests may not want to venture outdoors. Tea and coffee are served here, and if the day is hot, iced tea. The punch bowls will probably be outdoors. When we cater such a party, we sometimes serve Fruit Juice Frappes. These frappes are very colorful and pretty when they're passed on trays. They're simple concoctions.

Fruit Juice Frappes

Begin with shaved ice in a parfait glass. Then simply add any of the following combinations:

Apricot Nectar with a Scoop of Pineapple Sherbet, plus Soda.
Lemonade, Lemon Ice, and Ginger Ale.
Lime Juice, Lime or Mint Sherbet, plus Soda.
Grape Juice, Pineapple Sherbet, plus Soda.
Cranberry Juice, Red Raspberry Ice, plus Soda.

The ginger ale and soda should be iced in advance to make the drinks more palatable.

Iced Persian Chocolate is one of our favorite debutante punches:

Iced Persian Chocolate

4 quarts chocolate milk (ice cold)	1 12½-pound block of ice
	1 pint coffee ice cream
2 quarts *strong* coffee (ice cold)	1 pint vanilla ice cream
	1 pint chocolate ice cream
2 ounces unsweetened chocolate, melted	

Blend the chocolate milk with strong black coffee. Add melted chocolate. Fill punch bowl and add the block of ice. The three pints of ice cream should be added at least 45 minutes to one hour before serving so they melt partially into the liquid. This is very palatable if served *icy* cold in punch glasses. Serves 30 to 36.

Refer to the chapter in Part Two on "Afternoon Tea" for suggestions as to what food to serve for the tea.

Recently a grandmother gave a party for her two granddaughters. Since this family spent winters in Nassau and loved the Bahamian atmosphere, they wanted to transport some of that atmosphere to Cleveland. A famous British decorator designed the layout with colored sketches sent from London. Through the display department of a local department store, we were able to duplicate the drawings to perfection.

The color scheme was apricot and white and green, with the center poles of the tent decorated as palm trees. The material used was only homely muslin, but the effect was breathtaking.

One of the most striking debutante settings I've ever seen was created in a single-pole tent. The entire tent top was lined with a soft apricot flannel-like material. Around the pole was a huge circular chandelier, almost sixteen feet in diameter, with a Della Robbia effect provided by loads of oranges and grapes and a few apples. The fruit was plastic, but because they were up so high they looked real. At night this huge "wreath" was illuminated by many twinkling electric tapers. On little apricot-covered café tables around the edges of the tent were centered small but high compotes of fresh fruit. Similar centerpieces were on the tables on the screened-in terrace where the supper was to be served. Using fruit as a change from the usual flower decorations was truly delightful and different.

Not to be overlooked when you're planning a debutante tea is the parking problem. Local police should be notified and asked to have one or two officers on hand to take care of the extra traffic. Nearly every city has professional car parkers who will take the ladies' cars at the curb or at the front door, if there's a circular driveway. One man should be able to handle fifteen to twenty cars. For an afternoon affair, you can figure 1½ guests per car.

Surprisingly little food is consumed at these parties unless men are included. But so much depends on the weather at every party. If it happens to be a cool, nippy day, appetites are so sharpened that the average guest will consume 3½ to 4 canapés and sandwiches, and perhaps 1½ sweets. We usually figure 4 to 5 canapés a person, and 2½ sweets, since we never want to look skimpy or run short.

As far as the caterer is concerned, the bigger the crowd at the party, the less they eat; the smaller the number, the greater the consumption. Consequently, if more people show up than you originally anticipated, there's still likely to be enough and no eventual embarrassment.

CHAPTER 7

THE ENGAGEMENT ANNOUNCEMENT

Your daughter's engaged. "How shall we break the news?" is the question parents ask us, when they've decided to give a party to announce the event. Answering that question provides an opportunity for real originality.

One of the most unusual cakes we ever made for such a party was a set of books, made entirely of sheet cake built up and carved. The titles of the books disclosed the engagement, and although I don't remember all of them, these will give you the idea:

A TALE OF TWO CITIES

BOY MEETS GIRL

HELEN

JOHN

FALLING IN LOVE

WEDDING BELLS WILL RING

We made every effort to be sure that the titles were legible, and reading from left to right, there was no doubt that Helen and John had fallen in love and were announcing their engagement. A cake like that, of course, is strictly a centerpiece until late in the evening, when the family can cut it.

I've also seen pictures of the happy couple blown up to life size and put in heart-shaped "frames" of bright red ribbon or a border of red roses and set up side by side over the fireplace mantel.

We often use a big heart or overlapping heart cakes in the center of the dining room table, with the names or nicknames written on them. Usually the hearts have gold or silver arrows sticking in the sides of the cake.

If the two young people are fond of sailing, you might have a big paper or toy plastic sailboat bearing dolls dressed in nautical attire, with the names of the couple pasted on them. If they happen to be mountain climbers, depict a mountain with two hikers. Very often, in these days of winter sports, the romance will have blossomed on the ski slopes, and in that case you could have a ski slope built up with cotton, a small cardboard Swiss chalet with the name of a favorite ski resort, and again boy and girl dolls on skis, bearing the couple's names. Anything, in fact, that they're mutually interested in can be adapted as a centerpiece.

It presents no difficulty, however, if their interests are different. Suppose the young man is a radio announcer and his bride-to-be a nurse. Simply use a boy doll at a microphone and a girl in nurse's uniform and cap.

Another unusual centerpiece is a large engagement ring ornament on a raised pedestal, covered with fluffy pink maline. This device is often placed on a sheet cake, or a two-layer round cake, again with names, and in the lower corner a sketch in icing of Cupid with his bow and arrow.

Besides the centerpiece, most families order personalized napkins, usually white with pink, green, blue, or yellow printing. Normally silver and gold printing is avoided; that is saved for the wedding. If a centerpiece cake is not used, it's easy to order a few frosted cakes, heart-shaped or oblong, with the couple's names on them. Many people order flat wafer- or heart-shaped mints with names, of course in keeping with the color scheme.

Here's another idea. If it's just a small cocktail party to announce the engagement, an icebox cream cheese sandwich loaf can be ordered. It will have layers of chicken salad, ham salad, crab meat or tuna and egg salad, or pimiento olive cheese. The names can be written in pink cream cheese and garnished with red pimiento hearts. This dish must be kept cold, to slice easily, and forks must be used. It isn't a practical thing for large parties.

If you're having a good-sized crowd, on the other hand, it's best to have finger food with hors d'oeuvres. Finger sandwiches would be good, perhaps with olives and celery. If you want to use chafing dishes, choose items the guests can spear with a toothpick. I have some suggestions for this kind of food in Part Two, Chapters 3 and 4, on teas and cocktail parties.

Sometimes there are family circumstances which preclude a big wedding, and so the engagement announcement party turns out to be a larger affair than the wedding itself, particularly if the events are not too far apart. I remember one party where it was decided to have 600 or 700 people, with the wedding limited to half that many. In spite of its size, or perhaps because of it, this turned out to be a very informal affair and much fun. These people had such a gay time at the June engagement announcement that they didn't feel slighted when they were not included in the September wedding.

We took our inspiration from the fact that the prospective groom was a member of the Canadian National Equestrian Team, and his bride-to-be was an equally enthusiastic horse lover.

The setting was a farm in the country on which was erected a bright red and white striped tent which resembled the arena for a real horse show. A full-sized artificial horse was procured and placed in the middle of the tent, with boy and girl mannequins dressed in riding attire on which the couple's names were pinned, standing one on each side of the horse. Bales of hay and horse blankets were placed around the huge tent. The tables had red, white, and blue clothes with crossed Canadian and American flags.

We served the guests a simple buffet supper:

*Cold Whitefish à la Rhine**
Standing Ribs of Beef
*Mushroom Pie**
Cauliflower Salad Platter
Coffee Ice Cream
Maple Leaf-shaped Cookies

For the Cauliflower Salad Platter, cook whole heads of cauliflower until tender. Chill. Just before serving, smother the cauliflower with a dill remoulade. Surround the cauliflower with canned braised celery and white asparagus that have been marinated in a vinaigrette dressing. Wedges or slices of tomato and generous tufts of watercress or Bibb lettuce swathe the outer edge of the platter.

The ice cream was in the shape of horses' heads. The cookies bore the couple's names.

CHAPTER 8

PRE-NUPTIAL PARTIES:

The Trousseau Tea and the Wedding Shower

A trousseau tea is usually given only for one's closest friends, so the guest list will probably not exceed 20 or 30. It is, in brief, a rather intimate affair as parties go. No special color scheme need be used, but if you do use one, select one of the bride's favorite colors *other* than the one you plan to use at the wedding.

This kind of tea gives you the opportunity to be very feminine and dainty. Since the wedding is so near and so much is going on, the refreshments ought to be extremely simple—as simple as a decorated cake. When we do one of these cakes, our artist may sketch a girl standing in front of a clothes closet with an array of dresses and suits hanging inside. Part of a bed is shown in the corner, with a pile of linen and two suitcases and a hatbox on the floor. The cake can be angel food, chiffon, or yellow, with a fresh strawberry filling.

Bread and butter sandwiches are good, if the bread is really paper thin. Cold sliced chicken sandwiches with crisp lettuce and a little mayonnaise will probably be the first choice. With them you can serve the cake (with forks), or tiny cupcakes, or very thin cookies. That's enough! The idea is to keep it as simple as possible.

Wedding Showers

Showers are a traditional part of pre-nuptial entertaining. When it's possible, the bride enjoys these most if they come a few weeks in advance of the last round of parties. Some girls are so popular they're feted with six or eight showers, while others get one spectacular "cloudburst."

If there are fifty to eighty guests at a shower, it will probably be an evening affair, or perhaps a Sunday afternoon. The most practical centerpiece is a parasol or fancy umbrella with fresh flowers and ribbon on the handle. I've heard of a party where ice cubes were fastened inside the umbrella, and they gradually dripped into a large bowl of ferns and flowers underneath, but it seems a little too tricky to me.

We often get our ideas for the centerpieces from the invitations. For example, if they happen to have an umbrella or a sprinkling can, we have a large sheet cake decorated in the center with an enlarged replica of one of these utensils. If it's a parasol, we suggest lumps of loaf sugar, with assorted colored icing ribbons to look like wrapped presents, and then the artist makes raindrops above and on the sides with drops of thin Karo syrup.

If you use individual iced cakes instead of the sheet cake, these too can be decorated with the same motif. Another small but effective touch is to place small plastic umbrellas on each serving of cream cheese sandwich loaf.

In most cases, it's a rule of thumb that the larger the shower the simpler the refreshments should be. This is true especially for an evening affair when ice cream, cake, mints, nuts, and coffee are perfectly proper, and sufficient. Slices of ice cream can be "dressed up" a little by placing several sauces on the buffet—chocolate, burnt almond, butterscotch, and red raspberry sauce. We like the latter, rather than strawberry sauce, because the raspberry is more tart.

There are alternatives to sliced ice cream. We suggest medium-sized bowls filled with three or four kinds of sherbet and ice cream, topped with a perky bouquet of fresh mint. Lime, pineapple, and grapefruit sherbet with vanilla ice cream make a pleasing combination. If you do this, it will help to have a freezer in the house because it will then be possible to make these bowls in advance and simply bring them out when you're ready to serve. Always pleasing are chocolate or chocolate chip and mint sherbet. Another combination is pistachio and apricot or orange sherbet. Sometimes we add such fruit as mandarin oranges. If the shower emphasizes a pink color scheme, use strawberry and vanilla ice cream, unsweetened frozen or chopped fresh strawberries, and raspberry or strawberry sherbet. Top the individual dishes with a big *whole* strawberry. You can also make individual parfaits. For a big crowd, even paper cups are permissible. Should you happen to have old-fashioned glasses, or finger bowls, these always look pretty.

Shy away from whipped cream for a girls' party. It's too fattening. They'll appreciate your thoughtfulness in omitting it.

We find it hard to get fancy ice cream molds, but if you happen to use them, be sure to put the molded ice cream on a washed lemon leaf or sprig, or orange blossoms, because they slide off the plate very easily.

For ladies' gatherings, you can't improve on fruit. A simple fresh fruit salad with Paprika Dressing, accompanied by Parmesan and/ or Sesame Melba Toast, is most refreshing. To make the toast, brush thinly sliced white bread with butter and sprinkle with grated Parmesan cheese. To keep the toast from curling, use fresh bread. To make Sesame Melba Toast, sprinkle with sesame seeds instead of the cheese. The bread may be cut in shapes with a cookie cutter. If there's to be a large crowd, it's much faster to have the fruit arranged in individual lettuce cups so each guest has only to slip one onto her plate. Serve petits fours for dessert.

There are always people who, for various reasons, want cold meat and cheese platters and potato salad. The latter at least can be made more interesting, if you have the time, by molding it in several sizes of large cake pans that have been greased with butter or salad oil. Unmold them after they are very cold, one on top of the other, so that your potato salad is in the shape of a tiered wedding cake. Then decorate the whole thing with radish roses, carrot flowers, olive slices, and parsley. But remember, the potato salad must be *ice cold* and firm, or the "cake" will fall apart.

"Best Wishes to a Peach of a Pair" was the theme for a shower at which both men and women were present. We catered this shower immediately after the New Year, a time when everyone is particularly calorie-conscious, so we wanted to use fruit for that reason, as well as to be in keeping with the theme. We had a small tree as a centerpiece, with lemon leaves wired on it, and also plastic peaches and pears. The girl's name was spelled out with white letters on each peach; the boy's name was written out on the pears.

Into small finger bowls we put half of a canned pear and the larger half of a frozen peach (thawed). Between these two we poured a teaspoon of frozen red raspberries (thawed), to which were added pineapple and lemon sherbet. A decorated cake was placed under the tree. The decoration was a combination of a peach and a pear carved out of cake, each with flirtatious eyes, nose, and mouth.

When the bride is marrying a Canadian, you can depart from the conventional pastel color scheme and use red, white and blue. Try to get little Canadian and American flags, and use red, white, and blue candles, napkins, and mints.

We once did a shower of this kind near the July Fourth weekend. The sheet cake depicted a car with a trailer crossing the border over a bridge at Sarnia, Ontario. On one side was the Canadian flag, on the other, the American. Refreshments were finger sandwiches, cherry tomatoes stuffed with cream cheese, and fancy finger sweets with cherry and fresh blueberry tarts.

If a smaller group than usual is having the shower, it is often convenient to have a luncheon with a definite theme. I remember one, a bathroom shower for about twenty-four ladies. Four tables with pastel bathroom-colored cloths and napkins were set up in the garden. First we served chicken salad, with seedless grapes added, and Melba toast made to look like toothbrushes. To do this, you must make your own Melba toast, carving it in advance in the shape of the toothbrush and then using white solid Swiss cheese cut both ways with a sharp, thin knife to make the bristle effect.

We bought small pink and blue plastic toy bathroom sets, using the washstands as nut cups and serving the sherbet dessert in the bathtubs, along with little oval pastel cakes made to look like bars of soap. But the toothbrush Melba stole the show!

For a kitchen shower, we make a rolling pin cake. Any kind of thin sheet cake (the bride's favorite is a good idea) can be rolled up like a jelly roll and frosted. A small wooden dowel pin is inserted at each end to make the handles, and a few sprigs of icing orange blossoms will make the whole thing look much prettier than the homely household article. We also add some homemade poetry:

> After the wedding din,
> Get out your rolling pin:
> If you can't bake a pie
> At least you can try
> To make him obey with a grin!

Our artists devised another design for a kitchen shower to put on half a sheet cake. It shows a slender young cook standing with her hands over her head while a kettle of food is burning on the stove and smoke billows in the kitchen—a jocular forecast of what may lie just ahead for the bride.

For a kitchen luncheon shower, it might be fun to have the buffet in the kitchen itself and serve the main dish or salad on foil pie tins. Use mixing bowls and Pyrex dishes for the food at the buffet, serving it on colorful breakfast-table linen or gingham cloth. The menu for such an affair can be extremely simple and informal.

You can even do it potluck. Have each guest bring one of her own favorite recipes.

Another idea, and an unusual one, is to let each guest make her own salad. Take all the ingredients for a huge chef's salad and put each one in a separate mixing bowl: Bibb or Boston lettuce, ice cold; julienne ham or tongue, breast of turkey, and Swiss cheese; chopped hard-boiled egg, capers, sliced ripe olives, cherry tomatoes, anchovies, and slices of avocado. At one end of the table place several cruets of dressings and several medium wooden salad bowls so each girl can toss her own salad and then put it back onto her foil pan. Serve hot popovers or rolls and the cake, and that's all there is to it.

For a bedroom shower, a novel idea is to wash thoroughly a toy doll bed, line it with lettuce and fill the bed with a fresh fruit salad. Then get a toy dresser and have the drawers partly opened, filled with relishes. The cake could be made to resemble a box of linen, with fancy folded pillowcases, or it could depict the bride putting up her hair in curlers in front of a dressing table.

Some fortunate young couples these days start married life by buying a small home of their own. If that's the case, you can plan a garden tool shower. Use fresh fruit in clay flower pots, with a fresh flower sticking up in the center and serve with thin scalloped butter cookies, decorated with colorful flower petal designs in icing.

If you can find a toy wheelbarrow, fill it with shaved ice snow and pile it up with raw vegetable relishes. A regular wheelbarrow can be filled with ice snow and piled with splits of ginger ale, 7-Up, Coke, and grapefruit juice. We have also made topiary trees —styrofoam balls covered with green foil—and put an array of garden relishes on toothpicks into the balls to create a relish-and-pickle tree. Get a few wicker trays, line them with grape leaves or geranium leaves, washed and dried ahead of time, and serve your sandwiches on them.

Most brides are showered with luxury items, but how many do you know who are equipped for a crisis? The crisis shower presents include a fire extinguisher, adhesive tape, aspirin, light bulbs, flashlight, frozen steaks, paper dishes and cups, mousetraps, toothpicks, rust remover, a box of clean rags, a ball of string—the list of items with which to meet any crisis could go on ad infinitum. A large wash basket filled with cleaning necessities might be used for the centerpiece.

CHAPTER 9

PRE-NUPTIAL PARTIES:

Introducing the Future Daughter-in-Law

A woman who has no daughters in her family is deprived of the excitement of a wedding, which is part of being the bride's mother. To compensate, however, she may have the opportunity of giving her son's fiancée a tea, to introduce her to the friends of her future husband's parents. This is especially appropriate if she happens to be from out of town.

Like the debutante party, this kind of tea is often held in two sections. The first part comes in early afternoon, from 2 to 5 P.M., and is for the mother's friends, an older group. This becomes a cocktail party from 6 to 8 P.M. for the younger set. It makes a long day for a girl who has to meet so many new people in a short time, so you may think it better to attempt only the afternoon tea and let someone else entertain the younger ones.

These teas are meant to be rather special affairs, because the mother wants to give her future daughter-in-law a royal welcome to the family, and to make a favorable impression, but since they are so frequently given, the task is to vary them so they won't seem monotonous. I have several suggestions.

One is a pink and white tea, best perhaps in warm weather. Use a pretty pink tablecloth if you have one. Sometimes we use pale pink nylon net pleated over ballerina pink Indian head cotton, with a pink satin band around the top. A bowl of pink roses and white stocks or larkspur will look delightfully feminine. You might also use dainty pink sweet peas or pink and white carnations.

Don't use pink gladioli and/or white mums. These are extremely overworked flowers, and a florist has to be very clever to come up with an arrangement that will not look trite.

If you're having fifty or sixty guests, pale pink or white paper napkins are permissible. Again, we recommend putting the girl's first name on them, in deep pink, or in white on pink.

Serve iced tea or pink lemonade, as well as hot tea and coffee, if the day is hot. We would recommend placing the silver service at one end for both coffee and tea. At the other end will be the iced tea or lemonade, in a pretty glass bowl surrounded with tall 10-ounce glasses for the cold drinks. Have wheels of lemon hanging on the edge of the glasses, and fresh sprigs of mint in each glass.

Here's a menu for the occasion:

> *Crab Meat Salad with Pink Remoulade Dressing in Cream Puff Shells*
> *White Meat Turkey with Watercress Mayonnaise Finger Sandwiches*
> *Chopped Tongue Open Danish Sandwiches*
> *Zippy Watercress Rolls*
> *Minced Ham or Tuna Pinover Sandwiches*
> *Heart-shaped Open Canapés*
> *Bar-le-Duc Oval Open Sandwiches*
> *Fresh Strawberry Open Canapés*
> *Small Pastries*
> *Mints   Bing Cherries*

Pink Remoulade is a pink-tinted mustard mayonnaise.

Use a flower-petal cutter to make the Chopped Tongue Sandwiches.

For the watercress rolls, grate a rind of lime into the filling; the bread can be tinted a delicate pink, or else use white bread.

Pinover Sandwiches (see illustration next page) are made on thinly sliced bread about 2¼ inches square. Remove crusts. Butter just two of the four corners and put the filling on the bread diagonally. Then pin over the buttered corners so that the filling can be seen at each end.

In the open canapés, put red caviar on one side and black on the other; edge them with pink cream cheese.

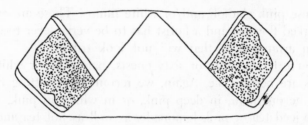

Bar-le-Duc is a tasty currant jelly; make the sandwiches with this and cream cheese on whole wheat bread.

When you make the Strawberry Open Canapés, spread bread with chopped mint, cream cheese, and butter mixture; slice off part of the berries sideways so they won't roll.

As a garnish for the sandwich trays, take little paper soufflé cups, spread the outside with a royal icing, and dip them in pink sugar. Ribbon handles can be cellophane-taped inside the cut. Fill the cups with dainty baby's breath or pink rosebuds. These are called Pink Sugar Baskets.

You might use loaf sugar decorated with little *hard* pink rosettes on them.

For an added sweet touch, small frosted petits fours, with the girl's name on each one.

Another enticing sweet would be Tiny Coconut Snowballs— cakes dipped in pink-tinted and white coconut, half and half, with white rosettes on the pink ones and vice versa.

Other alternative or additional sweet possibilities: Mocha Gau-frette Cornucopias*, pink mint chocolate Bavarian tarts, or dainty pink marzipan, 1 by 1½ inches, in Florentines.

Serve pink and white mints, half with names on them, and half with the ends dipped in dark chocolate. You can also dip a few dark sweet Bing cherries, with the stems on, in melted pink pastel chocolate.

To serve all this, you should have two waitresses for fifty people, but if you plan to have hot sandwiches passed, it would be better to have three helpers.

While the pink and white tea is nice for warm weather, a similar event in the fall or winter calls for something else—perhaps a brown and white tea (PLATE VII). You may want to have this kind of affair regardless of the season. After all, not every girl is the pastel type, and taking into consideration the new earthen color tones in home decoration, in some houses the brown and white scheme without any other color is very striking.

For this tea, cover the table with a colorful brown and white bold print material. It can have a white linen skirt overlaid with cocoa pleated nylon net. A band of dark brown velvet ribbon is drawn around the top, separating the print from the soft net. Dark brown and white candles should be used.

Yes, I know Emily Post is against the idea, but I use candles any hour of the day or night if there isn't brilliant sunlight flooding the room. Candles give height and importance to the table. If the tea is in fall or winter, the day may well be dull and cloudy.

Paper napkins and matchbooks should be white, with the girl's name printed in metallic brown.

The centerpiece could be white flowers with dark brown oak leaves in the autumn. In January, use white narcissus and pussywillows; in February or March, white hyacinths or white tulips and pussywillows, but in any case, use only brown and white.

In arranging your sandwiches, place them *diagonally* in rows across your platters—a row of whole wheat, then a row of white, then a row of Boston brown bread and again a row of white. When you arrange the sweets, do it the same way.

Here is the sandwich menu:

Boston Brown Bread Sandwiches
Chopped Olive Cream Cheese Sandwiches
Chicken Salad Envelope Sandwiches*
Whole Wheat Egg Salad Pinwheels or Tuna White
Watercress Rolls
Pumpernickel, Lettuce, and Swiss Cheese Sandwiches
White Asparagus Pinovers*
Hot Toasted Mushroom Sandwiches*
Hot Whole Wheat Orange Marmalade Sandwiches

The hot whole wheat orange marmalade sandwiches should be brushed with butter and toasted.

The tray garnish can be white sugar baskets with brown ribbon handles, made like the Pink Sugar Baskets*, or white Turnip Roses. Use dried brown oak leaves or brown seed pods under the turnips.

Turnip Roses in Six Quick Easy Steps

1. Select turnips 3–4 ounces apiece if possible. A 4-ounce turnip will make approximately 4 roses. Leave the purple skin on the turnip, but scrape the rough surfaces off as well as the root. Slice the turnip crosswise as thinly as possible—use a meat-slicing machine if one is available (your butcher may oblige you).

2. Roll the first few slices into a tight funnel shape with bottom held very tightly and the top much looser.

3. Keep building up your flower by overlapping the petals—making sure to cover the openings. On the average, you will use 8 to 10 turnip slices.

4. When your rose is the desired size, fasten with 2 toothpicks crosswise and tighten the bottom with rubber bands.

5. At room temperature the turnip petals are soft enough to curl the top edge down to give the pretty open rose effect.

6. Toss the finished roses in glass jar of water. Tint with vegetable coloring to make any shade you wish. Keep in refrigerator until you are ready to garnish platter. Then remove and drain on paper towel before nestling them in little beds of parsley.

Sweets for this occasion make a menu in themselves:

Chocolate Pecan Fudge Balls
or
Chocolate Rum Balls
White Coconut Snowballs
Brandy Snap Lace Cookies
Chocolate Chip Meringue Drops
Fudge Brownie Fingers
French Twirls* with Coffee Cream
White Iced Petits Fours
Chocolate-centered Daisy Mints
White Wafer Mints
Almonds   Pecans

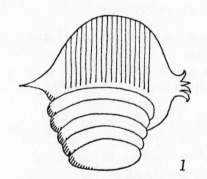

1

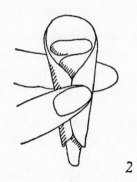

2

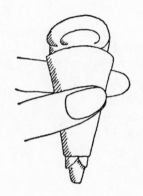

3

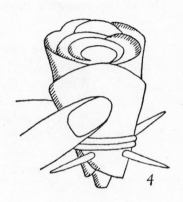

4

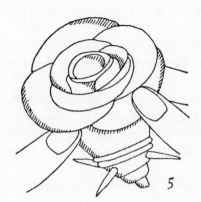

5

6

Each of the petits fours would have the girl's name in chocolate, and so would the white wafer mints.

Dip the ends of the almonds in melted dark semi-sweet chocolate, and the ends of the pecans in melted white chocolate.

Another variant would be an olive, avocado green, and aqua tea.

Use an aqua cloth with olive-green net and olive-green velvet band around the top. Napkins and matches would be printed in avocado green. Use olive-green and aqua candles.

For the centerpiece, Bells of Ireland, white stocks, and baby's breath, with fresh aqua-colored daisies. Some white flowers may be sprayed a delicate aqua, but be *sure* it's delicate.

This is the sandwich menu:

Shrimp Salad in Cream Puffs
Avocado, Chopped Mint, Lemon Rind Pinover Sandwiches*
Watercress Cream Cheese Mounds
Chicken Salad Pinwheels
Open Asparagus Canapés
Orange Bread Fingers
Avocado-green and Pastel Aqua Mints
Almonds   Salted Pecans

The cream puffs have slices of green olives across the top.

Tufts of watercress should extrude from the Pinover Sandwiches.*

Two whole cashews should be tilted into the watercress cream cheese mounds.

Use a stuffed-olive center for the chicken salad pinwheels.

Use a parsley, mayonnaise, and cream cheese spread for the open asparagus canapés.

Spread a mixture of candied ginger and cream cheese at each end of the orange bread fingers, and dip in chopped pistachio nuts.

To garnish the trays, use large limes made into baskets and filled with forget-me-nots, or, as an alternative, baskets made of green apples.

Half the mints should bear names, half should be miniature mints in fancy shapes.

Dip the ends of the almonds in melted pale aqua chocolate, then dip them again in pistachio nuts.

Here is the accompanying sweets menu:

White Petits Fours
Filled Chocolate Macaroon Fingers
Chocolate-dipped Mocha Mounds
Seedless Grape-filled Tiny Tarts
Orange Pastry Cinnamon Fans

Half the petits fours will be trimmed with aqua forget-me-nots, and half with olive-green names.

The mocha mounds have chopped pistachios on top.

Cinnamon fans are made of puff pastry.

A last suggestion: If you really want to go all out, have some frilly organdy tea aprons made to match the tea color scheme for the waitresses. After the party is over, have them freshly laundered and give them to your future daughter-in-law. You might have her first name embroidered on them.

CHAPTER 10

PRE-NUPTIAL PARTIES:

The Spinster Dinner

Usually the spinster dinner includes all the bridesmaids, the mothers of the bride and groom, and a very few close friends who may be hostesses at the church punch tables. When they are all together, the normal number is twelve to sixteen ladies, but occasionally there will be as many as twenty. If I am doing the catering, I prefer this to be a seated dinner, with all the guests at one table or two. Sometimes a T-shaped table can be arranged.

An apt theme for the spinster dinner could be "lavender and old lace." It's an occasion for merriment and joking. We often create a large round layer cake for a centerpiece, depicting an old maid. The artist shows a bespectacled old maid knitting in a rocking chair, with a canary in a cage, a bowl of goldfish, and a cat playing with her ball of yarn. She is wearing a lavender-and-old-lace costume, and looks to be about ninety. Inside the cake are fortune-telling trinkets wrapped in wax paper. Following is a list of the tokens and their symbols:

KEY TO FORTUNES

1. *Professor's Head:* Sign of knowledge; you should be a Phi Beta Kappa. There are brains in the family.
2. *Wishbone:* Success in the near future.
3. *Thimble:* Either you'll be an old maid or you'll have to live with one!
4. *Four-leaf Clover:* You're in for good luck!

5. *Fleur-de-lis:* Birds of a feather flock together. You're "flowery" and you'll live with "flowery" people.
6. *Anchor:* You're a tenacious person.
7. *Heart:* You're an affectionate person and will enjoy romance ahead.
8. *Wedding Ring:* A sign of matrimony. There'll be a wedding in the family this year.
9. *Penny:* Wealth ahead—through thrift. "Watch the pennies (be thrifty) and the dollars will take care of themselves."
10. *Button:* Bachelor. We do have to have them around.
11. *Jockey on Horse:* Beware of the racetracks. You're sure to lose your bets.

These are arranged around the cake, with red dots on the lace doily so that each guest will get a trinket in her piece of cake.

The meal itself does not have to be too heavy. Here is a suggested menu:

Deviled Egg Halves with Mushroom Sherry Sauce
Breast of Chicken with Grape Sauce*
Broiled Tomatoes
Zucchini and Water Chestnuts
Little Cinnamon Rolls
Spinster Cake
Ice or Sherbet

Serve the ice-cold deviled egg halves with a thin, piping-hot mushroom sherry sauce.

Herb butter goes with the zucchini and water chestnuts.

The ice or sherbet is optional.

I recall a spinster dinner where the couple planned to honeymoon in Hawaii, so the parents hit upon the idea of giving the dinner as a luau. If you want to carry out this idea, see the Hawaiian menus in Part Four.

At a Canadian party, some of the girls pooled their resources and made a scrapbook that was a "This Is Your Life" compilation for both the bride and groom. They cut out magazine ads, articles, and pictures to re-create the childhood, college, and courtship days, and presented the book at dinner.

CHAPTER 11

PRE-NUPTIAL PARTIES:

The Bachelor Dinner

While the spinsters are having their dinner, the bachelors are customarily celebrating at their own party. This is, of course, a stag affair, with ordinarily about ten or a dozen men present, and so the meal should be served by a male waiter. It *can* be buffet, but since toasts are usually involved, it's more convenient to have a sit-down meal.

It isn't hard to figure out what men like to eat best. This is a tried-and-true menu:

Shrimp Cocktail
Boston Strip Steaks, T-Bone Steaks,
or Standing Ribs of Beef
Hashed Brown Potatoes
Broiled Tomatoes with Mustard-buttered Bread Crumbs
Head Lettuce or Tossed Green Salad
Thousand Island or Russian Dressing
Crisp Hard Rolls or Hot Buttered French Bread
Apple Pie

The pie can be open Dutch apple or two-crust with cheese.

If cake and ice cream or sherbet are served instead of pie, we have made a custom decoration for the cake but it's a little expensive. The cake is usually a quarter or half sheet cake. The decoration depicts a man in a barbershop chair getting a haircut.

A beautiful blonde is manicuring his nails and a porter is shining his shoes. The inscription on the top reads, "It won't be long now 'til wedding bells ring." An alternate design is a picture of a terrified young man in his shorts and bare feet, standing on a block of ice. Next to it is a frying pan, and beside it a bonfire. The inscription across the top is, "Don't get cold feet," and below it, "Out of the frying pan into the fire!"

Corny? Well, yes, but it seems the cornier we get at the bachelor dinner, the more our clients like it!

CHAPTER 12

PRE-NUPTIAL PARTIES:

The Rehearsal Dinner

Since this occasion often falls on a Friday night, we have had to make sure in the past that, if it does, we make allowances for Catholics who may be present and cannot eat meat. Now that the Church has largely removed this restriction, it is easier to plan a menu in most cases, but since not all Catholics embrace the new doctrine, the hostess should decide what she wants to do about this matter.

The rehearsal dinner is most often a buffet, but even so, it's nice to seat everyone within hearing distance of one another, so that toasts can be offered. Guests usually number between 18 and 25, a figure that rises when important out-of-town guests arriving early in the city are included.

These dinners are often given by the groom's parents, and whether they want to go all out customarily depends on their financial circumstances. Certainly it is just as permissible—and we've catered them—to give the guests delicious, tasty box suppers to be served outdoors, if the weather permits.

For such affairs I try to avoid serving anything with garlic or a great deal of onion. After all, it's very close to the wedding by this time. One hears that this idea is old-fashioned, and perhaps it is, but people still embrace and kiss each other at weddings, and it's hard to believe they enjoy strong-smelling breaths.

The time of serving depends on what time the rehearsal is held. Obviously, people are more relaxed if the rehearsal can take place

at 5 or 6 P.M. and then eat afterward. Thoughtful people will try
to have the party break up at a sensible hour so that everyone
doesn't look bedraggled on the wedding day.

Whatever floral centerpiece is used, the one thing it must not do
is take away anything from the splendor of the wedding. It's
better, consequently, to stay away from the colors being used at
the ceremony.

Once in a while we use boxed groom's cakes, if they're not being
used at the wedding reception. One seldom sees them now except
at very large affairs. These are usually fruitcake wrapped in foil
and put in white boxes with the couple's initials and the date
imprinted, then tied with white satin ribbon. They are particularly
nice if the groom is from out of town; they make a pretty souvenir
for guests to take home.

Since most rehearsal dinners are buffet, we'd like to suggest
our favorites—always remembering that the groom's parents should
check to see what other meals are planned. If there is to be a
wedding breakfast or dinner next day, the food served the night
before should not duplicate any main entrée. In our work, menus
on the wedding day take precedence, and we plan the rehearsal
food so there will be no conflict.

Here, then, are two menus:

MENU NO. 1

Cold Poached Salmon
Caper or Cucumber Sauce
Beef Stroganoff
Cold Turkey
Spinach Noodle Casserole with Buttered Cracker Crumbs
Tossed Green Salad with Avocado
Molded Vegetable Aspic with Cottage Cheese
Assorted Rolls
Two-tone Wedding Molds of Vanilla Ice Cream and
Pineapple Sherbet with Strawberry Sauce
Macaroons   *Pralines*

MENU NO. 2

Chicken à la King
Baked Ham or Canadian Bacon
Hot Seafood Newburg
French-fried Carrot Balls*
Fordhook Lima Beans Vinaigrette
Platter of Slices of Pineapple, Red and Yellow
Tomato, and Rings of Red Sweet Pepper
and Green Pepper
Thin Jewish Rye Bread   Small Parkerhouse Rolls
Orange Blossom Trees*
Bell-shaped Butter Cookies

Serve the chicken à la king in patty shells or pie pastry shells. Roll the Carrot Balls in cheese bread crumbs before frying. Toss the lima beans with chopped pimiento or pickle relish. Hand-cut the cookies, and spell out the names of the bride and groom on them.

Remember, for this kind of dinner the food should be planned to suit a variety of tastes and not be too fancy. Notice, however, that in both these menus the dessert is fancier than anything else. That's because I believe it's the place for something a little special that is refreshingly cold and looks pretty as well.

CHAPTER 13

THE WEDDING

At last the day arrives. The best advice, and the hardest to take, is to be relaxed and poised on this important day in the family's history. People ought not to worry, unless of course they enjoy it, because very few weddings go off without some minor mishap. Real major catastrophes are exceedingly rare, however. The mishaps are easily minimized.

One way to avoid most of them is plan the event at least six months ahead, if possible, and get the details out of the way as fast as you can—although sometimes a wedding planned in two weeks turns out to be the smoothest of all.

In any case, choose a reliable caterer, and if the date is June, July, August, September, or December, you had better get on his books six months ahead. Don't call him in December to go into detail about a June wedding; simply give him a firm date and the approximate number of people you expect. Then, in January or February, you can begin to plan in more detail.

If possible, decide early what color the attendants are going to wear. Consult the florist early too, if you can. It's not always possible to guarantee that any certain flower (delphinium, for example) will be available. It helps the caterer if a color scheme can be agreed upon at least a month in advance.

The reason color is so important is that people go to many more weddings in the course of a year than they used to. If every wedding was traditionally white and green, they would soon be old hat and so monotonous the guests would be bored to tears. Naturally, I'm not advocating departures so far from the usual that the result is garish, but the event will always be more interesting if there are some innovations or little embellishments.

For example, I remember a wedding at which certain traditions of a Philadelphia family were carried out. On top of the wedding cake was a small tiered "planter," with each tiny pot having a sprig of fresh white begonia. It was sweet and simple.

I remember, too, a country wedding for which the florist used loads of pink geraniums. The buffet was especially beautiful, with this quaint flower used in graceful garlands over the main buffet and the wedding cake trimmed in white-icing geraniums, and topped with a couple of fresh geraniums. It was perfect for an informal country reception.

Daisy weddings in the summer are becoming more popular, but be sure the flowers hold up. Daisies need lots of water and wilt very quickly. To me it is an informal flower and should not be used at a formal evening wedding, but it's most appropriate for daytime and particularly for outdoor weddings. For a "daisy wedding," we like to decorate the cake either in garlands of icing daisies on the side of each tier, use them in clusters, or make four diagonal cascades of daisies showering over the tiers in a graceful flowing design.

There are two basic cake constructions. One is the kind whose tiers are not separated, one placed immediately on the other, with only a few wooden skewers or dowel pin supports. The other type, called the pyramid, has the tiers separated by either white gum paste drums or pillars or swans.

One of the newer ideas is to use inverted champagne glasses between the tiers, with an icing camellia-like rose or a fresh flower under each glass. The problem with pyramid cakes is that they are much more difficult to deliver, and in many cases the baker must send a cake decorator to the house to assemble the cake on the spot. This, naturally, increases the cost.

But no two people are alike, and we always try to express the individual tastes of the bride or her mother. We draw the line, however, when it comes to using bird cages with real lovebirds in the center of the cake, or small fountains. The trend today is to be less ornate, but at least fifty per cent of our wedding cakes have a touch of color. Not red, though. Recently a bride asked for red poinsettias on her cake for a Christmas wedding, but when she saw the cake, she was horrified. It was much too garish. As a result, I had to get into my car and deliver another one—a seventy-mile round trip. You can see why I try to talk people out of red. If it's December, we use white-icing poinsettias outlined in green.

Color *is* important, and certainly the cocktail paper napkins, coasters, and matchbooks can all be monogrammed or have printed names in a color that will blend with the main theme. Silver printing for weddings is still the most popular. Close behind is gold, and then green, aqua, and pink.

Since the wedding cake is usually not cut until almost the end of the reception, it is often practical to have some petits fours or a few kinds of sweet pastry. These are more popular at evening weddings than at late afternoon affairs, and they are used more often at church weddings with non-alcoholic punch than they are at champagne weddings. Children love them, and in any case it's nice to have a few because they do make the table more decorative.

These sweets can also carry out your color scheme. So can the candy mints. On occasion we dip fresh fruits in melted pastel chocolate to make an interesting compote. These are mainly strawberries, Bing cherries, pineapple chunks, and little seedless grapes —the latter often in clusters of three.

I don't like to see a wedding look like an ordinary cocktail party, so I discourage too many chafing dishes, full of things like cocktail wieners and tiny meatballs. A wedding ought to be a little more dressy. At an evening reception I like to see more finger sandwiches and fewer hors d'oeuvres or canapés. To make the sandwich trays prettier to look at, we like to garnish each tray with fresh curly parsley and fresh flowers, or flowers made from sliced turnips or grapefruit skins, dyed to match the color scheme.

Sometimes we have our waitresses wear yellow organdy or blue organdy tea aprons (they usually wear white uniforms), if the wedding has a dominant color scheme. And featuring a certain color *does* help to make a wedding outstanding. As a rule we don't use tinted breads. Every effort should be made to keep foods looking homemade, appetizing, and neat. I should add that the use of color is far from an invariable rule. We still do all-white weddings, or ones in green and white.

Here's a reminder about something you may not have thought about, if the wedding is going to be outdoors. Most tents are white, and if the day is bright the sun will shine through the fabric (most of them these days are plastic) and create far too much glare so there won't be enough contrast. Since there is likely to be green grass and green shrubbery all around, green table-cloths won't provide much contrast, unless it's a light mint green —a most attractive color.

If the wedding is in early summer, it is wise to order a tarpaulin spread over the grass. Ladies' spike heels ruin both the lawn and the heels. In the tent we like to provide some tables and seating, perhaps for twenty-five to forty per cent of the expected guests. The size of the tent depends on how much clear space you have. Sometimes the landscaping precludes a big one. You should dis-cuss this problem in advance with the man who's going to supply the tent.

There are times when the only practical thing to do is to have the wedding in a club, hotel, or rented hall. The advantage of a home wedding is that it's much more personal, and the hope is that your friends will remember it much longer. If you have a nice home and an attractive yard, why not use it?

Often the best plan is to have the big reception for two or three hundred people at a church and then bring back only a few, say forty or fifty, to the house for a buffet afterward. With after-noon weddings becoming so much more popular, this is a practical solution in many cases and is certainly more economical. The bride's family usually feels obligated to see that all the out-of-town friends and relatives are given some kind of supper before they leave the city, and this kind of crowd can be handled more easily back home, where they can be served more than just canapés, sandwiches, and cake.

Now, with these details out of the way, we can get on with the menus.

The Wedding Breakfast

MENU NO. 1

Eggs Benedict on Toast or English Muffins
Canadian Bacon Baked in Spiced Crab Apple or Peach Juice
Spiced Fruit Tray or Fresh Fruit Tray
Sesame Melba Toast*
Orange Marmalade or Strawberry Jam
Tiny Pecan Rolls   Small Danish Pastries

For the eggs benedict, use foil tart pans with a little melted butter in them, and bake in the oven on cookie sheets. Make a good Hollandaise sauce to pour over the eggs, adding chopped parsley or chopped watercress. Often a teaspoon of creamed spinach is used along with the Hollandaise.

MENU NO. 2

Fruit Juice Bar
Warm Baked Ham
Scrambled Eggs Sprinkled with Chopped Chives and Parsley
Tiny Hard Rolls or Toast
Assorted Jellies
Assorted Kuchens or Fancy Doughnuts

MENU NO. 3

Fruit Juices
Crisp Crumbled Bacon over Creamed Goldenrod
Eggs on Melba Toast
Spiced Prunes, Spiced Watermelon, and Cantaloupe Rind
Tiny Pecan Rolls and Tiny Danish Pastries

Alternate two kinds of fruit juice.
Cut additional Melba toast into heart shapes or triangles.

The Wedding Luncheon

MENU NO. 1

Fresh Fruit Cup or Plate
Boned Breast of Chicken
Watercress Sauce* or Currant Wine Sauce*
Giant Mushroom Caps Stuffed with Spinach or Peas
Tomato Aspic
Hot Tiny Sweet Rolls
Hot Tiny Parkerhouse Rolls
Sherbet and Ice Cream
Wedding Cake
Mints

The fruit can be in a thinly sliced cantaloupe ring, or a half of a grapefruit, or a third of a whole pineapple shell. Garnish with fresh mint.

Make the tomato aspic in small crinkled tart pans. An alternative would be a colorful vegetable aspic.

Butter the rolls ahead of time.

Use bowls for the sherbet and ice cream, and pile it high.

MENU NO. 2

Stuffed Eggs in Madrilene Aspic*
Heart-shaped Parmesan Melba Toast*
Boned Breast of Chicken Maryland
Mushroom Sauce
Orange Rice Balls*
Spiced Peach and Sheaf of Watercress
Tiny Assorted Rolls
Individual Wedding Ice Cream Molds
Wedding Cake
Mints

To decorate the stuffed eggs in aspic, use fresh shrimp or a teaspoon of crab meat salad or a little caviar. Garnish with lemon wedges and curly endive.

Serve the chicken Maryland on thin slices of country ham. Garnish the ice cream molds with fresh flowers.

MENU NO. 3

*Individual Rings of Crab Meat in Madrilene Aspic**
Cheese Pastry Straws
Turkey Hash on Triscuits or Cheerios
Long Green Beans with Toasted Almonds
Spiced Pears
Porcupine Celery   Olives*
Tiny Assorted Rolls
Wedding Cake
Ring of Lime Ice with Honeydew Melon Balls

Fill center of the crab meat rings with seedless grapes, and surround them with a good, zippy Pink Remoulade*.

An alternative to the cheese pastry straws would be long, pencil-shaped sticks of Parmesan Melba Toast*.

The green beans may be served with chopped hard-boiled egg instead of toasted almonds.

Mint ice may be served instead of lime ice, and strawberries instead of melon balls.

MENU NO. 4

Small Stuffed Hothouse Tomatoes
Finger Crackers Wrapped in Bacon
Half Breasts of Chicken
Yellow Country Chicken Gravy
*Spinach Croquettes**
Celery   Olives   Watermelon Rind
Tiny Rolls
Strawberry Sherbet and Strawberry Ice Cream
Wedding Cake

Peel the tomatoes and stuff them with crab or shrimp salad. Garnish with lemon wedges.

Finger Crackers Wrapped in Bacon are oblong saltines spread on both sides with a little peanut butter or soft Cheddar cheese and wrapped in ½ strip of very thin bacon. These are put on a wire rack in a 350° F. oven for 20 minutes and just before serving are put under the broiler.

Bone the chicken breasts. An alternate dish would be chicken Kiev.

Spinach tarts may be substituted for the croquettes.

Garnish the sherbet and ice cream with fresh mint and fresh strawberries.

MENU NO. 5

Fresh Fruit Cup
Chicken à la King
Hot Peas in Tomatoes
Perfection Salad
Green Goddess Dressing
Flat Princess or Parkerhouse Rolls
Butterscotch Caramel Loveknot Rolls
Wedding Cake
Watermelon Sherbet

Serve the fruit cup in a half large orange shell, a whole lemon opened into flame petals, or half of a cantaloupe.

The chicken à la king is served in a pie pastry shell or patty shell.

Skin the tomatoes, scoop out insides, then bake whole 15 minutes at 325° F., and stuff with peas.

Make the salad with *new* cabbage.

Serve the sherbet in sherbet glasses with a sprig of fresh mint.

MENU NO. 6

Jellied Shrimp Salad with Diced Avocado
Mustard Remoulade
Charcoal-broiled Filet Mignon
Creamed Peas and Mushrooms in Tart Shells
Celery   Olives   Radish Roses   Carrot Sticks
Buttered Princess Rolls
Tiny Hard Rolls with Sesame Seeds
Wedding Cake
Individual Molds of Lime or Mint Sherbet with
Honeydew Melon Balls

The steaks should be four or five ounces each.

An alternative to the creamed peas and mushrooms would be a tart shell filled with creamed spinach and crisp chopped bacon.

MENU NO. 7—BUFFET

Cold Sliced Turkey
Warm Baked Ham
Cold Sliced Roast Beef
Condiments
Mushroom Pie*
Spinach Pie*
Platter of Fresh Fruit
Platter of Fresh Tomatoes
Thin Party Breads
Tiny Pecan Rolls
Wedding Cake
Assorted Finger Sweets and Pastries

Hot Canadian bacon may be substituted for the baked ham.

The pies can be tarts if preferred.

Tomatoes should be thinly sliced, with Rose Toth Dressing* sprinkled over them, then *heavily* sprinkled with chopped parsley.

Some of the party breads should be buttered.

MENU NO. 8—BUFFET

Chicken Mandarin*
Orange Rice Balls*
Vegetable Wheel Vinaigrette*
Spiced Fruit Compote
Wedding Cake
Ice Cream and Sherbet   Mints

Hot creamed chicken and mushrooms may be substituted for the Chicken Mandarin*.

Arrange the vegetables for the salad in sections, so that the platter looks like a wheel with spokes.

The ice cream and sherbet is two tone marbleized, and is served in fancy crepe paper soufflé cups.

MENU NO. 9—BUFFET DE LUXE

Cold Sliced Turkey
Cold Rare Filet of Beef Tenderloin
Cold Lobster Salad
*Green and White Vegetable Salad**
Flat Princess Rolls
French Croissants
Tiny Butterscotch Loveknots
Wedding Bell Molds of French Vanilla Ice Cream
Chocolate Wedding Cake
Mints   Almonds   Pecans

Instead of lobster salad, you might serve a seafood salad of shrimp, lobster, and crab meat.

Be sure to serve the princess rolls piping hot.

Put the ice cream molds on sprigs of fresh flowers.

The Afternoon Reception

This appears to be the most popular kind of reception today. It is held usually from 4 or 4:30 P.M. to 7 P.M., with a supper afterward for about forty, fifty or sixty very close friends and guests from out of town. The supper is served about 8:30 or 9 P.M. By this time the bride and groom will probably have made an exit, but if they aren't going far, sometimes they return and eat supper with the family. Often, however, it's necessary for them to leave before too long, because the majority of guests won't leave until they do.

Here is a menu for the afternoon reception:

*Chicken Breast Pinover Sandwiches**
Tiny Lettuce and Roquefort Brownberry Sandwiches
Hot and Cold Canapés
Fancy Sweets and Tiny French Pastries
Mints   Nuts

Brownberry is a trade name for a kind of coarse, dark cracked wheat bread with a nutty flavor and a firm texture that makes it easy to slice very thinly. Spread with a mustard mayonnaise blended

with soft butter and use finely chopped iceberg lettuce and Roquefort cheese for the filling.

The cold canapés could be lobster, crab, or shrimp. You can
choose three or four kinds of hot canapés from a list that might
include Hot Toasted Mushroom Sandwiches*, shaved ham and
sesame fingers, bacon-wrapped olives or chestnuts, Cheese Soufflé Dreams*, Cheddar cheese rolls, heart-shaped hamburgers, crab
Lorenzo, and so on.

Only a few small fancy sweets are necessary.

We seldom serve coffee during the hot summer months.

If this reception is served in late afternoon, it will be the time
of day when people appear to be most hungry, so we often figure
on six canapés and sandwiches and two sweets per person.

Here are some wedding buffet suppers for those who stay on:

MENU NO. 1

Cold Meat Platter of Ham, Turkey, and Roast Beef
Hashed in Cream Potatoes* in Casserole
Platter of Fresh Fruits
Celery   Olives   Watermelon Rind
Thin Buttered Party Breads
Wedding Cake

MENU NO. 2

Chicken à la King or Chicken Mandarin* in
Pie Pastry Shells
Fresh Fruit Platter
Hot Parkerhouse Rolls

Butter the rolls ahead of time.
No dessert is served with this menu.

MENU NO. 3

Beef Stroganoff
Rice Ring
Vegetable Wheel Vinaigrette*
Hot Rolls
Wedding Cake

In this menu, as in Menu No. 1, I'm presuming that there will be leftover wedding cake.

MENU NO. 4

Standing Ribs of Beef
Mushroom Pie*
Stuffed Tomatoes
Hot Rolls

The beef will have to be roasted elsewhere and brought in. If the reception guests smell it ahead of time, they'll never leave.

Tomatoes are peeled, scooped out, and stuffed with cottage cheese blended with grated Roquefort cheese.

Serve the rolls piping hot. And no dessert.

If the bride and groom are motoring and leave about seven o'clock, we often pack a honeymoon basket with fresh fruit salad, turkey or roast beef sandwiches, a piece of wedding cake, mints, and nuts for them to enjoy all by themselves in their motel or in their car. We understand they greatly appreciate it.

The Formal Evening Wedding Dinner

MENU NO. 1

Crab Meat or Shrimp in Madrilene Aspic
Bell-shaped Parmesan Melba Toast*
Fresh Boned Breast of Chicken
Currant Wine Sauce*
Orange Rice Balls* or Spinach Croquettes*
Peas with Artichoke Hearts
Porcupine Celery*
Ripe and Stuffed Olives
French Sesame and Plain Croissants
Sweet Butter Balls
Lemon Sherbet Baskets
Wedding Cake
Fancy Mints   Almonds and Pecans

This is a sit-down, served dinner.

Place seedless grapes or fresh, flaked pineapple in the center of the crab or shrimp aspic.

A substitute for the peas with artichoke hearts might be creamed peas and finely diced braised celery sprinkled with toasted pecans.

The Lemon Sherbet Baskets* are whole lemons scooped out and filled with lemon ice or mint ice cream and lemon sherbet, on a sprig of fresh mint or lemon leaves.

MENU NO. 2

*Watercress Soup**
*Heart-shaped Sesame Melba Toast**
Filet of Beef Tenderloin
*Glazed Artichoke Sherry Sauce**
Individual Timbales of Potato Soufflé
Fresh Green Beans
Bibb Lettuce Salad
Tiny Rolls
Ice Cream Bombes
Wedding Cake
Fancy Mints   Almonds   Pecans

This, too, is a formal sit-down dinner.

The soup is made with a chicken stock base. A dab of whipped cream floats on its surface, along with fresh chopped watercress. It must be served piping hot.

Béarnaise sauce is an optional substitute for the Glazed Artichoke Sherry Sauce*. The beef is garnished with cherry tomatoes or glazed apricots.

The timbales of potato soufflé, with chopped mushrooms added, are baked in custard cups.

Cut the green beans in half-inch pieces and add macadamia nuts or almonds.

Add a few leaves of Belgian endive to the lettuce salad. If endive isn't available, use two stalks of white canned asparagus or two small stalks of braised celery heart.

There should be one ice cream bombe for each table; serve with macaroon curlicues decorating the sides, and accompanied by fresh fruit. Use your favorite ice cream flavors.

Of all the weddings I have catered, two formal ones I remember vividly. One was a pink and American Beauty wedding—a sit-down breakfast for about 300 to 350 people. Since the tent tops were white, we used light and deep pink tablecloths, deep pink chair covers, and American Beauty napkins. The flower center-pieces were light and deep pink.

I recall the first course well. It was a fresh fruit cup. We scraped the yellow skins off the thick-skinned grapefruit and then made fancy flowers like water lilies out of the grapefruit shells. These were dyed a deep pink with vegetable coloring and filled with fresh fruit—on galax leaves. Beautiful!

As I remember, we then served small-sized Cornish game hens with Currant Wine Sauce*, creamed spinach, and garnished the plates with tiny Harvard beets. Dessert was watermelon sherbet piled up with strawberry ice cream and darker red raspberry sherbet, to get the shaded effect. It was passed in silver bowls.

A wedding of about the same size held a year later was done entirely in shades of blue. The mother of the bride had always dreamed of a blue wedding for her daughter; even the bridal gown was ice-blue satin.

So it was to be a blue and white wedding. How could I make it unusual? My mind turned to the beautiful English Wedgwood china that belonged to my sister-in-law—a blue laurel pattern with a basket of fruit in the center. I bought a piece of it, and blue laurel became the theme. New blue chair covers and tablecloths were made, but we used white napkins. Happily the tent top was white; I remembered several summer parties I had done in blue tents, and the complexions of the guests looked terrible.

The florist cooperated. He ordered a great supply of mountain laurel roping and sprayed it a deep blue. He made square laurel "trees," like pyramids, for each table centerpiece. These were of blue laurel and white roses.

The wedding cake had garlands of white-icing laurel around each tier, and each leaf of laurel was outlined in a dainty blue piping. Thus the cake was strikingly simple but exquisite in design. Since the bride was passionately fond of chocolate, the cake was a rich moist chocolate inside, iced outside in white butter icing.

It was a morning wedding, so we served the sit-down luncheon at 2 P.M. The first course was on the table when the guests sat down. We had white plastic flower pots with a specially made decal that copied the blue laurel theme from the china. These were put on the pots by the decal maker. The pots themselves were filled with fresh fruits, including ripe blue plum sections, seeded blue Italian grapes, and fresh blueberries. There was a single, short-stemmed fresh white rose in the center of each pot.

Special blue menus had been printed and each guest was given a matchbook covered in blue satin and decorated with a cloth lily-of-the-valley sprig. Blue and white mints were on the table.

I don't recall the remainder of the menu, except that the main course was boned fresh breast of chicken with Orange Rice Balls* in cornflakes.

What I remember most happily was how the guests oohed and aahed all afternoon. Blue skies and a bright sun framed the whole picture. It was a truly lovely wedding in every way.

CHAPTER 14

WEDDING ANNIVERSARIES

Every married couple knows about anniversaries. The first few are observed with real freshness and spark. Then they begin to seem not so important, and merit nothing much more than a dinner out together. Still, it's possible to liven them up by making a little extra effort. We've done it, when people have asked us how, and following are some of the things we've told them about how to mark milestones.

First Anniversary—Paper

This is usually a small party. Make everything as easy as possible: paper tablecloth, napkins, paper dishes, and a paper centerpiece or a cake. Sometimes we design a quarter of a sheet cake to look like a local or rural newspaper, and write on it items like these:

The Weather—mild and sunny

Outlook—more sunshine

Then, in addition, headlines describing recent events in the lives of the celebrators, such as "Smiths Buy New Car," or anything else that's occupying their interest at the moment. Some of them are unashamedly corny, like "Mary and John Mark 1st Anniversary," with a subhead reading, "John Says Married Life Great Success."

For decoration, paper bells can be made, with the anniversary dates crayoned on them.

As for food, the first anniversary budget often can't stand too expensive fare, so we recommend a casserole dish, such as Lasagna Ercole*, or meatballs and spaghetti, green salad, French bread, sherbet or ice cream, and the cake.

Here's another idea if you have a dining-room chandelier. Get a wire hoop and fasten it up with string toward the ceiling. Cover the wire hoop with crepe paper streamers to make a gay paper chandelier. A round hatbox can be made into a dummy cake and used as a centerpiece. Doesn't matter how amateurish it looks.

Second Anniversary—Wood

Use as much wood as possible in setting your table, even if you have to splurge and buy a few pieces. Individual wooden salad bowls and wooden-handled steak knives can be used. Flowers are arranged in a wooden bowl.

Again, the meal should be simple and the group kept small. If the budget permits it by this time, steak is a good suggestion for the main entrée. Dessert would be a chocolate whipped cream roll, made in the shape of a wooden log. With the prongs of a fork you can rough up the chocolate butter cream icing to look like the bark of a tree. Serve with or without extra chocolate fudge sauce.

Tenth Anniversary—Tin

This can be an informal party, with red and white checked tablecloths, 9-inch foil pie pans for plates, tin cups from the dime store, and a tin centerpiece.

For decoration, we cut silhouettes of a man, woman, and children out of heavy kitchen foil. Foil bells can be molded to hang from the light fixtures. Make the table look as tinny as possible. Arrange the flowers in a tin coffee can.

First course is a soup served right out of tin cans, preferably low ones, like those canned sweet potatoes come in. Then serve a savory beef stew. Salad comes in small 6-inch foil tart or pie tins.

Dessert is "tin roofs"—that's old-fashioned ice cream sundaes with sauce and peanuts on top. If you serve cake, have two or three dimes wrapped in wax paper baked in it, and warn guests as they consume it to look out for money, a sign of good luck.

Fifteenth Anniversary—Crystal

This time let's have a buffet table set with everything in crystal or glass, even if you have to rent glass plates and punch glasses from the caterer. Six-ounce glass punch cups can even be used to serve coffee. Glass cake stands and antique crystal bowls will give the table some height. Use glass candlesticks or candle holders and tall tapers.

If it's an evening party, it might be fun to have only a sweet table. The invitations in that case would read: "Come for dessert and coffee." Let people pick and choose from an array of tempting desserts, forgetting their calories for once.

Here is a sweet table menu that will help them forget:

Hungarian Nut Torte
Profiteroles
Lime or Lemon Chiffon Pie
Little Cherry or Strawberry Tarts
Angel Food Cake
Macaroons
Coffee Cake or Butter Tea Ring
Salted Nuts   Mints

Profiteroles are little cream- or custard-filled puffs, with a delightful caramel glaze and powdered sugar; serve chocolate sauce on the side.

Make the pie with a graham cracker crust.

The cake should be a large one. Decorate it with small cordial toast glasses tucked into the top. And you might put a bottle of crème de menthe next to it.

It doesn't have to be macaroons. Any cookie will do.

Twentieth Anniversary—China

Five years later, and now let's set the table in china. If it's an evening coffee hour, like the crystal party, everything can be in china.

This time you may want to serve a seated dinner or buffet supper. That calls for a decorated cake, so let's use a plain sheet cake and decorate it with some new china demitasse cups and saucers that perhaps you've wanted to invest in for a long time. Or maybe you received some for a wedding gift and they've been collecting dust all these years. Have the inscription on the cake read, "Our 20th Anniversary." When it's time to serve, take the cake out to the kitchen, wash off the saucers and serve your guests demitasse coffee, for a change. The cake can then be cut in the kitchen.

Here's another idea. Get a big angel food ring cake with a large hole, big enough to hold a china vase, an antique one or a fancy china pitcher, and fill it with fresh flowers. A clever cake decorator can duplicate an icing border on the ring cake that matches your best set of china. Of course you'd have to risk taking a piece in to the bakery for him to copy!

Dessert could be pots de crème, served in those attractive little china pots. You may have to borrow some if you have more than six or eight people.

Twenty-fifth Anniversary—Silver

This, of course, is the first big one. To some people that means a big party to match; others prefer a small dinner. In any case, if you're having an at-home, take extra care so that guests won't think you've planned the affair just to get presents.

Actually, most silver anniversary parties appear to be arranged by friends of the couple, or relatives, rather than the celebrants. That provides an opportunity to play up the silver idea, while it has to be played down if the couple give it themselves.

Let's assume, then, that it's going to be a real silver party. If you want a truly elegant table, use all silver appointments—coffee and tea service at one end, silver punch bowl at the other. Use silver candelabra if available. Often in a home we use the tiered silver anniversary cake for a centerpiece, but if hot food is to be put on the table, then I prefer having the cake on a buffet, a server, or a special small table.

The color scheme depends on the general decor of the house. Pink and silver, apricot and silver, white, blue, and silver are all nice and, generally speaking, have more interest than plain white and silver. If the couple happen to be Scottish in background, you could use a plaid cloth and have red roses with eucalyptus sprayed in silver, or use blue and white delphiniums with the silver-sprayed foilage and some heather.

If the number of guests is small, you may want to have a small double bell cake (carved out of sheet cake) or double hearts. Occasionally we make an open book with silver bookmark and silver-edged leaves, with "Another page in Kellys' family history" written on the cake.

People aren't supposed to eat the silver paint used on these cakes. Be sure to cut it off and discard it before you serve.

If you have a big open house or reception, serve the same kind of food you would for a wedding. Hot canapés are always popular, along with a few cold canapés and some sandwiches.

At a small sit-down dinner you can be a little fancier. Use silver matchbooks and small silver-trimmed nut dishes as favors. During the cocktail hour or gathering period before dinner, one might display pictures of the couple mounted on a board or screen covered with silver foil, tracing the romance, engagement, and married life, with pictures of the children. That will promote much reminiscing about old times.

You can use silver doilies under the first course or under the dessert. The candy compotes should be silver, and I like to use a few silver-wrapped Hershey kisses or bells with the mints to carry out the theme.

Here's a silver and blue menu:

Avocado in the Snow*
Parmesan Melba Toast*
Crown Roast of Lamb
Pea Soufflé
Broiled Giant Mushroom Caps
Green and White Vegetable Salad*
Tiny Mint Biscuits
Pineapple Sherbet with Fresh Blueberries
Bell-shaped Petits Fours
Mints Chocolate Bells

Make the Parmesan Melba Toast* bell-shaped.

On top of each rib in the crown roast place a silver paper frilled cap, and put sprigs of mint around the whole platter.

Whole peas are added to the soufflé before cooking.

Put a spiral of mashed potato in each of the mushroom caps, and dust with coarsely shaved Cheddar cheese. Top with a small silver onion.

Mint Biscuits are regular baking powder biscuits with chopped mint added to the biscuit dough. Split and spread them with butter and mint jelly, and reheat.

Write a blue "25" on each of the petits fours.

The mints are blue and white, bell-shaped. Chocolate bells are covered with silver foil.

I recall a twenty-fifth anniversary party at which the couple had met on a Pennsylvania Railroad train. The lady passenger offered the gentleman a red apple. The friend who was giving the affair decided to use that as the theme. It was a seated dinner for 30 people in his huge front hall. A large oval table was erected, and running around the center of the table was an olive-green electric train, with "Pennsylvania Railroad" painted on the passenger cars. Graceful swags of fern surrounded the train track, along with dozens of the biggest red apples money could buy.

We borrowed a conductor's uniform and a red cap from a Pennsylvania Railroad employee. The honored couple and the guests were called for in one of those little automobile trains one sees in American Legion parades.

Real PRR tickets were obtained and the stubs were fastened to the backs of the chairs. Guests had to match the ticket stubs they were given to find their seats and dinner partners. I don't recall the entire menu, but I do remember the exquisite cake, which was a pink and silver train, bearing an appropriate greeting. Apples and trains certainly made that celebration unique!

Probably you'll never do anything so elaborate, but it will give you an idea of how to plan a special party for this special anniversary. How did the couple meet? What are their common and major interests?

Facts like these will give you ideas. I recall one couple who were always talking about Wooster College, where their two children had gone to school. For them we used a red and yellow Scotch plaid cloth (school colors); red and yellow candles, flowers, and so on. Since Wooster was famous for its kiltie band, we even hired a bagpiper to come and play a *short* concert, particularly "Here Comes the Bride."

If the party is for people who are much interested in their church, or if it is the minister and his wife who are having the anniversary, it's appropriate to make the cake in the shape of a large Bible. On one side the inscription congratulates the couple with names and dates. On the other is a verse appropriate to the occasion. For example, use Deuteronomy 2:7 written out for a fortieth milestone.

Fortieth Anniversary—Ruby

Don't wait for your fiftieth. If you're alive and healthy, make a big occasion out of the fortieth.

We catered a party for a prominent Cleveland couple who called the affair "Forty Rosy Years." Both were civic-minded and had been active in social and educational projects. Their cake was a large two-tiered one, with "40 Rosy Years" written on it in dark ruby red. Eight clusters of five icing roses each were arranged gracefully on it. Surrounded with garden pachysandra, it made an impressive centerpiece.

Incidentally, we often put fresh greens around a cake for two reasons: First, the doily under a cake often gets crumpled or soiled and doesn't lie flat enough; second, the contrast of the green fern makes the white frosting stand out more.

Naturally, one thinks of using Happiness dark red roses, one of the prettiest flowers, but if the celebration comes in fall or late summer, you can use dark red cosmos, glamellias (plucked glads), dark red snapdragons, or cockscombs. All these come in brilliant ruby-red shades but are quite scarce.

To get a little red in your menu, you can use Cherry Horse-radish Beets*, or julienne or sliced beets for that matter. To cook them Harvard style tends to make them look redder. A tomato aspic can be made redder by using strawberry gelatin with the tomato; this makes it very palatable as well.

Serve vanilla ice cream with red raspberries or sauce. Any one of our dinner menus can be used as a starter for planning.

One thing we *don't* recommend is red icing on petits fours. It just doesn't taste good, and of course tints the mouth when you eat it. Because red roses symbolize love, we are quite often forced to decorate cakes with them, but if you want the trimming really to taste good, you should use white roses *edged* in red—a sort of two-tone rose.

Fiftieth Anniversary—Golden

A few years ago I spent three weeks in India and was fascinated with the outstanding display of brass in the shops there. How lovely for a golden wedding, I thought, and bought several brass trays on the spot. Now we can set a fiftieth anniversary table completely in brass, which looks so like gold. We have antique brass French candelabra, even a pair of brass punch ladles I found in Hong Kong. We do a good many of these parties. People live longer now, and we find ourselves catering many more golden wedding receptions than we once did.

Most of these parties tend to be open house, but it depends on the health of the couple whether the celebration is in their own home or in the house of one of the children, or in a church or rented hall. Whenever it's possible, I believe it's better to have the party in the couple's home, especially if they have lived there a long time and have many memories associated with it. If they're in good health, they'll enjoy it; most older folks thrive on a little excitement.

If possible, I think it's better for someone else to give the party. Don't bother the celebrants with too many details. Let them sit back and enjoy it, and see their old friends without having any worries. Sometimes, of course, the couple are natural planners and want to do it all themselves because they enjoy the planning itself. If so, by all means make them part of the whole business.

Older people don't like to stay up too late, so late afternoon is probably the best time for a reception—say from 4 to 7 P.M., with a small dinner afterward for the immediate family. You may be interested to know that our records show a higher rate of acceptance for a golden wedding party than for a regular wedding; often the figure is as high as 90 per cent. On the invitation one can say, "Your presence but no presents please," but still many like to send bouquets of flowers or plants, or some small remembrance.

Gold, yellow, and white are the favorite colors for the fiftieth anniversary reception. If the couple is very popular and likely to get lots of yellow flowers, such as roses and mums, you may want to use gold and white only and keep out the yellow.

We usually use golden-yellow Indian head cloths with gold napkins for the round tables, white or yellow chair covers, or gold-painted folded chairs. A brass bowl hurricane lamp is used if the supper is to continue after dark. If you use pachysandra with a little gold-sprayed huckleberry, you won't need too many flowers. One thing I've learned is that daisies don't hold up in oasis because they don't get enough water. Yellow and white mums and marigolds do keep nicely in commercial oasis which one obtains from his florist.

Here are a half-dozen golden anniversary menus:

MENU NO. 1

Cantaloupe Halves
Wedding Ring Melba Toast
Small Rock Cornish Game Hens with Bread, Orange,
and Pecan Stuffing
Apricot Glacé Sauce*
Yellow Wax Beans, Yellow Summer Squash, Whole-kernel Corn
Molded Artichoke Salad
Tiny Corn Muffins
Lemon Sherbet and Vanilla Ice Cream
Wedding Cake
Mints   Nuts

Make pointed edges around the cantaloupe halves and fill them with honeydew balls and fresh pineapple; or make a ring of cantaloupe with these fruits accompanying.

For the wedding ring Melba, use a doughnut cutter to cut out the bread, and butter it before toasting. Sprinkle with celery seed.

Add grated orange rind and toasted pecans to a bread and celery dressing for the Rock Cornish hens.

Combined cooked beans, summer squash, and corn and sauté in melted butter. Or serve with Hollandaise sauce.

For the salad, use sliced artichokes, a few sliced raw mushrooms, lemon gelatin, and a few small yellow pear tomatoes. If you can't find pear tomatoes, use cherry tomatoes cut in half. Serve with a mild curry mayonnaise dressing.

If you don't want corn muffins, have tiny orange buttercream rolls or butterscotch loveknots.

Put the sherbet and ice cream in Lemon Baskets* on lemon leaves.

MENU NO. 2

Fresh Fruit Cup
*Cheese Soufflé Dreams**
Boned Half Breasts of Chicken with Orange Sauce
Mushroom Noodle Croquettes
*New Orleans Carrots**
Tomato Salad
Tiny French Croissants
Butterscotch Loveknots
Vanilla Ice Cream
Fresh Peach Sauce
Mints   Almonds   Pecans

Serve the fruit cup in scooped-out halves of small grapefruit placed in a glass finger bowl filled with yellow-tinted ice, or with green ice for contrast.

The hot Cheese Soufflé Dreams* are passed.

You'll need two small noodle croquettes for each serving of chicken. Put a spiced peach on each plate.

Make the salad a small one, composed of two small slices of tomato spread with egg salad, on Bibb lettuce.

Loveknots are a gooey brown sugar caramelized sweet roll—similar to a Philadelphia sticky bun, but no raisins are used.

The ice cream is a bell mold.

Obviously, this will be a sit-down dinner.

MENU NO. 3—BUFFET

Lobster Capon Madeira* on Bell-shaped
Melba Toast or in Saffron Rice Rings
Filet of Beef Tenderloin
Mushroom Pie* or Spinach Pie*
Cold Stuffed Tomatoes
Cucumber Aspic
Tiny Pecan Rolls   Tiny Butter Rolls
Coffee Baked Alaska*
Wedding Petits Fours
Mints   Almonds

Carve the beef tenderloin at the table.

Scoop out the small tomatoes and fill them with curried egg salad or with artichoke hearts and white asparagus vinaigrette.

Sliced oranges go with the cucumber aspic, or you might have avocado aspic with grapefruit sections instead.

MENU NO. 4—BUFFET

Cream of Celery Soup
Flaked Fresh Salmon in Aspic*
Open Mushroom Tarts
Carrots Newburg
Celery and Olives
Tossed Green Salad
Slender Bread Melba Sticks
Cantaloupe Rings
Wedding Cake or Petits Fours
Mints

Put a dash of curry in the soup and sprinkle with toasted slivered almonds. Make it quite thin and serve it on the terrace before guests come in to the buffet.

Garnish the salmon in aspic with yellow tomato wedges or yellow pear tomatoes.

The tenderloin is carved at the table.

Fill the mushroom tart shells with creamed mushrooms, and if you like, add diced zucchini.

Instead of carrots Newburg, you may want carrots and grapes, Harvard style.

The celery and olives are in shaved ice.

Sprinkle the salad generously with mandarin oranges.

Spread the Melba sticks with a thin coating of melted Cheddar cheese.

The cantaloupe rings should be thin. In the centers put lemon or pineapple sherbet, or a vanilla ice cream ball with a teaspoon of grated pineapple over the top.

MENU NO. 5—BUFFET

Lobster or Seafood Salad
Hot Creamed Chicken
Saffron Rice Balls
Baked Ring of Butternut Squash
Fresh Cut-up Fruit
Fancy Finger French Pastries

For the salad, add a dash of curry and yellow mustard to the mayonnaise. Sprinkle grated egg yolk lightly over the top.

Serve the creamed chicken with grapes and water chestnuts or toasted almonds.

Add a little mashed potato to the squash ring before baking (to give firmness) and fill the center with cooked peas.

Cut up the fruit and put it in a glass bowl.

MENU NO. 6—SIMPLE BUFFET

Cold Meat Platter
Potato Salad
Platter of Sliced Yellow Tomatoes and Pineapple
Assorted Thin Breads
Relish Tray
Finger Pastries
Mints   Nuts

Sliced baked ham, tongue, turkey, and Swiss cheese garnished with parsley and marigolds make up the cold meat platter.

Garnish the potato salad with a wreath of deviled egg halves.

Alternate the sliced yellow tomatoes with sliced pineapple. In the center of this platter, have a pile of big black spiced prunes stuffed with a yellow-tinted cream cheese, or cream cheese mixed with a mustard artichoke relish.

If you don't want a relish tray, olives and celery will do.

The Sixtieth Anniversary—Diamond

Few people are fortunate enough to reach this milestone, and quite often they will not feel up to having a big party. However small it may prove to be, we suggest the diamond motif.

The wedding cake can be diamond-shaped—one or two tiers will probably be enough—with a diamond-shaped plaque sticking up from it, bearing the numeral 60. If the couple is still very active, you may want to order a sheet cake (or a half sheet) and make the trim humorous. Something like a gay old couple in an open, sporty convertible speeding down the road with a cloud of dust behind, the driver with one arm around his girl, and above it the inscription: "At Your Sixtieth Still Going Like Sixty! Congratulations!" Sometimes we use a cake in the shape of the numeral 60. The numbers can have a floral trim, with names and year dates. Just be careful it doesn't come out looking like a tombstone.

The party will probably be an open house buffet. Cut the sandwiches with a diamond cutter, or else cut that shape with a knife—sort of an even parallelogram. Several kinds of open canapés on diamond-shaped pieces of bread will be very attractive.

Napkins and matchbooks can be personalized. Mints should have "60" on some, and initials or first names on the remainder.

If the couple should happen to come from a foreign country, be sure to have the national foods dear to their hearts.

CHAPTER 15

HOUSEWARMINGS

America is always on the move. Most of us move every three to five years, and wherever we move, the day often comes when the new owners or tenants feel like having a good old-fashioned housewarming. People often invite their friends to see their new home, if they've just bought one. It may be more fun, though, to have a housewarming given by friends of the new homeowners. It seems to me we don't have as many surprise parties as we used to, and now and then it can be really fun.

A housewarming can be a potluck affair, with everyone assigned to bring an item. If someone makes wonderful chili, that's her assignment. Sometimes, though, it may be easier to call a caterer, and everyone contributes a certain amount to the total cost.

If it's a house with a fireplace, have a fire in it after the surprise entrance, unless of course it happens to be summer. A fire on the hearth is traditionally linked to a housewarming. Remember the old Scottish expression, "Long may your chimney send up smoke."

The cake artist will make you a house cake. It may not duplicate the one being warmed, but you should specify when you order whether your house is a two-story colonial, split-level, ranch, Georgian, or modern. The cake itself can be chocolate, spice, or white. Often we put the old Scottish saying on the roof of the house.

Let's keep the menu simple:

MENU NO. 1—SUPPER

New England Baked Beans or Baked Succotash
Baked Ham Loaf
Molded Figs, Spiced Prunes, and Cottage Cheese in Lemon Aspic
Pickle Tray   Blueberry Muffins
Housewarming Cake
Coffee Ice Cream
Peanut Brittle   Chocolate Pecan Bark

Chili con carne may replace the baked beans, if you like.

Serve croutons and cheese atop the baked succotash.

The ham loaf can be a large one, or an individual one for each guest. In either case, serve it with gingersnap gravy (raisin sauce with crushed gingersnaps).

With the ice cream, serve crème de cacao and toasted coconut in a side dish, to be added as desired.

MENU NO. 2—BUFFET

Swedish Meatballs in Sour Cream Mushroom Gravy
Rice and Creole Shrimp Casserole
Salami Cornucopias
Four-bean Salad
Crusty Parsley-buttered French Bread
Decorated Sheet Cake
Puffed Rice Candy

Place stuffed green olives in the center of the cornucopias.

Four-bean salad is made with Fordhook limas, yellow and green beans, cooked, with a few kidney beans vinaigrette, and a few slices of red onion, very thinly sliced.

If you don't want a sheet cake, how about hot gingerbread with lemon sauce?

MENU NO. 3—LATE BUFFET

Large Fresh Fruit Platter
Toasted Cheese or Grilled Ham and Cheese Sandwiches
Hot Toasted Mushroom Sandwiches*
Assorted Cookies and Brownies

This is a buffet menu to serve at about 10 P.M.

The fruit platter can be served with the fruit arranged in separate sections, or together.

Have the sandwiches prepared, ready to grill at the last minute.

Instead of the assorted cookies and brownies, you may want a decorated cake.

CHAPTER 16

PARTIES FOR LONG SERVICE

Many business firms like to recognize the long-time service records of their employees with some kind of celebration, and considering the nature of this achievement, when a man has completed forty or fifty years with the same company we like to use the theme, "Something to crow about."

This party may well be a big group, forty to eighty people, so a finger-food buffet is the most functional. Fitting in with the usual business day, a 5 to 7 P.M. party is ideal.

Red and white rooster cocktail napkins are easy to get, and we also use red and white checked tablecloths. For a centerpiece, a big paper rooster (or one in ceramic or styrofoam) on a piece of driftwood or a split rail fence. A few sprigs of Queen Anne's lace or field daisies or cockscombs will make the rooster look a little less stark, particularly if it's an amateur creation.

In our kitchens we have several copper rooster molds. We like to make a chicken liver pâté mold, sometimes rubbing it lightly with egg salad. After it's unmolded on a platter, we garnish it with red pimiento for the coxcomb and the wattle ("gobbler") below. Surround the mold with party rye, Melba toast, or crackers.

A second rooster mold can be made with ham salad or ham mousse. Deviled pullet eggs or halves of deviled eggs are popular with men—and don't overlook turkey and ham sandwiches, because they're always acceptable.

Spread thin rare roast beef with a horseradish, cream cheese,

PLATE I

LEFT:
   Caviar in a "Daisy" of
      Cucumber Boats

BELOW:
   Cold Hors d'Oeuvres:
      California Snow Pea
         Pods
      Filled Cherry
         Tomatoes
      Stuffed Artichoke
         Hearts

PLATE II

Zucchini Squash Casserole

and mayonnaise spread and roll up. It's to be eaten with the fingers, like dried beef rolls.

A chocolate sheet cake or layer cake can depict a rooster strutting forth, holding an Oscar. Inscription: "Congratulations, George, on 35 Years with Smith Bros."

If the men don't want to eat the cake, it's given to the honored gentleman to take home to his family. If coffee is being served, it would be easy to make egg-shaped petits fours in the company's colors, with the man's initials and "35 Years" on each one.

CHAPTER 17

THE SWAN SONG RETIREMENT PARTY

Retirement is one of those inevitable things we don't like to face, but eventually it happens to most of us. Today, happily, many people are able to retire at a relatively youthful age so they can do the things they've always wanted to do. In any event, a retirement party ought to be a swan song without melancholy overtones. Try to make it as gay as possible.

I remember a lady who was retiring after many years as private secretary to the president of the Chamber of Commerce. Her friends were planning a farewell and we were given the task of designing the cake. We asked what she intended to do after retirement and were told that she meant to work part time in an antique store. That gave us our cue.

On a flat sheet cake, our artist depicted a quaint antique store, with furniture, glassware, china, and old Tiffany lamps—even a few cobwebs and a mischievous spider in the corner. The honored guest was so pleased she wouldn't permit her cake to be cut, and proudly showed it to all her friends for the next month.

But of course not everyone knows what he's going to do after retirement. Sometimes the decision is fairly sudden. For these occasions, the swan song theme is always useful and appropriate.

You can rent a fountain or water pond and plastic swans very reasonably at a display store or florist, either to be used in the center of the buffet table or in the front hall or family room. If you have a pond, plastic water lilies with altar candles can be used, and a few bunches of slender cattails at the edge will make your pond more decorative.

If guests gather outside on a terrace, you might even have very small frogs' legs, French-fried crispy golden brown, for an hors d'oeuvre. We usually identify them by using little ceramic frogs on a bed of parsley, so guests will know what they're eating. It's surprising how many people have never tasted them. Before they're passed, squeeze a little fresh lemon over them and it's a good idea to serve a zippy tartar sauce.

With a retiree group we recommend that you have a sit-down dinner, or at least tables to sit at if you serve buffet. Use light blue or aqua cloths, and white and blue, yellow and blue, or pale coral and blue flowers. If you don't want to go to the expense of flowers, make a cardboard swan, finished on both sides, and be sure you have it on a heavy base so it won't blow over if it's breezy.

Here is a menu for this sit-down retirement party:

Lump Crab Meat Salad
Fish-shaped Melba Toast with Herb Butter
Breast of Capon or Chicken under Glass
Fresh Plum Sauce
French-fried Parsnips* or French-fried Cauliflower*
Hot Cinnamon Buns
Salad
Della Robbia Swan-shaped Cream Puffs
Aqua and White Mints

Serve the crab meat salad in "water lily" cups, using grapefruit shells opened up like a water lily.

Boneless breast of duckling may be substituted for breast of capon or chicken.

Add grated lemon or orange rind to the fresh plum sauce.

Sprinkle the parsnips with rosemary.

Dip partially cooked cauliflower in flour, then in raw egg, and then in fine bread crumbs before French-frying (PLATE IV).

Make individual salads with a big slice of beefsteak tomato, a slice of pineapple, a thin ring of green pepper, a teaspoonful of cottage cheese, and crisp, crinkled bacon. Serve with Paprika Dressing*.

As for the cream puffs, many bakers can fashion the swan heads and necks with a plain pastry tube. Just cut off the top half of the cream puff and break in two parts for the wings. Fill with sliced peaches, berries, cherries, and toasted pecans folded together with whipped cream. If you prefer, you can fill the cream puffs with any ice cream. Be sure to dust the cream puff with powdered sugar. Mr. Arthur's Butterscotch Sauce* or pistachio sauce may be served.

Put the mints in little plastic swan dishes.

After dinner, if each guest has brought humorous dime-store presents, you can construct a makeshift fishpond. Let the honored guest fish up the various gifts to help him retire. Bits of jocular advice could be on the cards.

It may sound corny, but it's turned out to be fun more than once: get someone in the group to compose a "Swan Song" poem set to the tune of "Way Down upon the Swanee River."

With retirement there is sometimes a major move to another part of the country—California or Florida, New England or the Bahamas. To make a gay party gayer, the centerpiece decorated cake can depict a moving van heading west or south, or else a car with a little trailer piled high with belongings. The inscription: "Westward Ho!" or "California, Here We Come!" along with a few purple mountains, cactus plants, and orange groves to enhance the pastry scene. Sometimes we make a sketch of two gray-haired people sunning themselves in deck chairs.

Make the table setting casual if the new home is to be in California. If it's New England, you could dream up a Yankee menu of boiled dinner, or molasses baked beans, frankfurters, and Boston brown bread sandwiches.

Inspiration increases if you know your geography. Or turn elsewhere. There are always people who have such pronounced hobbies as golf or fishing, and these can be played up with a cake in the shape of a golf bag or a huge swordfish.

And do suggest to the speechmakers that they be funny, brief, and not too sentimental.

CHAPTER 18

BON VOYAGE PARTIES

There are all kinds of reasons for bon voyage parties, since there are all kinds of reasons for people to go abroad these days. Mother and Dad may be taking a long trip, now that the kids are out of college and married. The bachelor career girl may be going to Spain, or Portugal, or Hawaii. The favorite aunt and her friend may be starting out on a Caribbean cruise. The couple next door may even be going around the world. Whatever the reason, everyone deserves and likes to have a send-off with a bon voyage party.

Destination and mode of travel are important in planning. If people are going abroad by boat, you can order a boat carved out of cake to look like a steamship. It can be personalized a little more if you have the name of the ship. Maybe the travel agent can provide a picture, and the smokestack can be the same color as the actual boat.

If you're clever at making mobiles, they're always interesting. One might depict various kinds of travel—jets, steamships, mules, rickshaws, whatever—and hang the mobile from the dining room chandelier.

Travel agents are usually willing to give you posters of the area being visited. They are fine for a recreation room, porch, or mantel, but don't get your living room into the act; they'll look too garish. If the place is to be Japan or the Orient, use Japanese lanterns. In Part Four, in the section "Nationality Menus," you'll find one you may want to use to give the tourist a foretaste of what delicacies are in store for him.

The nautical theme can be accentuated with aqua, turquoise, or royal blue tablecloths and napkins. Anchors of styrofoam, plastic lifeboats, and plastic captain's steering wheels are available from a display house.

For a centerpiece, a boat dock can be created with a pile of luggage on it. The centerpiece cake could be made to look like two or three suitcases with icing travel stickers bearing Rome, Paris, or London labels, or the names of famous hotels.

If it's a dinner, you might type up the menu as though on a ship or in a restaurant, and though your fare may not be as elegant, you can have fun making even the homeliest items sound French or Italian.

If it's to be Europe, you can always make a cardboard Eiffel Tower. Our artists have made several Arcs de Triomphe and Eiffel Towers, but it's too much work to make a three-dimensional Tower of Pisa. Any of these, in fact, are much less expensive and easier to sketch on a flat sheet cake or a round layer cake than to create in three dimensions.

If you don't want a cake centerpiece, an alternative is to decorate individual petits fours with pennants saying, "Bon Voyage," along with anchors and little steamships.

I remember doing a dinner party for a couple going to Australia and New Zealand. Our artist made a cardboard kangaroo for one table and a kiwi bird (the famous symbol of New Zealand) for the other. Both of these were surrounded by unusual foliage and a wild sweet grass flower not commonly seen.

We did a welcome home party for a couple whose children wanted to observe their thirty-ninth wedding anniversary, and used the theme "Around the World in Eighty Days." They made up the menus themselves with a picture on the cover of two people sitting in an old-fashioned blimp. Little balloons were centerpieces on each table, along with red carnations.

This was the menu:

HORS D'OEUVRES FROM AROUND THE WORLD

Hawaii	Macadamia Nuts
Japan	Snow Pea Pods Stuffed* with Crab Meat
Hong Kong	Egg Rolls
India	Curried Lamb Balls
Turkey	Stuffed Grape Leaves
Russia	Caviar
Italy	Prosciutto Ham with Honeydew Melon
France	Pâté de Foie Gras
Africa	Bananas Wrapped in Bacon
Spain	French-fried Shrimp
Holland	Edam Cheese
Germany	Sauerkraut Balls
Scandinavia	Herring in Sour Cream
England	Fresh Smoked Salmon
Mexico	Enchiladas
United States	Wimpies

DINNER MENU

Hot Mushroom Bouillon
Parmesan Melba Medallions
Whitefish à la Rhine*
Tossed Green Salad Oahu
Lemon Mint Dressing
Filet of Beef Tenderloin
Béarnaise Sauce
Potatoes Suzette
Artichoke Bottoms with Spinach*
Coffee Baked Alaska* with Crème de Cacao
Mints

CHAPTER 19

GROUND-BREAKING CEREMONIES

As people advance in the world, they often dabble in real estate projects and find themselves consequently on building committees for churches, lodges, and social institutions. This calls sooner or later for attending or planning ground-breaking ceremonies and cornerstone layings. These milestones are now observed with re-freshments, if it's only hot coffee and doughnuts. More often than not, it seems, the weather is cold, damp, and raw, with snow or rain. These are brief ceremonies, fortunately, but as quickly as the speeches are over and the cameras click, there should be some provision for the brave souls who have stood their ground and listened despite the weather.

Here are 4 quick menus for these stouthearted people:

MENU NO. 1

Piping-hot Coffee
Assorted Raised, Glazed Doughnuts
Fried Cakes and French Crullers

MENU NO. 2

Hot, Double-strength Beef Bouillon
Ham Sandwiches on Rye Bread
Turkey Sandwiches on Whole Wheat Bread
Corned Beef Sandwiches on Pumpernickel Bread
Hot Coffee

Add mushroom broth to the bouillon.

MENU NO. 3

Hot Chocolate   Hot Coffee
Ham Salad Sandwiches
Roast Beef Sandwiches
Dill Pickles   Gherkins
Petits Fours

The petits fours can have toy shovels stuck in them, or you might have a sheet cake cut up, with a shovel in each piece.

MENU NO. 4

Hot Tomato Bouillon
Tiny Hot Barbecued Hamburgers
Cookies
Coffee

Add a little pea soup to the bouillon, for body.
Decorate the cookies with icing shovels.

Cornerstone Laying

I recall doing a large church dinner following the ceremony of laying a cornerstone for a million-dollar new church sanctuary.

Each long table had three red bricks, overlapping, with a small trowel. We used bright green cloths and small individual clay pots of bright red Irene geraniums placed on top of the brick pyramid. It was most effective as a decoration. Glasses of red tomato juice enlivened the color scheme.

The menu was extremely simple—a layered casserole on each table. In the bottom layer was cut-up fresh julienne beef, then loose brown rice cooked in consommé, then mushrooms, and on top, green buttered peas. An individual jellied salad in a lettuce cup was placed at one corner of the dinner plate. There were plenty of rolls and a simple dessert, a choice of warm honey spice cake with lemon sauce or cherry tarts.

CHAPTER 20

THE AFTER-FUNERAL BUFFET

With transportation so rapid today, memorial services and funerals are usually well attended. Relatives from long distances away are able to attend, and because they have traveled so far, it is only proper to see that they have some food before they leave. Consequently we are often called upon to assist the bereaved family when they need help most. Frequently, too, more people come back to the house after the funeral than one would normally anticipate, so it is a good idea to plan generously, no matter how simple the menu. The food should be not only simple but nourishing, with as little fuss as possible.

In winter months we recommend hot soup as soon as the guests return. There is no colder place than a cemetery in rainy, snowy, or cool weather.

Here are menus appropriate for after the funeral.

MENU NO. 1

Hot Cream of Tomato Soup
Cold Meat Platter
Potato Salad or Hot au Gratin Potatoes
Pickle and Relish Tray
Assorted Thin Breads
Butter and Condiments
Sheet Cake or Square Cakes

The soups should not be too creamy. If you don't have enough bouillon cups, use regular coffee cups.

Ham and turkey are a must on the cold platter. Corned beef, roast beef, and Swiss cheese would be optional.

Cake, or cakes, can be chocolate, white, or coconut.

MENU NO. 2

Chicken Bouillon
Warm Baked Ham with Mustard Sauce
Scalloped Potatoes or Hashed in Cream Potatoes*
Cole Slaw
Pickles
Buttered Parkerhouse Rolls
Apple Pie with Cheese or Ice Cream

Add celery to the bouillon. Watercress Soup* is an alternative. Baked beans are optional to go with the ham.

You may also want to have a fresh fruit platter.

MENU NO. 3

Hot Cream of Mushroom Soup
Cut-up Fried Chicken
New England Baked Beans
Chili Sauce
Molded Fruit Salad
Poppy Seed Dressing*
Cloverleaf or Butter Rolls
Fruit Tarts

For the soup, be sure to grind the mushrooms very finely.

MENU NO. 4

Vegetable or Minestrone Soup
Hot Roast Turkey
Mushroom Pie* or Spinach Pie*
Platter of Sliced Tomatoes
Pineapple with Cottage Cheese Bowl
Paprika Dressing*
Assorted Small Hard Rolls
Assorted Layer Cakes

The turkey should be large, depending on the approximate number of people you expect, and of course should be served with stuffing. In summer you can serve it cold.

Place the cottage cheese bowl in the center of the pineapple slices.

The layer cakes may be coconut, chocolate, or spice.

MENU NO. 5

Mushroom Bouillon or Chicken Bouillon
Standing Ribs of Beef or Sirloin Butt Roast of Beef
Hashed in Cream Potatoes*
Broccoli Croquettes* or Green Beans with Almonds
Tossed Green Salad
Rose Toth Dressing*
Baked Custard, Coconut Meringue, or Lemon Meringue Pie

MENU NO. 6

Hot Corn Soup or Hot Old-fashioned Bean Soup
Platter of Sandwiches
Deviled Egg Halves
Relish Tray and Spiced Fruit
Hot Macaroni and Cheese Casserole
Assorted Cupcakes

Make the bean soup thin if you use it.

The sandwich platter is made up of shaved ham, roast beef, turkey, chicken or tuna salad sandwiches.

In summer, you may substitute macaroni salad for the casserole. A fresh fruit platter is optional.

The cupcakes can come from your baker.

Part Two

Entertaining at Home Around the Clock

CHAPTER 1

BRUNCH

The task of planning meals goes on from early morning until late at night. I won't have anything to say here about breakfast. It's one meal people choose for themselves, and nearly everybody has decided ideas concerning it. There are nearly as many variations in breakfast menus as there are people. The tendency is to eat pretty much the same thing day after day, unless one is entertaining or eating away from home. Even then, I've noticed that it is easier for people to order breakfast in a restaurant than any other meal.

Let's skip breakfast, then, and begin with that in-between meal we call brunch. In the past five years the brunch has become more popular. People seem to have more time early in the day; ladies, especially, seem more at leisure and like to wear informal clothes to these affairs. Brunch is usually, in fact, an informal gathering, relaxed and fresh. Hostesses like it because it's easier at midday to get guests who may have too many invitations later on.

We have several popular menus for brunch, and here they are:

MENU NO. 1

Chicken Pancakes
Pickled Watermelon Rind   *Porcupine Celery**
Fresh Fruit Platter
Poppy Seed Dressing*
Sesame Melba Toast*   *Tiny Pecan Rolls*
Tiny Danish Pastries

The pancakes are regular Swedish crêpes, filled with chopped creamed chicken and mushrooms, and served with a hot Watercress Sauce*.

MENU NO. 2

Spinach Crêpes
Mushroom Sauce
Sesame Melba Toast
Raw Vegetable Tray
Spiced Fruit Compote
Piping-hot Coffee Rings

Add freshly chopped spinach to the crêpe batter before frying. Fill with chopped creamed chicken.

Get two or three varieties of coffee rings from your baker.

MENU NO. 3

*Mushroom Fritters**
*Spinach Sauce**
Hot Canadian Bacon
*Molded Fresh Fruit Salad or Bing Cherry Salad Mold**
Parsley-buttered Melba Toast   Cheese Sticks
Pink Grapefruit Sherbet
Thin Shortbread Cookies

MENU NO. 4

Hot Corned Beef Hash
Curried Eggs
Melba Toast   Toasted English Muffins
Cantaloupe Wedges

The eggs should be mildly curried; they are simply creamed hard-cooked eggs with curry powder added to cream sauce. Goldenrod eggs may be substituted.

Serve ice cream or sherbet with the cantaloupe.

MENU NO. 5

Turkey Hashed in Cream
Ham Cornucopias
Tiny Sweet Rolls   Corn Sticks
Bunch of Grapes Salad
Peach or Cherry Cobbler

To form the cornucopias roll up thinly sliced ham with rice to which grated orange rind and diced onion have been added.

For the salad, rub pear halves with chutney cream cheese or with cream cheese blended with Worcestershire sauce, candied ginger, and orange rind, then cover with grape halves.

Make the cobbler with biscuit dough.

MENU NO. 6

Broiled Little Sausages
Sautéed Chicken Livers in Onion Butter
Cottage Cheese Blintzes*
Crusty Zwieback or Holland Rusks
Honeydew Melon Wedges
Benne Seed Cookies

Serve the blintzes with bowls of sour cream, blueberries, strawberries, and tart orange sauce.

MENU NO. 7

Orange Baskets
Crisp Bacon Strips
Scrambled Eggs
Chicken Livers
Toast
Heated Kuchen

Fill the orange baskets with cut-up fresh oranges.

Chicken livers are optional, sautéed with butter and onions.

Butter the toast lightly.

MENU NO. 8

Small Ham Steaks
Rice and Cheese Balls
Broiled Tomatoes
Cracked Wheat Bread Toasted with Peanut Butter
Assorted Melon Balls with Chopped Mint
Tiny Sweet Rolls

Barbecue or charcoal-broil the ham steaks.
Roll the rice and cheese balls in cornflakes or Rice Krispies.
Sprinkle mustard bread crumbs on the broiled tomatoes.

MENU NO. 9

Shish Kebab
Crisp Fried Cornmeal Mush
*Rhubarb Strawberry Mold**
Hot Danish Pastries

Make the shish kebab of cubed ham, chunks of chicken breast, and mushroom caps. Add a kumquat or spiced peach if you wish, and charcoal-broil.

Serve syrup with the cornmeal mush. Fried hominy may be substituted.

CHAPTER 2

LUNCHEONS

Luncheon may be the most varied meal in the whole culinary scale, particularly in America. What is eaten depends much on the kind of gathering and its purpose. Many a businessman tortures his stomach with the usual indigestible business lunch. Ladies lunching together are great salad or sandwich eaters. To many people, a lunch is a sandwich and coffee, or Coke, or a malted.

Entertaining at luncheon does provide a hostess with an opportunity to use considerable ingenuity and adapt her menu to the mood of the moment as well as to the guests. There is always the danger of repeating standard formulas, but since we have catered so many hundreds of luncheons, I think I can recommend here a wide variety of them which will not be commonplace.

MENU NO. 1

A Bouquet of Salads

On a dinner plate arrange three lettuce cups. Fill them with any of the following combinations:

Chicken Salad	*Chicken Salad*
Fruit Salad	*Fruit Salad*
Tomato Aspic with Cottage Cheese	*Mixed Cooked Vegetables Vinaigrette*

Crab Meat Salad
Fruit Salad
Whole Tomato scooped out,
and filled with Cottage
Cheese

Shrimp Salad
Vegetables Vinaigrette
Cucumber Aspic with Cottage
Cheese

Fresh Salmon Salad
Cucumber Aspic with Cottage
Cheese
Asparagus Vinaigrette

Chicken Salad with Apple
Tomato Aspic with Diced
Cauliflower
Melon Balls

Chicken Salad with Grapes
Waldorf Salad with Pineapple
Tomato Aspic with Egg Salad

Chicken Salad with Almonds
Fresh Fruit Salad
Perfection Molded Aspic

Any of these bouquet luncheon plates can be put on the table ten minutes or so ahead of time, to make the tables look bright and appetizing with a minimum of fuss. You can put half a stuffed egg in the center if you wish. Be sure the lettuce is really ice cold and crisp. It's always enhanced with tufts of watercress.

Little else is needed, whether this luncheon is served to ladies or to men. Even men are weight watchers at noon and businessmen get drowsy if they eat too heavily. In cooler months, the salad bouquet lunch can be introduced with a small cup of hot double-strength beef consommé, tomato bouillon with a thin slice of orange, chicken soup, or even thin cream soup. But always serve it only after it reaches a rolling boil!

Any kind of bread or roll is acceptable with the salads. Sometimes it's a change just to make bread and butter sandwiches, or have a bread tray with three or four varieties. People sometimes get tired of rolls—they have them so often—and the breads, if fresh and crusty, are a tempting change.

Since the salad plate is fairly hearty, desserts can be a problem. For ladies, I often serve no more than a macaroon, a French Twirl*, lace cookies, or chocolate-covered mints. But some ladies are always disappointed if you don't serve desserts. Any kind of sherbet is acceptable but it's a much overworked idea.

One of my favorite desserts in cold weather is Crème Brûlée. This is a rich custard baked in very shallow Pyrex dishes heavily covered with brown sugar and put under the broiler until quite dark. It should be passed in the dish so that the diet-conscious can take only a small portion. A strained Tart Red Raspberry Sauce* is a delightful topper. A newer version is Angel Food Crème Brûlée*.

Another light dessert at noon is cake, either angel food, chiffon, or coconut. Sometimes I think we make a mistake in not offering more cake desserts at noon. The portions can be very small. And some women are really fond of petits fours.

MENU NO. 2

Ladies who visit tearooms at noon are familiar with the frequent use of cheese rarebits. They're good, particularly during the winter months. This is a favorite combination:

Cheddar Cheese Rarebit over Melba Toast
Slivered or Whole Toasted Almonds
Crinkled Crisp Bacon
Small Fruit Salad or Vegetable Aspic
Tiny Party Cupcakes

The unfrosted cupcakes are scooped out well and filled with your favorite ice cream or custard filling.

MENU NO. 3

*Artichoke Rarebit**
*Kumquat Orange Molded Salad**
*Paprika Dressing**
Chocolate-covered Mints

Add a dash of sherry to the rarebit if desired, and serve over dry Melba toast.

MENU NO. 4

Baked Half Breasts of Chicken with Dried Beef in Cream Sauce
Giant Mushroom Caps
Melon Ball Salad
Tiny Sweet Rolls   Tiny Scones
Miniature Fresh Strawberry Tarts

Add a few sweetbreads and water chestnuts to the breasts of chicken.

Insert a slice of tomato in each mushroom cap.

MENU NO. 5

Chicken Mushroom Timbales
Grape Sauce*
Salad
Poppy Seed Dressing*
Cherry Curly Rolls
Fresh Pineapple Wedges

You can omit the mushrooms in the timbales if you like.

Spinach Sauce* may be substituted.

Make the salad with sliced oranges, cucumbers, and chopped chives.

Stiffened cherry pie filling is rolled into the sweet roll dough to make cherry curly rolls.

MENU NO. 6

Little Glazed Ham Balls*
Spinach Timbales
Molded Apple Waldorf Salad
Tiny Cheese Biscuits
Chocolate Coconut Macaroons

Serve the Ham Balls* in a thin mushroom gravy made with consommé as a base. A ham loaf may be substituted.

Bake the timbales in custard cups.

Add seedless grapes or maraschino raisins to the salad. These can be purchased at any gourmet food shop.

MENU NO. 7

Ham and Celery Pie
Tomatoes Stuffed with Seedless Grapes Vinaigrette
Sesame Hard Rolls or Sesame Melba Sticks*
Chocolate Chiffon Cake

This is how to make the pie. Into a cheese pastry crust, layer braised julienne celery, diagonally cut, that has been cooked in consommé with chives. Add slices of ham and a mushroom sauce. Sprinkle mustard bread crumbs on top. Peas may be added if you wish.

Skin tomatoes, scoop out and stuff with a mixture of seedless grapes, diced avocado and diced celery which has been mixed with a vinaigrette dressing (PLATE VI).

MENU NO. 8

Individual Ham Loaves
Creamed Diced Celery
Broiled Tomato Halves
Philadelphia Sticky Buns
Fresh Sliced Peaches

Put just a whisper of curry—*very* delicate—in the celery and sprinkle it heavily with toasted pecans.

MENU NO. 9

Hungarian Gulyás*
Fluffy Rice
Tossed Green Salad
Crusty French Bread with Sesame Butter
Pineapple Chiffon Pie

MENU NO. 10

Shrimp Salad
Tomato Wedges
Relish Tray
Broiled Grapefruit Halves

Omit celery from the relish tray.
Lemon meringue pie may be substituted for the grapefruit.

MENU NO. 11

Hot Cream of Mushroom Soup
Sandwiches
Relish Tray   Sliced Tomatoes
Blueberry Tarts

Make the sandwiches man-sized: corned beef on rye, turkey on whole wheat, shaved roast beef on white.

Serve the blueberry tarts with a small scoop of ice cream.

MENU NO. 12

Watercress Soup*
Toasted Shaved Ham Sandwiches on Rye Bread
Hot Toasted Mushroom Sandwiches* on White Bread
Grapefruit and Avocado Salad
Paprika Dressing*
Rice Pudding with Strawberries

MENU NO. 13

Finger Sandwiches
Assortment of Finger Sweets

This is called a petite luncheon and is popular with lecture groups. Serve trays of the sandwiches made with whole wheat and white bread: chicken salad, tuna fish, egg salad, dried beef, cottage cheese and watercress, plain watercress, Avocado Pinovers*, ripe olive cream cheese with toasted pecans or almonds.

MENU NO. 14

English Grill
Crusty Hard Rolls   *Poppy Seed Rolls*
Sweet Butter
Salad
Fresh Strawberry Tarts

This menu is for an important business lunch.

The English grill consists of (for each person) one double loin lamb chop, one little sausage, one chicken liver, one or two mushroom caps stuffed with stems, bread, and onion; and a slice of broiled tomato. Garnish plate with a sheaf of watercress or, if you like, serve broiled pears and have a tomato and cottage cheese salad.

The tarts should be medium-sized. As alternatives: very small pieces of baked custard pie or slender pieces of Dutch apple pie or blueberry tarts.

MENU NO. 15

Melon Wedges
Individual English Meat Pies
Crusty Hard Rolls
Swiss Cheese Salad*
Snow Pudding

Another menu for the important business luncheon.

Melon wedges should be small. As an alternative, serve cantaloupe and honeydew wedges in ice.

Serve the meat pies in glass casseroles, with pastry crust only on top. Omit potatoes. Be sure the meat is of high quality and tender, and include carrots, mushrooms, and braised celery, with a few peas.

A horseradish mayonnaise dressing accompanies the salad.

Put a few blueberries on the snow pudding.

MENU NO. 16

Fresh Bing Cherries
Swedish Meatballs
Brown Mushroom Gravy
Noodle Casserole
Relish Tray
Coconut Cream Tarts

Serve the cherries with stems on. An alternative: fresh strawberries with stems on, dipped in powdered sugar.

Instead of the casserole: noodle croquettes rolled in cornflakes.

MENU NO. 17

White Salad
Poppy Seed or Caraway Melba Toast
Crusty Dill Bread
Tangerine or Apricot Sherbet

This is a big salad. Make it with slivers of chicken breast, raw fresh mushrooms, marinated artichoke hearts, braised celery, peeled crisp apple in a white mayonnaise with sour cream added, and plenty of celery seeds. Garnish with white asparagus spears. It will be especially grandiose if you have a perky stalk of Belgian endive sticking up.

The Melba toast should be pencil slim.

If this menu is served in winter, add a *thin* pea soup, blended with celery soup, beef consommé, and tomato.

Garnish the sherbet with mandarin oranges.

MENU NO. 18

Cold Stuffed Tomatoes
Deviled Egg Halves with Avocado Stuffing
Hot Popovers
Lime Pie

Skin the tomatoes, scoop out and fill with julienne tongue, peas, celery, and artichoke hearts, or Artichoke Mustard Relish. This relish is sold in food stores in Georgia and South Carolina. If it is not available in your neighborhood, grind mustard pickle and artichoke hearts together and you will have an approximation of the relish.

MENU NO. 19

Stuffed Celery
Chopped Sirloin of Beef Hamburgers on Toasted Buns
Salad
Vanilla Junket

Stuff the celery with soft Cheddar cheese and toasted almonds.

Make the salad with horseradish julienne beets (*see* Cherry Horseradish Beets*), celery, and raw apple in consommé aspic, with a dash of vinegar added. Serve with Russian dressing.

MENU NO. 20

Crab Meat Salad in Avocado Halves
Cherry Tomatoes
Melba Toast Triangles
Strawberry Chiffon Cake

Fill the avocado halves with crab meat salad and sprinkle with grated orange rind.

Serve sliced tomato garnish instead of the cherry tomatoes, if you like.

Put fresh strawberries on the cake.

MENU NO. 21

Grilled Ham Steaks
Gingersnap Gravy
Hot Apple Fritters with Powdered Cinnamon Sugar
Grapefruit and Orange Salad
Paprika Dressing*
Thin Corn Sticks
Chocolate Fudge Brownies

The ham steaks should be small, or you can use half a larger one.

Gingersnap gravy is made by adding gingersnap crumbs to a traditional raisin sauce.

Put mint fudge icing on the brownies.

MENU NO. 22

Braised Lamb Shoulder Stew
French-fried Cauliflower*
Spiced Peaches
Butterscotch Pie

The stew should be really brown. Serve with baking powder biscuits made with chopped green onion in the dough.

Make the pie with a graham cracker crust.

MENU NO 23

Hot Ground Beef Pastry Turnovers
Spinach Sauce* or Mushroom Sauce
Mexican Vegetable Salad Aspic*
Broiled Peach Halves

Serve the aspic on a slice of tomato.

Horseradish sour cream and brown sugar are spread on the peach halves.

MENU NO. 24

Hot or Cold Whitefish à la Rhine*
French-fried Cucumbers*
English Pea Timbales*
Plain Tomato Aspic
Fresh Coconut Chiffon Cake

Sprinkle rosemary on the cucumbers.

Add whole peas to the pea timbales.

The aspic goes on a slice of orange; add grated orange rind to the mayonnaise.

Layer cake may be substituted for the coconut chiffon cake.

MENU NO. 25

Stuffed Chicken Breasts
Baked Bananas
Pumpernickel Watercress Sandwiches
Fresh Fruit

Stuffing for the chicken breasts is bacon, pecans, and orange rind, with bread and celery.

Dip the bananas first in egg and Rice Krispies, quickly French-fry them, then bake. Dust with cinnamon and nutmeg.

Fruit may be served either whole or cut up.

MENU NO. 26

Medium Sliced Ham Cornucopias
Celery Sauce
Peas with Chopped Fresh Iceberg Lettuce
Toasted Peanut Cinnamon Buns
Chocolate Tarts

Fill the cornucopias with mashed potatoes to which Cheddar cheese has been added.

Add flakes of finely shaved apple to the celery sauce.
Add the iceberg lettuce to the peas at the last minute.
Chocolate chiffon pie may be substituted for the tarts.

MENU NO. 27

Layered Cheese Meringue Casserole
Crusty Rolls or Hearth Bread
Blueberries and Sherbet

To make the casserole, line a deep pie dish with a regular pie
shell and bake. Then fill with layer of ground beef (already browned
with onion), a layer of creamed spinach or broccoli. Beat egg whites
as though to make meringue, add a pinch of curry powder, a little
dehydrated cheese, and a pinch of salt. Pile up high and bake until
golden brown. When pie is removed from oven, dust lightly with
Parmesan cheese or with herbs. This is a meal in itself, but you
could add wilted lettuce with bacon.

Sprinkle the blueberries over the sherbet.

AFTERNOON TEA

Now that so many people spend their holidays in those parts of the West Indies with a British tradition, or have fallen in love with London (a current American passion), the tea and high tea are experiencing a popular revival in coffee-loving America, after nearly a century of neglect.

Tea *does* give you a pickup, coffee drinkers notwithstanding. The afternoon tea can be, and usually is, a simple affair, but there is also the much more elaborate high tea, better known abroad than here.

There are all kinds of idiosyncrasies in tea-making. Some of the British pour in the cream or milk first, then the tea. Others prefer lemon, or thin slices of lemon with clove. One way to satisfy everybody is to make the tea fairly strong. Even if you use teabags, *always* use a teapot, and never offer the guest a cup with a teabag in it. Have a pot of hot water handy to dilute the tea to exactly the right preference for each person. To my mind, there is no substitute for fine English bone china. Tea never tastes the same in thick pottery cups. Don't save your expensive collection for posterity; use it daily to delight yourself and your friends.

Here are some simple suggestions for tea. I won't dignify them as menus by numbering them.

Heated Rye Krisp
Tart Orange Marmalade or Currant Jelly
Wedges of York State Cheese
Jelly Ribbon Pound Cake

Lightly butter the Rye Krisp.

Toasted Cinnamon Bread
Creamed Cottage Cheese with Chopped Dried Beef Sandwiches
Plain Pound Cake or Florence Cake

Toasted Raisin Bread
Triscuits with Cheddar Cheese
Macaroons

Raisin bread is lightly buttered.

Toasted Pecan Bread
Unsweetened Dried Prunes and Apricots
Tiny Assorted Fruit Tarts

Toasted English Muffins
Longhorn Cheese and Crackers
Thin Peanut Butter Cookies   Chocolate Chip Cookies

With the muffins, serve plain or parsley butter and greengage plum jam.

Anise Bread with Cream Cheese
Whole Wheat Bread with Honey Butter
Coconut Macaroons

Use plain butter with the anise bread, if you prefer. Serve as open-faced slices.

Orange Cranberry Bread
Watercress Rolls on White Bread
Chocolate Macaroons   Lace Cookies

Banana Bread with Butter or Cream Cheese
Ham Salad Pinwheel Sandwiches
Tiny Chocolate Cupcakes

Lettuce Sandwiches on Whole Wheat and White Bread
Ripe Olive Cream Cheese Sandwiches
Tiny Spice Cupcakes or Spice Squares

For the lettuce sandwiches, use crisp iceberg lettuce, with chopped chive or green onion and mustard mayonnaise.
Dust the cream cheese with toasted sesame seeds.

Tiny Scones
Toasted Macadamia Nuts
Chocolate Thin Mints

Break the scones with a fork and toast them. Brush with lemon butter.

Cheese Buns
Peanut Butter Spread
Little Wedges of Fruit Cake   Chocolate Macaroons

Split, toast, and butter the cheese buns.
The spread is made with peanut butter, crisp bacon bits, and honey. Serve it separately.

Boston Brown Bread Sandwiches
Pimiento Cream Cheese or Olive Cream Cheese Sandwiches
Fruited Meringue Kisses

Tiny Blueberry Muffins
Crackers with York State Cheese
Lemon Snap Cookies

Spicy Hot Gingerbread
Fresh Bing Cherries

The gingerbread may be plain or frosted with lemon icing.

Hot Whole Wheat Muffins
Apple Butter and Regular Butter
Puffed Rice Candy

Crusty Fresh Poppy Seed Bread
Cherry Tomatoes Stuffed with Chicken Salad
Oatmeal Cookies

Serve the bread very thinly sliced, and buttered.

I could go on with a hundred other simple suggestions like these, but perhaps I've given enough to inspire you to make your own tea combinations, if you don't find what you like here or want to add to the list.

High Tea

In England people often are sparing with the dessert at luncheon and wait until four or five o'clock (sometimes even later in Scotland) for a high tea. This kind of entertaining can be done if you feel you don't want to have a full dinner for your guests, but nevertheless would like to have something a little special. There are also still a few people in the world who don't drink, although their ranks seem to be growing thinner, and for them the high tea is a splendid substitute for a cocktail party.

In Barbados, my father's birthplace, it is quite customary to seat everyone at a very long table loaded with goodies, and the guests pass trays around and around. That may not be practical here, so probably you will want to have a buffet tea table with your close friends pouring.

Not everyone likes tea—this is particularly true in larger groups—so we recommend serving coffee as well. In summer, do offer iced tea too, or Iced Persian Chocolate*.

As you can see from the menus that follow, the high tea is really a meal in itself.

MENU NO. 1

Sliced Corned Beef Sandwiches
Breast of Turkey Sandwiches
Watercress Rolls
Tiny Ground Beef Pastry Turnovers
*Tiny Hot Toasted Mushroom Sandwiches**
Small Stuffed Cream Puff Shells
Fresh Coconut Layer Cake
Little Shortbread Cookies
Tiny Jam Tarts
Unblanched Salted Almonds   Pecan Pectin Jellies

Make the corned beef sandwiches on pumpernickel or rye bread. Use loads of cress for the watercress rolls, and plenty of cream cheese and butter. Leave tufts of cress extruding.

Dust the turnovers with sesame seeds.

Stuff the cream puff shells with crab meat or shrimp salad.

MENU NO. 2

Hot Tiny Mushroom Tarts
Toasted Apricot Sandwiches
Closed Peanut Butter and Crisp Bacon Sandwiches
*Cold Chicken Salad Envelope Sandwiches**
Roast Beef Sandwiches with Horseradish Butter or Mayonnaise
Stuffed Artichoke Hearts
*Lettuce and Roquefort Brownberry Sandwiches**
Chocolate Cake Squares
Filled Finger Macaroons
Cinnamon Puff Pastry Fans   Pastel Mint Wafers

Soak dried apricots a couple of hours to make them soft. Add a lump of butter, brown sugar, and cinnamon. Place on small rounds of toasted whole wheat bread and broil until butter bubbles.

For the peanut butter and bacon sandwiches, be sure the bread is really thin.

Roast beef should be pinkish and shaved thin.

Stuff the artichoke hearts with minced corned beef.

Chocolate Cake Squares are baked in a single layer pan, iced with penuche boiled icing, and sprinkled with shaved semi-sweet chocolate.

The Puff Pastry Fans are made with brown sugar.

MENU NO. 3

Little Shrimp Biscuits with Artichoke Mustard Relish*
Hot Open Wimpies
Ivy League Triangles*
Caramelized Bacon*
Cucumber Sandwiches
Stuffed Celery
Flemish Cornucopia Sandwiches
Butterscotch Tarts
Whole Giant Strawberries
Hermit Fruit Drop Cookies
Angel Food Cake
Almonds

For the Shrimp Biscuits, make baking powder biscuits, split, and butter. Insert a tiny shrimp and a sliver of green onion in each one.

Wimpies are little hamburgers on toast or in buns.

As an alternative to the bacon you might like cold wedges of roast pork, lean and tender, with gooseberry chutney dip—a real delicacy.

Make the cucumber sandwiches with cream cheese and chives on whole wheat bread.

Stuff the celery with olive cream cheese, or with ripe olive cream cheese, and sprinkle with toasted sesame seeds.

Flemish Cornucopia Sandwiches are made with dried beef, cottage cheese, loads of watercress, a few capers, and black pepper. Use a thin carrot stamen.

Put little drops of meringue on the butterscotch tarts.

Dip the giant strawberries in melted pastel chocolate.

For the angel food cake, use seafoam boiled icing or divinity fudge icing with lime added.

Dip the almonds in melted pastel chocolate.

MENU NO. 4

Fresh Mint Sandwiches
Strawberry Canapés* Open on Pineapple Cream Cheese
Rolled Asparagus Sandwiches
Curried Chicken Salad Open Canapés
Dried Beef Rolls with Horseradish Cream Cheese
Tiny Hot Biscuits
Crab Meat in Hot Buttered Bread Cups
Broiled Stuffed Mushroom Caps
Oysters Wrapped in Bacon
Plain French Twirls*
Lemon Crunch Cake
Coffee Custard in Chocolate Cups
Maple Nut Meringues

Make the mint sandwiches with loads of chopped mint, lemon rind, and cream cheese.

When making the Strawberry Canapés, slice off part of the berries sideways so they won't roll.

With the hot biscuits, used minced country ham or deviled ham.

Fill the bread cups with crab meat Dewey or creamed crab meat with sherry.

Mushroom caps can be stuffed with stems, bread, and onion, or with chicken livers.

Graham cracker crumbs are baked into the sides of the lemon cake.

The coffee custard is of the little pot de crème type, and is served in semi-sweet chocolate cups.

MENU NO. 5

Hot Asparagus Pinover Sandwiches*
Chicken, Fine Noodle, and Mushroom Croquettes
Little Wieners in Pastry
Cheddar Cheese Fondue Squares
Cranberry Orange Bread and Butter Sandwiches
Open Tomato and Cucumber Canapés
Salami Cornucopias
Open Lobster Canapés
Walnut Spice Cookies
Tiny Cherry Tarts
French Twirls* with Mocha Cream
Little White Cupcakes

Brush the asparagus sandwiches with sesame butter and broil lightly on both sides.

The wieners are wrapped in regular pie pastry or cheese pie pastry and baked.

For the Tomato and Cucumber Canapés, spread rounds of bread with anchovy or chive cream cheese and top with thin slice of tomato and thin slice of cucumber.

Use green pepper cream cheese in the cornucopias, which can also be made with summer sausage instead of salami.

Use a mustard remoulade spread and capers on the lobster canapés.

Frost the cupcakes with vanilla and chocolate icing.

MENU NO. 6

Hot Pecan Croquettes*
Broiled Sausages Wrapped in Bacon
Hot Shaved Ham and Sesame Sandwiches
Cheese Soufflé Dreams*
Chopped Tongue Open Danish Sandwiches*
Swiss Cheese and Lettuce Sandwiches
Egg Salad Sandwiches on Whole Wheat Bread
Tuna Fish Cornucopias   Tiny Fruit Tarts

Bananas wrapped in bacon could be a substitute for the sausages.

Make the Swiss cheese and lettuce sandwiches with shaved Swiss cheese and mustard mayonnaise.

Make the egg salad sandwiches Envelope* fashion, rolled, or as fingers.

Tuna fish salad can be served in bread cornucopias (sometimes called calla lilies).

MENU NO. 7

Hot Banana Fritters
Toasted Canadian Bacon Sandwiches
English Muffins
Rolled Chicken Salad Sandwiches
Kumquat Halves with Walnut Cream Cheese
Cucumber Chunks Stuffed with Salmon
Ladyfingers or Sponge Drops
Chocolate Chip Mint Meringue Drops
Rice Krispie Cookies
*Tiny Coconut Snowballs**

Serve the banana fritters (or apple fritters if preferred) with brown sugar syrup, with a dash of spice added.

To make the Canadian Bacon Sandwiches, shave the bacon very thin and layer it 4 or 5 slices thick. Moisten with mild mustard mayonnaise, butter and melted cheese. Place under broiler.

Spread the English muffins with onion, parsley and soft Cheddar cheese, and broil until cheese bubbles.

Add pimiento to the chicken salad sandwiches.

Add a bit of Worcestershire sauce to the walnut cream cheese.

Scoop out the cucumber chunks and fill with salmon salad.

Fill the ladyfingers or sponge drops with tart currant jelly.

MENU NO. 8

Thin Wedges of Cooked Chicken Breast
Miniature Meat Pies
Sweetbreads and Dried Beef in Little Bread Cups
Toasted Raisin Cinnamon Bread
Spiced Meat Wedges
Chiquita Rolled Sandwiches
Fresh Spears of Pineapple
Avocado Dip with Pistachio Nuts
Cheese and Cracker Tray
Plunketts with Custard
Gaufrettes* Rolled with Chocolate Buttercream
Almond Brittle   Thin Chocolate Mints

Dip the chicken in beaten egg and crushed cashew nuts. French-fry quickly and then keep hot on cookie sheet.

Fill the bread cups with creamed chopped sweetbreads, dried beef, and mushrooms.

To make the Spiced Meat Wedges, take 6 slices of thin bologna and spread with green watercress cream cheese. Stack slices and let them get firm, then slice into wedges.

Make Chiquita Rolled Sandwiches with ripe olives, chopped green onions, green pepper cream cheese, American cheese, and catsup.

Plunketts are little round unfrosted white butter cakes. They are often made in crinkled tart pans and served with a vanilla custard sauce.

MENU NO. 9

Little Cottage Cheese Blintzes*
Toasted Scones with Corned Beef
Open Mushroom Sandwiches* with Crisp Bacon
Dill Cream Cheese Sandwiches
Tiny Open Date Butter Sandwiches with Walnut Halves
Stuffed Tender Raw Carrots
Little Chocolate and Maple Eclairs
Tiny Whipped Cream or Marshmallow Lady Locks
Tiny Gooseberry Tarts
Apricot Jam Cookies

You may use plain crêpes for the blintzes. In either case, serve them with bowls of sour cream, lingonberry or blueberry sauce, raspberry or strawberry sauce.

Spread the toasted scones with minced corned beef and sweet pepper relish.

Put a slivered dill pickle on top of the dill cream cheese sandwiches.

Scoop out the carrots and fill with cold curried pea purée.

Lady Locks are standard bakery products called cream horns in some parts of the country; they are made with puff pastry wrapped around metal tubes.

MENU NO. 10

Tiny Fresh Parkerhouse Rolls with Ham
Stuffed Celery
Tiny Apricot Tarts

Fill the rolls with shaved ham and sweet pickle relish.

Stuff the celery with mashed avocado and lemon rind, with a little cream cheese added for body.

CHAPTER 4

THE COCKTAIL HOUR

Many caterers, I believe, feel the same way I do about the cocktail party—that Americans, especially, tend to linger too long and then don't appreciate or can't enjoy the food prepared for dinner. If people are going to drink, they should eat, which is the reason for having food at cocktail parties. Yet the hors d'oeuvres ought to be kept light and dainty if supper follows. If no supper is being provided, however, and there are no dinner plans at all, then the snacks can be heartier.

Several items in the suggested menus that follow will appear more than once in this book. The idea is that if you miss them in one place, you'll certainly see them in another.

If dinner is being planned, we like to complete that menu first because we don't want to take anything away from it by whatever we might be serving at the cocktail hour. For instance, if you're planning to serve ham or roast loin of pork for dinner, obviously no ham or bacon should be used for the canapés or hors d'oeuvres.

One of the most common questions we hear is, "What's the difference between a canapé and an hors d'oeuvre?" To some extent they are used synonymously, but in our own terminology, when the appetizer is without bread, it's an hors d'oeuvre. Most canapés have a bread base. Diet-conscious people object to bready canapés, but the fact is that bread isn't nearly as fattening as whatever is put on it.

If the hostess has to make her own canapés well in advance, say in the morning, it's far better to use firm bread than crackers. The latter get limp very quickly and will be difficult to pick up if they have moist fillings, not to mention the departure of their appeal.

Certain kinds of canapés are better if the bread is day-old or if it is toasted. A variety of shapes is desirable. We've found it much quicker to use bread sliced thin, lengthwise. In our kitchens we spread the long slice of bread first with the salad mixture, then cut with the cutters. After that, the filling left on the skeleton bread is scraped off, not to be wasted. Our company is especially famous for its hors d'oeuvres and canapés. As I've mentioned before, we have made as many as 80,000 in a day at the holiday season.

Can canapés be frozen? Many of the hot variety can be, but we don't recommend the freezing of cold canapés. Once they are thoroughly thawed they become very limp and soggy. Many can be prepared twenty-four hours ahead and simply kept in a regular refrigerator, but *not* a freezer.

Nearly everything listed here as a French-fried item is planned so that it can be made early in the day and reheated. We know that some things taste marvelous when they're French-fried at the last minute, but it isn't practical for most hostesses, or for the help in the kitchen. In addition, frying produces smoke and very few kitchens can get rid of smoke entirely. Personally, I don't object to items *very quickly* fried in vegetable oil, but they should be in the hot grease just long enough to seal them over, if they're croquettes or balls, and to get crispy brown. Then, just before serving, they can be placed on cookie sheets and heated piping hot and made browner, if need be, under the broiler.

If you live in an apartment or in small quarters and have quite a few bacon-wrapped items, do these ahead of time too. It won't hurt them to be done three or four hours ahead. Drain off as much of the bacon fat as possible, then put them under the broiler to get crispy. A little aroma of bacon or ham is pleasant, but try to avoid smoke and fumes.

And that's enough for preparation. Here are fifteen cocktail party menus:

MENU NO. 1

California Snow Pea Pods, Stuffed*
Stuffed Artichoke Hearts
Stuffed Short Stalks of Celery
Macadamia Nuts
French-fried Mushrooms
Smoked Sturgeon Blintzes*
Tomato Cheese Rounds

Canned artichoke hearts are acceptable. Cut them in half, drain on paper towels, and stuff with a dab of sour cream and Danish caviar, or with deviled tongue (PLATE I).

Stuff the celery stalks with anchovy cream cheese, sprinkle with chopped parsley, and lay an anchovy filet on top, or chop up the anchovy filet in the cheese.

Dip the mushrooms in egg and cracker crumbs. Dust lightly with Lowry salt as they come from oven.

The miniature blintzes can be made ahead, put in a foil pan or on a cookie sheet, and heated at the last minute.

The Tomato Cheese Rounds are made with a slice of tomato and a thin slice of American cheese. Use firm but not overripe tomatoes.

MENU NO. 2

Mr. Jiggs's Brussels Sprouts*
Cold Chunks of Lobster on Picks
Deviled Egg Halves
Halves of Shrimp Wrapped with Hot Bacon
Hot Montreal Sardines
Hot Baked Chicken Legs
Whole Pecans

Serve mustard remoulade sauce as a dip with the lobster chunks. For the deviled egg halves (they can be deviled egg rings), put a small dab of caviar on some and tiny pickled onions on others.

To prepare the shrimp, put a small mound of curried wild rice on a half shrimp, wrap in bacon, and bake on wire racks at 300° F. for 20 to 25 minutes. It keeps people guessing.

To make Hot Montreal Sardines, spread bread fingers with American or Cheddar cheese, top with a small silver sardine, add hand-grated orange rind, and sprinkle with caraway seeds. Run under broiler to heat.

For the Hot Baked Chicken Legs, use tiny broiler-size legs, dip them in beaten egg and chopped cashew nuts, French-fry them early, then reheat on a cookie sheet.

The pecans may be plain or done with garlic salt.

MENU NO. 3

Stuffed Radish Roses
Stuffed Short Stalks of Celery
Crab Cucumber Ring Canapés
Hot Sauerkraut Balls
Hot Tiny Biscuits with Ham
Hot Onion Rings
Mixed Salted Nuts

Stuff the radish roses with chicken liver pâté, then dust over with finely grated egg yolk.

Stuff the celery with a mixture of dried beef, cream cheese, watercress, and capers.

For the Crab Cucumber Ring Canapés, spread whole wheat bread with chive cream cheese and top with cucumber rings filled with crab meat salad.

Fill the hot tiny biscuits with shaved salty ham and spread with Dijon mustard.

Hot Onion Rings are made by spreading the mixture for Cheese Soufflé Dreams* on rounds of toast, topping with thinly sliced raw onion rings. Put melted butter on the onions and broil until cheese puffs.

MENU NO. 4

Fresh Figs with Prosciutto
Orange and Green Pepper Cream Cheese Canapés
Egg Salad on Whole Wheat Bread Canapés
*Finger Crackers Wrapped in Bacon**
Bread Cups Stuffed with Lobster

If figs are in season, cut them in quarters and wrap them in prosciutto ham. Out of season, use thin chunks of honeydew melon.

Spread rounds of bread with a green pepper cream cheese spread, place a thin orange slice on it, and top with a button anchovy.

Edge the egg salad canapés with chopped parsley.

Spread some of the finger crackers with peanut butter, some with Cheddar cheese.

Brush the bread cups with butter and fill with lobster Newburg. You must cut the lobster finely for this.

MENU NO. 5

Ripe Avocado Slivers
Filled Cream Puffs
Filled Cherry Tomatoes
Prune Halves Wrapped in Bacon
Tiny Curried Meatballs
Miniature Shish Kebabs Hawaiian

Serve long slivers of ice-cold ripe avocado that have been dipped in frozen lemonade. They are to be dipped in a chafing dish filled with a mixture of spicy catsup, brown sugar, and Worcestershire sauce (see sauce for Avocado in the Snow*).

Cut off the tops of the cream puff shells and fill them with a bit of fish salad. Garnish with olives.

Put a dab of onion-flavored sour cream and Danish caviar in cherry tomatoes that have been lightly scooped out (PLATE I). In fall, use yellow miniature tomatoes.

Prunes may be halved or quartered. Put a tiny stuffed olive in the center of each prune, then wrap in bacon and broil.

Regular Swedish meatballs may be served instead of the curried meatballs.

The shish kebabs, no longer than three or four inches, are made with shrimp and ham cubes or with shrimp and chicken chunks.

MENU NO. 6

Ham Rolls
Spanish Artichoke Bottoms
Shrimp Canapés
Hot Curried Lamb Balls
Hot Frogs' Legs
Hot Cheddar Cheese Rolls with Sesame Butter
Fritos

Shave thin slices of ham, spread with a mixture of mustard (a few drops of Dijon) and cream cheese, and roll up.

Spanish artichoke bottoms are smaller than the French kind. Slice them and on each one put a dab of green onion sour cream and Danish caviar, or make half with black and half with red caviar.

Shrimp canapés will go further than a shrimp bowl. Spread diamond-shaped bread with green pepper cheese, add the shrimp and top with regular shrimp cocktail sauce.

Lamb balls can be served with or without the addition of chopped chutney.

Frogs' legs should be of the very small variety. They are French-fried and served with a tartar sauce.

MENU NO. 7

Raw French Endive and Raw Cauliflowerets
Miniature Pickled Corn-on-the-Cob Canapés
Smoked Salmon Canapés
Grilled Filet of Beef Tenderloin on Little Sesame Sandwich Buns
Hot Miniature Quiche Lorraine Tarts

For the endive and cauliflowerets, use a fresh dill dip with chopped shrimp and an herb salt dip.

For the Corn-on-the-Cob Canapés, we use half an ear of pickled corn sliced lengthwise, on bread spread with a mixture of dried beef, cottage cheese. watercress, capers, and black pepper.

Arrange strips of smoked salmon diagonally with onion cream cheese on dark rye or pumpernickel bread.

The beef filets should be two-ounce size. You can cook the filet on an electric grill right at the dining room table. Have three kinds of spreads: Artichoke Mustard Relish*, tomato barbecue sauce (thickened with cornstarch and not sweet), and horseradish sour cream sauce. As an alternative to the sandwich buns, use party white or party dill bread.

The tarts can be either plain onion or Swiss cheese with bacon added.

MENU NO. 8

Do-It-Yourself Canapés
Open Turkey Bread Canapé
*Chiquita Rolled Sandwiches**
Bacon-wrapped Small Chicken Livers
Chinese Egg Rolls
Cocktail Wieners or Sausages in Barbecue Sauce

For the Do-It-Yourself Canapés, simply provide flaked smoked salmon, little slices of fresh pumpernickel bread, a bowl of sweet butter, lemon juice, a bowl of capers and a pepper mill.

The turkey bread canapés are on asparagus cream cheese mixed with mayonnaise.

Insert in the chicken livers a slice of water chestnut dipped in soy sauce and brown sugar and broil.

Our Chinese egg rolls are usually made with egg salad as a base, chopped spinach, watercress, and green onion and chopped fresh shrimp. We dip these in raw egg and then in Rice Krispies or cornflakes and then French-fry them. Often we put a little whisper of curry in the mixture. They are a little less rich than egg rolls wrapped in pastry. It is our American version of the Chinese egg roll which one finds in oriental restaurants. Very often we serve a hot mustard sauce as an accompaniment.

MENU NO. 9

Roquefort Onion Cream Cheese Ball with Crackers
Egg Salad Mold
Crisp Party Rye Melba Toast
Garnished Whole Cold Salmon on Platter
Caper Mayonnaise
Dill Party Bread
Hot Tiny Crab Meat Croquettes
Small Barbecued Spareribs
Curried Chicken Balls

Garnish the cheese ball with chopped walnuts and chopped parsley.

Place caviar in center of the egg salad mold.

Roll the croquettes in Rice Krispies.

Spread the spareribs with sweet-sour sauce before broiling.

Roll the chicken balls in toasted coconut. Bake, don't fry.

MENU NO. 10

Open Cold Pork Canapés
Hard Apple Wedges
Open Watercress Cream Cheese Canapés
French-fried Poultry Dressing
Miniature Pizzas with Mushrooms
Crab Nips

For the Cold Pork Canapés, spread fingers of bread with parsley mayonnaise. Slice the pork quite thin.

Leave the skin on the Hard Apple Wedges. Dip the wedges in lemon juice to prevent browning. Prepare a soft Roquefort cream cheese dip, or you can put a little mound on each apple slice.

The Watercress Cream Cheese Canapés are on bread rounds, mounded and fortified with two whole salted cashews and a perky sprig of cress.

To make the Poultry Dressing, dip a small chunk of chicken or turkey stuffing in egg and then in crushed cornflakes. Fry ahead of time, and reheat on cookie sheets.

For the Crab Nips, add sour cream and Parmesan cheese to crab meat, then moisten with mayonnaise and pile on bread rounds.

MENU NO. 11

Tiny Wedges of Whitefish à la Rhine*
Small Open Danish Sandwiches
Pickled Beet and Goose Liver Canapés
French-fried Bluepoint Oysters with Tartar Sauce
Mushroom Caps Stuffed with Ground Beef
Hot Chiquita Rolled Sandwiches*

Put the whitefish on *firm* bread diamonds or else serve forks.

To make the Danish sandwiches, spread dark bread with butter to which you have added horseradish, add shaved corned beef or tongue, and cut in very small triangles.

Make goose liver canapés and stick a tiny wedge of cold pickled beet in each one.

MENU NO. 12

Pickled Button Mushrooms
Pâté Maison
Crab Meat in Dogwood
Hot French-fried Miniature Scallops with Tartar Sauce
Steak Cubes
Chicken Tart Shells

Of course there are many recipes for Pâté Maison. We like ⅓ goose liver, ⅓ chicken liver, ⅓ finely ground ham. Serve with crackers.

For the Crab Meat in Dogwood on bread rounds, make four small mustard cream cheese petals with a pastry tube and put a nest of crab salad in the center.

Cape scallops are best, if you can find them, but in any case they should be the smallest you can buy.

Take tiny 1½-inch cubes of top sirloin of Boston strip steak, broil with Lowry salt, and pass on toothpicks.

Heat together a sweet-sour pineapple onion sauce and chopped chicken and fill tart shell just before serving.

MENU NO. 13

Pickled Shrimp
Medium Sweet Pickle Boats
Raw Zucchini Slices
French-fried Chicken Livers or Chicken Liver Croquettes
Mushroom Pie Pastry or Puff Pastry Turnovers
Pastrami-wrapped Water Chestnuts

Dig into the center of the pickles lengthwise and make a ditch, or boat. Fill with Pâté Maison*. Be sure to have a level bottom so the boat doesn't rock.

Sprinkle Raw Zucchini Slices with Lowry salt after patting with a paper towel. Spread with crab meat salad or with mashed avocado and bacon bits.

MENU NO. 14

Crisp Dilled Long Green Beans
*Cold Turkey Pinovers**
Open Flying Sardine Canapés
French-fried Artichoke Hearts
*Miniature Blintzes**
Ice-box Cheddar Cheese Wafers

Prepare cold spears of turkey Pinover* fashion, and add celery-seed mayonnaise spread with parsley.

To make the Open Flying Sardine Canapés, take oblong rye bread fingers and spread with a mustard onion cream cheese with a pastry tube. Place the sardines erect in the cream cheese.

The Miniature Blintzes are finger-style, the size of a watercress roll. They are filled with cream cheese, chopped green onion, and red caviar.

MENU NO. 15

Corned Beef Pinwheels
Chicken Salad Ovals
Cold Salmon Chunks
Hot Tiny Muffins Stuffed with Shrimp
Broiled Sweetbread Slices
Hot Stuffed Grape Leaves

For the pinwheels, use pumpernickel bread and kosher corned beef salad mixture.

Decorate the chicken salad ovals with half of a Tokay grape in the middle and a seedless grape at each end.

Put the Cold Salmon Chunks on white bread on a cucumber spread, with grated egg white or yolk around the edge.

Bake hominy muffins with chopped onion and watercress in the dough, scoop out the centers, and fill with whole shrimp and Pink Remoulade* or with a shrimp salad mixture. Heat and serve.

The Sweetbread Slices are served with bacon bits on bread spread with a mild cheese.

Grape leaves are obtainable in cans or jars. Stuff them with a mixture of rice, ripe olives, green onion, and tomato paste. You may also add minced cold lamb, along with a little chopped mint and dill. Serve hot.

CHAPTER 5

DINNER

Dinner is by far the most popular kind of entertaining. A sit-down dinner is best. If there are to be only six, eight, ten, or twelve guests, we recommend that guests be seated even if you must resort to family style.

Whenever it's possible, we like to have things that can be prepared early in the day and reheated. Not many people today have much domestic help, if any, and most of the time the hostess is the cook. If that's your case, try to spend as much time as you can with your guests and as little as possible in the kitchen. Even if your meal is simple, it can still be elegant.

One more word to hostesses. Since so many people are conscious of the cholesterol problem, don't hesitate to substitute margarine in any recipe if you think it's advisable for your guests.

MENU NO. 1

Stuffed Eggs in Madrilene Aspic*
Filet of Beef Tenderloin
Glazed Mushroom Caps
Potato Puffs Rolled in Cornflakes
Green Beans "Extravagant"
Porcupine Celery*   *Stone Olives*
Tiny Salt Caraway Sticks
Coffee Baked Alaska*

Serve Triscuits with the first course.

Sauté the green beans with macadamia nuts. It's more work, but they're so much tastier when they're cut only in ½-inch lengths. Baked Alaska can be either individual or a large one.

MENU NO. 2

Eggs à la Russe* on Melba Toast with Bibb Lettuce
Boston Strip Roast
Giant Mushroom Caps Stuffed with Broccoli
Noodle Croquettes Rolled in Cornflakes
Yellow Wax Beans with Chive Butter and Water Chestnuts
Thin Sliced Dill Pickles
Hot Herb-buttered French Bread
Angel Food Cake Crème Brûlée*
Tart Red Raspberry Sauce*

Boston strip roast is sometimes called a New York sirloin cut.

MENU NO. 3

Hot Watercress Soup*
Sesame Melba Toast*
Standing Ribs of Beef
Artichoke Pan Gravy
Orange Rice Balls*
Spinach Ring
Cherry Horseradish Beets*
Tossed Green Salad
Rose Toth Dressing*
Small Poppy Seed Crescent Rolls
Swedish Gaufrettes* with Coffee and Chocolate Ice Cream
Crème de Cacao or Chocolate Sauce

Make the soup with chicken stock. Be sure to add extra fresh chopped cress just before serving so it will be nice and green. Rub the beef with Lowry salt before roasting.

For the gravy, use a double-strength beef consommé thickened with cornstarch and a few diced artichoke hearts. The frozen ones will do nicely.

Add a little cream sauce to the spinach ring and surround it with the beets.

Put a few raw mushrooms in the salad.

MENU NO. 4

Hot Mushroom Bouillon
Pencil-slim Melba Toast with Powdered Celery Seed Butter
Eye of Beef, Medium Rare
Hashed in Cream Potatoes*
Two-tone Bean Platter
Sliced Tomatoes with Artichoke Salad Dressing on Romaine
Small Loaves of Bread
Butter Pats or Rolls
Strawberry Biscuit Shortcake

Add a little beef consommé and thinly sliced mushrooms to the bouillon.

For the Bean Platter, use sliced green beans with water chestnuts sprinkled over them and yellow wax beans tossed with sliced olives and parsley butter.

Put the bread loaves on the table, piping hot, to be sliced on little bread boards.

Fresh peach shortcake may be substituted for the strawberry.

MENU NO. 5

Honeydew Melon with Prosciutto Ham
Boned Leg of Lamb
Potato Balls in Parsley Butter
New Orleans Carrots* and Peas
Raw Vegetable Dish
Herb Baking Powder Biscuits
French Cheese Cake with Cherry or Blueberry Sauce

Instead of ham, you can serve the melon with a teaspoon of lime sherbet.

Garnish the leg of lamb with French-fried pear halves, with mint jelly in each pear half.

The Potato Balls are cut out of raw potato with a melon ball cutter and boiled.

Serve the carrots in a ring with the peas in the center.

The raw vegetables are raw cauliflower, Porcupine Celery*, cherry tomatoes, and ripe olives.

MENU NO. 6

Individual Madrilene Aspic Rings
Broiled Double Loin Lamb Chops
Stuffed Giant Mushroom Caps
Broiled or Baked Peach Halves
Braised Hearts of Celery
Small Cloverleaf Rolls
Coffee Mallow

In the center of each aspic ring put cold, fresh flaked salmon and shaved cucumbers. Sprinkle with capers. Dressing is a blend of ⅔ mayonnaise, ⅓ chive sour cream.

Fill the mushroom caps with peas or purée of peas. Each guest gets two caps.

Add mint jelly to the peach halves.

To the celery hearts add chopped watercress and toasted, slivered almonds.

Sprinkle shaved semi-sweet chocolate over the coffee mallow.

MENU NO. 7

Asparagus Soup
Italian Bread Sticks
Leg of Lamb
Tower of Pisa
Peas with Diced Yellow Summer Squash and Chopped Mint
Small Molds of Perfection Salad
Tiny Blueberry Muffins
Angel Food Cake
Chocolate Chip Ice Cream with Pistachio Nut Sauce

No cream in the asparagus soup; make it with chicken stock base.

Leg of lamb may be either boned or with bone.

Tower of Pisa is spiral mashed potatoes put through fluted pastry tube and dusted with sesame seeds or chopped parsley.

Make the salad with green new cabbage and serve each one on a thin slice of tomato.

The angel food cake can be either a ring or individual shells filled with the ice cream and topped with sauce. For the sauce, add pistachios to burnt sugar sauce.

MENU NO. 8

Hot Tomato Orange Bouillon
Potato Flake Crackers
Chicken Paprikash
Buttered Farfel or Noodle Ring
Three-bean Dish
Grapefruit and Avocado Salad
Baking Powder Biscuits
Coffee Bavarian

Add orange juice to the bouillon in a proportion of 1 to 3, and place a thin slice of orange in each soup cup. We like a suggestion of clove, but be careful, it's very subtle and strong. One clove is enough for a whole kettle of soup.

Make the Three-bean Dish with Fordhook lima beans, finely chopped yellow wax beans, and a very few kidney beans for color. Go sparingly on the latter. Sauté all together in butter.

Add poultry seasoning to the biscuits, which should be light as a feather.

Sprinkle shaved semi-sweet chocolate over the coffee Bavarian.

MENU NO. 9

Hawaiian Streamlined Antipasto
Boned Chicken Breasts
Mushroom Sauce
Hot Julienne Buttered and Glazed Carrots
Vegetable Casserole
Corn Sticks
*Sherry Almond Mousse**
Sherry Custard Sauce

For the antipasto, a spear of fresh pineapple, 3 or 4 shrimp or 3 or 4 generous chunks of lobster meat with a soufflé cup of

Pink Remoulade*, one ripe olive, a sheaf of watercress or, if the weather is hot, curly endive.

Serve the chicken breasts on a thin slice of country ham.

Plain, rich chicken gravy can be substituted for mushroom sauce.

To the carrots, add either seedless or seeded Tokay grapes.

Make the casserole with sliced zucchini, diced yellow summer squash, water chestnuts, watercress, and parsley butter. I also like a whisper of onion.

MENU NO. 10 (PLATE VIII)

Hot Deviled Crab Meat
Celery Seed Crackers
Filet of Beef Tenderloin
Wild Rice and Mushroom Casserole
*Horseradish Mousse**
Caesar Salad with Croutons
Deep Blueberry Tarts à la Mode

Serve the crab in sea shells.

Surround the mold with little spiced cherry beets.

Instead of blueberry tarts, you might have red sour cherry tarts or deluxe deep dish apple pie. The pastry shells should be baked by spreading pie dough on the *backs* of cupcake tins.

Serve no bread with this menu.

MENU NO. 11

Small Rings of Tomato Aspic
Boston Strip Roast, Medium Rare
Fresh Corn and Wax Beans with Parsley Butter or
Brown Butter
Julienne Zucchini Squash
Tiny Rum Rolls
Tiny Butter Rolls
Ring of Watermelon Ice with Honeydew Melon Balls

Fill the tomato aspic rings with seedless green grapes and flaked crab meat in remoulade. Garnish with lemon wedges and curly endive.

Cut the fresh corn off the cob and mix it with fresh yellow wax beans cut in ½-inch lengths. Sauté.

With the squash, serve celery and tomato sauce with ripe olives and Parmesan cheese.

Raspberry ice may be substituted for the watermelon ice.

MENU NO. 12

Shrimp Cocktail Plate
Charcoal-broiled Boston Strip Steaks
Stuffed Baked Potatoes
Broccoli Croquettes*
Asparagus Aspic
Tiny Poppy Seed and Salt Caraway Sticks
Fresh Peach Melba

On each cocktail plate, put cocktail sauce in a soufflé cup in the center and surround with shrimp. Use 2 lemon wedges as garnish.

The strip steaks should be small, about 10 ounces.

Stuff and refill the baked potatoes. Small whole browned potatoes may be served instead.

For the aspic, use long asparagus (canned green) arranged in an oblong drip pan and cover with a chicken vinegar aspic. Add chopped asparagus and chopped watercress to the mayonnaise.

Make the peach Melba with fresh peach halves and Tart Red Raspberry Sauce* over vanilla ice cream.

MENU NO. 13

Chilled Apple Juice
Lamb Shish Kebabs
Spinach Pie*
Yellow Wax Beans with Chestnuts and Crisp Bacon
Stuffed Tomatoes
Pineapple Sherbet with Fresh Pineapple
Macaroons

Peel the tomatoes, scoop out, and fill with a mixture of cottage cheese, Roquefort cheese, and chopped chives.

After broiling the shish kebabs, dip into a glaze made with consommé and chopped mint thickened slightly with cornstarch to make the lamb shine attractively.

Put the sherbet in a bowl and add shaved *fresh* pineapple, which can be marinated in crème de menthe if you wish.

MENU NO. 14

Caviar California
Eye of Beef, Medium Rare
*Mushroom Pie**
Zucchini Squash Boats
*Bing Cherry Salad Mold**
Fresh Banana Layer Cake

Squash Boats should be well scooped out, then stuffed with a mixture of celery, grated red cabbage, chopped onions, bread crumbs, and chopped parsley.

Garnish the molded salads with pitted fresh Bing cherries in season.

MENU NO. 15

Salad
Old-fashioned Pot Roast of Beef
Brown Gravy
Buttered Farvel or Wide Noodles
Spinach Soufflé Ring
Julienne Harvard Beets
Garlic or Herb-buttered French Bread
*Frozen Grapes**

The salad is made with diced celery, avocado slices, crisp bacon, a little grated lemon rind, and chopped shrimp, crab meat, or chicken breast. Serve this as a first course, with Pink Remoulade*.

Use a rump roast for the pot roast.

Garnish the noodles with buttered cracker crumbs.

Put sliced sautéed mushrooms in the center of the soufflé ring.

Add horseradish to the beets if desired.

MENU NO. 16

Fresh Grapefruit Sections with Sherbet
Roast Boneless Loin of Pork
Little Silver Onions Baked in Currant Jelly
Creamed Spinach Casserole
Wilted Lettuce Salad
Tiny Cinnamon Rolls
*Peppermint Stick Mousse**

Place a teaspoonful of pink grapefruit sherbet or mint sherbet on the grapefruit sections.

Crown roast of pork may be used instead of loin.

Add raisins to the spinach casserole.

Serve the mousse with a thin dark chocolate sauce.

MENU NO. 17

Cucumber Boats
Hot Baked Ham
Mustard Sauce
Mashed Sweet Potatoes
Succotash
Heart of Palm Salad
Bran Muffins
Peach Mary Anns

Cut the cucumbers in half lengthwise, scoop out and shave the pulp (discard the seeds). Line with 5 or 6 shrimp in a row, and partly fill with cocktail sauce.

Add a bit of apple to the sweet potatoes and top with marshmallows.

Garnish the heart of palm with chopped egg yolk or grated orange rind and arrange on Bibb lettuce.

For the dessert, fill angel food shells with vanilla ice cream and top with fresh sliced peaches.

MENU NO. 18

Salmon Salad
Hot Baked Ham
Baked Bananas
Frenched Green Beans with Macadamia Nuts
Corn Sticks
Stuffed Tomatoes
Chocolate Ribbon Layer Cake

Put the salmon salad in the center of individual rings of cucumber and pineapple aspic.

Before baking, dip the bananas in beaten egg and Rice Krispies; dust with cinnamon and nutmeg.

Stuff small skinned tomatoes with seedless grapes, diced celery, and mayonnaise.

MENU NO. 19

Asparagus Aspic Rings
Filet of Beef Tenderloin
Eggplant Casserole
Green Beans
Small Poppy Seed Rolls
*Sherry Almond Mousse**
*Tart Red Raspberry Sauce**

In the center of small rings of cold asparagus aspic, put a teaspoonful of diced chicken, diced ham, or shredded crab meat that has been marinated in your favorite dressing.

Cut the green beans into ½-inch sections; serve with slivered almonds.

MENU NO. 20

Thin Hot Corn Soup
T-bone or Porterhouse Steak
Mushroom Pie*
Asparagus Spears
Tomato and Avocado Salad
Rose Toth Dressing*
Little Round Loaves of Dill Bread
Honeydew Melon with Blueberries

Tie the asparagus in little bunches before cooking if it is fresh, and remove the strings before serving. Serve with grated lemon rind and mustard-buttered bread crumbs.

Cut the dill bread at the table.

Pitted Bing cherries may be substituted for blueberries.

MENU NO. 21

Halibut Mousse with Seafood Sauce
Cucumber Vinaigrette
Peas with Diced Celery in Butter
Hot Cherry Tomatoes Basil
Crusty Sourdough Bread
Sliced Papaya with Lime Wedges
Benne Seed Cookies

Skin the tomatoes and warm them lightly so they won't lose their shape. Pour scalding-hot tomato sauce over them, and sprinkle with basil.

MENU NO. 22

Jellied Borsch
Lobster Thermidor
Baked Mushrooms
Three-bean Salad Vinaigrette
Watercress Whole Wheat Rolled Sandwiches
Red Raspberry Sherbet Parfaits

Add beef consommé to beet mixture for the borsch in proportions of 1 to 4. Serve with a dash of sour cream and chives.

The thermidor is served hot in lobster shells or lobster tail shells—or large seashells, as a variation. You can cut the cost by adding crab meat to the lobster.

Bake the mushrooms in tomato sauce and top with croutons. Serve the parfaits without whipped cream.

MENU NO. 23

Stuffed Tomatoes
Individual Rock Cornish Game Hens
Plum Sauce
Artichoke Bottoms with Broccoli*
Spiced Fruit Tray
Sesame Vienna Bread
Egg Nog Chiffon Pie

Stuff the skinned small tomatoes with grated raw vegetables and cottage cheese, topped with crisp crinkled bacon or dried beef.

Serve the game hens with dressing and a plum sauce made with wine.

The bread should be served in small loaves on boards at each table.

Garnish the pie with shaved semi-sweet chocolate curls on top. Rum chiffon pie may be substituted for the egg nog—either to have a graham cracker crust.

MENU NO. 24

Split Pea Soup
Hot Individual Ham Loaves
Glazed Kumquat and Apricot Sauce
Corn Pudding
Broiled Tomatoes with Herbs
Wilted Spinach or Tossed Salad with Spinach
Small Cranberry Orange Muffins
Cantaloupe Rings with Sherbet

Pea soup should be hot and thin. Add some beef consommé so it isn't too heavy.

Serve lime or mint sherbet in the cantaloupe rings.

MENU NO. 25

Caesar or Grecian* Salad
Miniature Cheese Rolls
Meat Loaf
Creamed Potatoes with Peas
Hot Buttered Cabbage
Fresh Peach Tarts

The meat loaf can be your favorite, whatever it is.
Celery cabbage or Brussels sprouts are alternatives to buttered cabbage.
No rolls are served with the main course.
The peach tarts may be served with ice cream.

MENU NO. 26

Jellied Madrilene
Veal with Fig Sauce*
New Orleans Carrots*
Braised Celery Virginia*
Tossed Green Salad
Flaming Cherries Jubilee

Serve the madrilene in bouillon cups with a dab of sour cream and caviar in the center, or plain with a thin slice of lemon.
A hot veal mousse with fig sauce may be substituted for the filet of veal. Put little mounds of loose brown rice around the platter.
Carrots may be grated rather than riced.
Add small raw cauliflowerets to the tossed salad.

CHAPTER 6

YEAR-ROUND BUFFET DINNERS

Buffet dinners are more popular today than ever before because so many people are concerned about their weight for one reason or another. The buffet is an extremely functional plan because it enables people to be selective. If the crowd is large, the items should be fork food so that no one will have to use a knife. For these big parties the hot foods should all be in chafing dishes with Sterno heat, which produces hotter temperatures than alcohol burners; or you can put them on one of the new electric hot trays.

We prefer to keep the buffet table in the center of the room, rather than against a wall. It's rarely possible to gain any additional floor space by pushing the table to one side, and if people can move down both sides of a buffet, the lines will go twice as fast. If seating is not provided and guests have to stand, they *prefer* to stand around the walls of the room rather than in the middle of the floor.

I've attended several buffets at which the light was so dim that guests actually could not see the display of food as easily as they might have liked. Use candles if you will, but be sure there are enough of them so your friends can identify the various dishes. Remember that many ladies refuse to wear their glasses at parties, and they need all the help they can get in the way of illumination. They won't be able to see the buffet "picture" you have created if you don't give them enough light. And every buffet should look as pretty as a picture, no matter how simple it may be.

I have twenty-five buffet menus for you.

MENU NO. 1

Cold Turkey   Cranberry Jelly
Lobster Salad
Hot Beef Stroganoff
Parslied Rice Ring
Artichoke Hearts and Green Bean Casserole
Stuffed Tomatoes
Tiny Assorted Rolls
Fresh Fruit Platter
Finger French Pastries

Garnish the salad with a whole lobster in the shell on a bed of parsley. To be adventuresome bake a 4- or 5-pound round or oval loaf bread, scoop it out, and spread the outside of the crust with a paste of flour, water, and paprika. After it dries, use it as the "body" of a giant lobster. Cut a fresh lobster in two and fasten the head on one side, the tail on the other. Fill this shell with the lobster salad.

Add water chestnuts and watercress to the artichoke hearts and green beans and toss all in chive parsley butter.

Stuff the tomatoes with cottage cheese and grated Roquefort cheese.

MENU NO. 2

Baked Ham
Chicken Salad
Hot Lobster Newburg
Melba Toast Points
Hot Beef Burgundy
Spinach Croquettes*
Vegetable Wheel Vinaigrette*
Hot Cheese Biscuits
Walnut Sponge Whipped Cream Roll
Caramel Rum Sauce or Mr. Arthur's Butterscotch Sauce*

Garnish the ham with crab apples.

The chicken salad can be sprinkled with grated Roquefort, or with toasted almonds, toasted pecans, and mandarin oranges.

MENU NO. 3

Seafood Salad
Chicken Mexican
Small Broiled Beef Shish Kebabs
Mushroom Fritters* with Spinach Sauce*
Braised Hearts of Celery
Coca-Cola Salad Mold*
Parkerhouse Rolls
Little Crêpes Suzette*

Make the seafood salad with crab, lobster, and shrimp, wreathed in a row of thinly sliced cucumbers.

Hot Chicken Mexican is baked chicken served with a ripe olive and tomato sauce.

Use four-inch skewers for the shish kebab.

Breaded French-fried Mushrooms* may be substituted for the fritters.

Add almonds and Tokay grapes to the hearts of celery.

Butter the Parkerhouse rolls in advance.

Serve lingonberry, blueberry, or orange sauce with the crêpes.

MENU NO. 4

Standing Ribs of Beef
Creamed Radishes*
Frenched Green Beans
Bing Cherry Salad Mold*
Grilled Hard Rolls
Pyramid Profiteroles with Chocolate Sauce

Surround the roast beef platter with broiled peach halves and little sprigs of fresh currants.

Garnish the salad with watercress and fresh Bing cherries with the stems left on.

Pyramid Profiteroles are tiny cream puffs filled with custard, whipped cream, or ice cream. Usually the bottom layer of these is arranged in a single layer of chocolate cake with center cut out, then the rest are piled up about 5 inches high. On top of the pyramid put the leafy top of a pineapple. Pass chocolate sauce. Figure on one pyramid for 6 to 8 guests, one to each table.

MENU NO. 5

*Chicken Mandarin**
Beef Stroganoff
Parslied Rice Ring
Tossed Green Salad
Sesame Dressing
Fresh Strawberry Mousse
Macaroons

Garnish the mousse with fresh mint leaves and fresh strawberries.

MENU NO. 6

Coq au Vin
*Orange Rice Balls**
Broccoli Soufflé Rings
French Croissant Rolls
Caesar Salad
Fresh Strawberries with Sour Cream and Brown Sugar

Coq au Vin, is, of course, cut-up chicken stewed in a wine sauce.

Fill the soufflé rings with water chestnuts and mushrooms, and sprinkle grated cheese around the edges.

Toss crisp bacon, croutons, and anchovies in the Caesar salad.

Place the strawberries under the broiler flame for two minutes, then place on flat Swedish Gaufrettes*, and top with sour cream and brown sugar.

MENU NO. 7

Boned Chicken Breasts
Seedless Grape Sauce*
Rice Balls*
Fordhook Lima Beans with Water Chestnuts
Apple and Mincemeat Waldorf Salad
Butterscotch Loveknot Rolls
Trays of Assorted French Pastries

Add Worcestershire and grated orange rind to the Grape Sauce*.
Put a dash of American cheese in the Rice Balls*.
Fold pimiento sour cream sauce into the lima beans.

MENU NO. 8

Small Rock Cornish Game Hens with Chestnut Dressing
Cranberry Sauce or Lingonberry Sauce
Lemon-glazed Carrots
Dilled Peas with Diced Celery
Broccoli Vegetable Aspic
Poppy Seed Dressing*
Sweet and Plain Rolls
Coffee Bavarian with Hot Chocolate Sauce

MENU NO. 9

Baked Squab
Hashed in Cream Potatoes*
Green Beans with Almonds
Mandarin Orange Salad
Poppy Seed Rolls
Cake and Ice Cream

Serve the squab with tart Bing cherry sauce.
Sliced olives can be substituted for almonds in the green beans.
The molded salad is made with mandarin oranges and grated
fresh orange rind in orange gelatin. Top with watercress mayon-
naise before serving.
The dessert may be a white butter cake shell filled with vanilla
ice cream and topped with blueberry or Tart Red Raspberry
Sauce*.

MENU NO. 10

Antipasto
*Gourmet Breasts of Chicken**
Ham and Mushroom Sauce
Yellow Wax Beans
Two-tone Tomato and Perfection Salad Aspic
Celery Seed Mayonnaise
*Chocolate Bourbon Mousse**

For the antipasto, use deviled egg quarters, raw cauliflowerets, celery stuffed with anchovy cream cheese, ripe and stuffed olives, shrimp or lobster chunks, cherry tomatoes, salami cornucopias, and dried beef rolls with horseradish.

Add water chestnuts and artichoke hearts to the wax beans and serve with watercress and parsley butter.

MENU NO. 11

Cold Borsch
Swedish Meatballs with Mushroom Brown Gravy
Roast Duckling
*Grape Sauce**
Sage Stuffing Ring
Kumquat Salad
Spiced Watermelon Rind
Melba Toast Sticks
Peach Almond Mousse

The borsch should be served as a separate course before guests come to the buffet table.

The duckling should be served as crisp and golden-brown halves, in a Grape Sauce*.

Make a ring of the regular traditional sage stuffing, in a buttered mold, and bake. Turn out on platter and in center of the ring put creamed celery (diagonally cut) and toasted pecans.

Melba toast sticks must be pencil-thin, half poppy seed and half caraway seed.

Make the mousse with fresh or frozen peaches, as available, and serve with a peach sauce.

MENU NO. 12

Crown Roast of Lamb
Potato Balls*
Creamed Peas, Mushrooms, and Braised Celery
Lime Mint Salad Mold
Whole Wheat Bread Pinover Sandwiches*
Swedish Gaufrettes*
Orange and Pineapple Sherbet
Mandarin Orange Sauce*

Place the crown roast, with frilled papers on ends of ribs, on a round platter, and fill center with Potato Balls* cut with a melon ball cutter, and be sure to have loads of parsley butter.

The peas, mushrooms, and celery are served in a mild cheese sauce.

For the salad mold, use honeydew slices and canned minted pears in lime gelatin. Use Paprika Dressing*.

Make the sandwiches with cucumber butter.

MENU NO. 13

Cold Turkey
Hot Baked Ham
Au Gratin Potatoes
Hot Vegetable Platter
Lemon Salad Mold
Thin Party Breads
Grapefruit Cake*

Use plenty of Cheddar cheese in the potatoes.

Hot vegetable platter consists of cherry beets, Harvard-style, in the center; surround with ring of glazed fresh carrots sprinkled with grated lemon rind, then a ring of French-fried cauliflower generously sprinkled with chopped parsley.

Make the salad with lemon gelatin, canned figs, pitted prunes, stuffed olives, and pears.

Include dill, rye, and whole wheat among the party breads.

Garnish the cake with fresh strawberries.

MENU NO. 14

Creamed Chicken Breast, Sweetbreads, and Mushrooms
in Pie Pastry Shells
Hot Canadian Bacon
Gingersnap Gravy
Butternut Squash Ring with Lima Beans
Corn Sticks   Blueberry Muffins
Stuffed Tomatoes
Paprika Dressing*
Angel Food Crème Brûlée*
Tart Red Raspberry Sauce*

Bake the pastry shells on the backs of cupcake tins.

Bake the Canadian bacon in crab apple juice.

Grease the mold well for the squash ring; it should be like a soufflé. In the center put Fordhook lima beans with julienne Swiss cheese and brown butter.

Stuff the tomatoes with a mixture of diced fresh pineapple, diced avocado, and finely cut celery.

MENU NO. 15

Hot Shrimp and Chicken Creole in Rice Ring
Tiny Glazed Ham Balls*
Mushroom Soufflé
Bunch of Grapes Salad
Tiny Hominy Muffins or Popovers
Broiled Peaches with Sour cream and Brown Sugar
Angel Food Cake or Ladyfingers

Place the soufflé ring on a platter surrounded with long, whole green beans and yellow butter beans sprinkled with grated lemon rind and buttered bread crumbs.

PLATE III

LEFT:
Cradles with Fresh
Fruit Salad
Cream Cheese Teddy
Bear and Crackers
with Relishes

BELOW:
The Butterfly Tea

PLATE IV

Arabian Nights Dinner

Arabian Nights Eggplant
French-fried Cauliflower
Tossed Greek Salad

MENU NO. 16

Hot Deviled Crab
Noodle Ring or Noodle Croquettes
Stuffed Mushroom Caps
Baked Stuffed Tomatoes
Four-bean Salad Vinaigrette
Poppy Seed Vienna Rolls
Apricot Sherbet
Praline Cookies

Serve the crab in little foil fish shells or seashells.
Fill the mushroom caps with chopped spinach and crisp bacon.
Scoop out the skinned tomatoes and fill them with whole-kernel corn and melted butter. They may be sprinkled with grated cheese if desired.

MENU NO. 17

Hot Baked Ham
Hot Queen Anne Cherry Sauce
Cold Turkey
Corn Soufflé or Corn Pudding
Spinach Noodles and Mushrooms with Pimiento Butter
Tiny Cinnamon Rolls
Cucumber Sour Cream Aspic
Filled Tiny White Cupcakes

Garnish the turkey with little clusters of seedless grapes.
Add a few green beans cut in ½-inch lengths to the noodles and mushrooms.
Surround the aspic with sliced tomatoes and clumps of braised celery hearts vinaigrette.
Scoop out the cupcakes and fill with coffee ice cream. Sprinkle with shaved semi-sweet chocolate curls.

MENU NO. 18

Cold Poached Salmon
Dill Watercress Remoulade Dressing*
Lean Briskets of Beef
Small Stuffed Baked Idaho Potatoes
Hot Celery Cabbage with Parsley Butter
Pickle Tray
Individual Roquefort Cream Aspic Rings with Fresh Fruit
Little Cucumber Sandwiches
Chocolate Ice Cream Roll

Add capers to the dill watercress sauce for the cold salmon.
Bake the briskets of beef slowly in onion soup.
Add caraway to the cabbage if you wish.
Spread mint ice cream on the chocolate cake and roll. Serve hot chocolate fudge sauce to pour over it.

MENU NO. 19

Creamed Dried Beef and Oysters
Hot Corned Beef
Mushroom Fritters*
Sautéed Beans, Corn, and Squash
Smothered Cauliflower
Jewish Rye Bread
Porcupine Pears or Fresh Pears

Slice the corned beef on a board at the table.
Sauté the yellow wax beans, whole-kernel corn, and diced yellow summer squash in green onion butter. Water chestnuts may also be added.
Smother the cooked cauliflower with Dill Watercress Remoulade Dressing* and surround with tomato wedges and Bibb lettuce.
Be sure the rye bread is fresh and warm. Or use crusty rye rolls.
Dip canned pears in brown sugar syrup. Stick slivered, toasted blanched almonds in their sides. Cinnamon-flavored cream may be served with these.

MENU NO. 20

Hot Corned Beef
Chicken Mexican* or Chicken Tetrazzini
Little Stuffed Cabbage Rolls in Tomato Sauce
Horseradish Mousse*
Frenched Fresh Green Beans with Plain or Herb Butter
Buttery Croissants
Swiss Cheese Salad*
Fresh Peach Pie à la Mode

Slice the corned beef on a board at the table.
Surround the mousse with pickled beet slices.
Instead of pie, you may serve peach ice cream with Kadota fig sauce.

MENU NO. 21

Hot Ham Cornucopias
Roast Eye of Beef
Broccoli Pie
Corn Pancakes
Green and White Vegetable Salad*
Tiny Salt Caraway Sticks and Sesame Rolls
Coffee Baked Alaska*

Fill the cornucopias with mildly curried chicken.
The beef should be medium rare, thinly sliced.
Make the Corn Pancakes with fresh corn, cut off the cob, and chopped parsley added to pancake batter.

MENU NO. 22

Breaded Pork Tenderloin
Spiced Apricots
Meatballs in Brown Mushroom Gravy
Noodles with Chopped Toasted Walnuts
Acorn Squash with Brown Sugar and Butter
Peas with Chopped Iceberg Lettuce and Chervil
Melon Ball Salad with Chopped Mint
Poppy Seed Dressing*
Toasted English Muffins
Open or Two-crust Apple Pie with Cheese Crust

Have the butcher flatten the pork tenderloin with a cleaver. Fold a little white sauce into the noodles and add walnuts just before serving.

Add the lettuce and chervil to the peas at the last minute. You might like to add a little pineapple to the acorn squash.

MENU NO. 23

Shrimp Jambalaya
Rice Ring
Cold Jellied Tongue
Dill or Mustard Sauce
Acorn Squash with Brown Sugar and Butter
French-fried Parsley*
Cole Slaw with Pineapple Tidbits
Celery Seed Bread
Pineapple Chiffon Pie

Sprinkle toasted pecans and crisp bacon on the squash just before serving.

Make the pie with a gingersnap crust.

MENU NO. 24

Clam Chowder
Baked Canadian Bacon
Pickled Kadota Figs
Sweet Potato Soufflé
Cheese Baking Powder Biscuits
Porcupine Pear and Cream Cheese Salad
Floating Island Pudding

Make the salad by rubbing canned pears with chutney cream cheese and orange rind, and stick slivered, toasted almonds upright in the cheese. Garnish with crisp dandelion greens if available.

Creamed tapioca pudding with a meringue topping may be substituted for the floating island pudding.

MENU NO. 25

Broiled Minced Ham Patties on Peach Halves
Rice Ring
Harvard Carrots
Hot Cherry Tomatoes Basil*
Molded Three-tone Aspic
Eggnog Chiffon Pie

Figure on two peach halves per person.

Add grated Cheddar cheese to the rice ring.

Make the Harvard carrots like Harvard beets. Add grated lemon rind.

Three-tone aspic is made with avocado aspic, tomato aspic with diced celery, and new cabbage in aspic.

Instead of eggnog chiffon pie, you may prefer a chocolate chiffon, with a crust made of crushed cornflakes, melted butter, sugar, and ginger.

CHAPTER 7

THE AFTER-THEATER BUFFET

By "theater" in this chapter, I mean any evening event that is followed by a buffet supper at home. I was first intrigued by this kind of entertaining when we were called upon to cater parties given by supporters of the Cleveland Symphony Orchestra—receptions and light suppers to honor special concert soloists and guest conductors. Since the same people were guests at most of these affairs, we were challenged to produce a variety of menus.

We discovered that our problem is really twofold. First, we have to provide something hot and substantial that will be hearty enough for performers who probably have not eaten before the concert. Second, we need to find something that will be tasty yet light enough for people who have to get up at a fairly early hour and go to work. These people want something more like a "snack." For everyone who requests it, we are also careful to provide decaffeinated coffee. More and more people seem to like it at a late supper because coffee keeps them awake.

Many of the suppers we cater are given in Severance Hall, the orchestra's residence, but sometimes the guests are taken home by the host, and of course the menus that follow could be served as easily one place as the other.

Most of the time we use a floral centerpiece, but on occasion we produce something special. For example, we made a cake in the shape of a grand piano when the party honored a pianist and, similarly, a cake in the shape of a violin on another occasion.

Different color schemes are used from week to week. When you do this kind of entertaining, remember that anything different from the regular routine is always welcome.

Here, then, is a substantial sampling of our late-evening buffet menus.

MENU NO. 1

Mélange of Meats
Dry Melba Toast
Grapefruit Platter
*Paprika Dressing**
Cheese Platter with Rye Bread
Butter Cookies

For the mélange use a mixture of creamed sweetbreads, breast of chicken, dried beef and mushrooms and serve on the Melba toast.

In the center of the grapefruit platter we fastened a treble clef sign made out of strong wire and strung with maraschino cherries or grapes. This was stuck upright into a whole grapefruit. For the rest, arrange sections of grapefruit on leaf lettuce and sprinkle pomegranate seeds or halves of seeded grapes over the whole design. The dressing is in a separate bowl.

For the cheese platter, consider French brie. Concertgoers seem to be particularly fond of it. It is best when taken out of the refrigerator 24 hours ahead and left at room temperature.

Butter cookies can be made violin-shaped, hand-cut, and decorated with a little thin "piping" of icing around the edge.

MENU NO. 2

Quiche Lorraine
Breast of Turkey Sandwiches
Jellied Asparagus Salad Mold
Short Celery Stuffed with Crab Meat Salad
Little Fruit Tarts
Brandy Snaps

When you make the Quiche Lorraine with layered Swiss cheese and bacon, use plenty of bacon.

Make the sandwiches on white and whole wheat bread.

Unmold the salad onto Romaine and watercress, garnish with Belgian endive, and serve with mayonnaise to which you have added chopped asparagus tips.

Fruit tarts might be apricot, cherry and blueberry.

MENU NO. 3

Avocado in the Snow*
California Snow Pea Pods, Stuffed* with Crab Meat
and Deviled Tongue
Toasted English Muffins
York State Cheese
Swedish Meatballs in Brown Gravy
Parslied Rice Ring
Dill Pickles
Jelly Ribbon Pound Cake

Use avocado-green cloths and a bouquet with fresh lacy dill in the center of the table.

Leave skin on the avocado halves and serve the sauce in a chafing dish.

Be sure the pickles aren't the garlic kind.

MENU NO. 4

Flaked Fresh Salmon in Aspic*
Hot Cheese Rarebit with Almonds and Bacon
Dry Melba Toast
Shaved Roast Beef Finger Sandwiches on Rye Bread
Dilled Pickled Mushrooms
Spicy Cookies

Again, use the dill centerpiece.

Make the Salmon in Aspic* in a curved fish mold. With it serve Dill Watercress Remoulade Dressing* with capers.

Serve slivered almonds and crisp bacon alongside the rarebit in separate bowls.

MENU NO. 5

Hot Crab Meat Casserole with Grapes and Water Chestnuts
Dry Melba Toast
Cold Sliced Filet of Beef
Thin Party Rye and Dill Bread
Brie Cheese and Crackers
Melon Ball Platter
French Twirls* with Mocha

The beef should be quite rare. Serve horseradish mayonnaise as an accompaniment.

MENU NO. 6

Artichoke Rarebit*
Dry Melba Toast
Kumquat Molded Orange Salad*
Paprika Dressing*
Chicken Salad Envelope Sandwiches*
Tiny Honey-Spice Cupcakes
Macaroons

Have a bowl of grated Parmesan cheese to sprinkle on the rarebit.
Frost the cupcakes with lemon and maple frosting.

MENU NO. 7

Vegetable Beef Soup
Open Danish Layered Shaved Tongue Sandwiches on Rye Bread
Open Chicken Salad Sandwiches
Roquefort Cream Aspic Ring with Fresh Fruits
Celery and Olives
Tiny Danish Pastries

Make the soup hot and thin.
For the chicken salad sandwiches, a dash of curry in the mayonnaise may be used if desired.
Surround the aspic ring with the fresh fruits.
Place the celery and olives in shaved ice.
Nut, jam, and cheese fillings in the pastries make for a varied choice.

MENU NO. 8

Chicken Mandarin*
Hot Toasted Mushroom Sandwiches*
Black Diamond and Gouda Cheese and Crackers
Bing Cherry Salad Mold*
Tiny Chocolate Chip Cookies
Coconut Macaroons

Serve the Chicken Mandarin* in deep pie pastry shells, and pass dry Melba toast.

Garnish the salad with fresh pineapple spears; serve a whipped cream dressing with grated pineapple.

MENU NO. 9

Creamed Chicken and Asparagus on Melba Toast
Toasted Finger Shaved Ham Sandwiches
Fruit Salad
Paprika Dressing*
Angel Food Pan Cake

Add cut-up fresh asparagus to the creamed chicken.

Brush sesame seeds and butter on tops of the sandwiches before toasting.

For the salad, use slices of apple (with skin), orange sections, and grapefruit sections tossed together and served on Bibb lettuce leaf.

Frost half the cake with thin strawberry icing, the other half with thin pineapple icing.

MENU NO. 10

Tenderloin of Beef Burgundy
Rice Ring
Green Salad
Cottage Cheese and Red Caviar Blintzes*
Miniature Chocolate and Maple Eclairs
Orange Puff Pastry Fans

The beef dish is made with tenderloin tips and browned mushrooms in wine sauce.

The Blintzes* should be small and hot and served with additional sour cream sauce, and with Danish caviar and chives on the side.

MENU NO. 11

*Hot Tomato Orange Bouillon**
Russian Ground Beef Roll
Fruit Platter
Hot Cheddar Cheese Puffs
Tiny Pecan Rolls

The Beef Roll is made with chopped hard-boiled eggs, ground mushrooms, onions, and chopped sirloin of beef rolled up in narrow puff pastry. Bake about 30 minutes at 380° F. and slice at the table. Serve with horseradish sour cream sauce.

For the fruit platter, arrange scooped-out fresh pineapple shells with the green tops pointing outward and fill with pitted Queen Anne cherries, pitted Bing cherries, fresh shaved pineapple, and fresh strawberries.

MENU NO. 12

Lobster Bisque
Hot Canadian Bacon
Party Rye Bread
Cheese and Fruit Tray
Praline Cookies

Serve your favorite crackers with the bisque.

On the cheese and fruit tray, have several kinds of cheese, little clusters of grapes, fresh pineapple spears, and big strawberries with stems. Crackers, too.

MENU NO. 13

Hot Chicken Mousse
Mushroom Sauce
Boeuf à la Mode
Toasted Cheese Bread or Cheese Scones
Green and White Fruit Salad*
Little Chocolate Cupcakes

Boeuf à la Mode is shaved jellied beef, with dill or horseradish dressing.

With the salad serve an Apricot and Mint Dressing, which is made by adding apricot purée and chopped mint to Paprika Dressing*.

Frost half the chocolate cupcakes with chocolate fudge icing and half with root beer icing. Root Beer Icing is made by adding root beer extract to a white divinity fudge icing.

MENU NO. 14

Hot Watercress Soup*
Bacon, Tomato, and Lettuce Sandwiches
Hot Broiled Peach Halves
Bowl of Cottage Cheese
Plain Butter Pound Cake
Fruit Bar Cookies

Make the sandwiches on thin, medium sandwich buns.

In the center of the peach halves, put butter, brown sugar, and currant jelly.

Add a *little* crumbled Roquefort cheese to the cottage cheese and mix well.

MENU NO. 15

Oysters Rockefeller
Hot Ham Pie Pastry Turnovers
Cheese
Molded Fruit Salad in Lime Gelatin
Tiny Chocolate Nut Fudge Balls
Tiny Coconut Snowballs*

Arrange the oysters on the shell on rock salt spread on cookie sheets. Cover edges of cookie sheet with parsley. Be sure to have oyster forks.

Use ground ham and Artichoke Mustard Relish* to fill the turnovers.

Serve two kinds of your favorite cheese.

MENU NO. 16

Lobster Newburg
Melba Toast
Sirloin Butt Beef
Stuffed Tomatoes
Buttered Party White Bread
*Swedish Gaufrette Cornucopias**

Beef should be shaved, pinkish, and sliced, served with a Dijon mustard spread.

Skin tiny hothouse tomatoes and fill with seeded grapes and diced celery moistened with sour cream mayonnaise.

Use a mocha filling with the cornucopias; dip the ends in shaved chocolate.

MENU NO. 17

Split Pea, Tomato, and Chicken Soup
Cold Shrimp Salad
Small Buttered Parkerhouse Rolls
Miniature Pickled Eggplant
Pickled German Corn on the Cob
*Miniature Lady Locks**
Little Whipped Cream Puffs

The soup is a blend of the three kinds of soup, cooked with apple, strained, then a dash of curry added.

Garnish the salad with tomato wedges and strips of avocado.

Mocha cream and pineapple cream filling are good choices for the Lady Locks*.

MENU NO. 18

*Ham and Celery Pie**
Open Breast of Turkey Sandwiches
Egg Salad Pinwheel Sandwiches
Jellied Madrilene Aspic
Chewy Date Bars
Spritz Cookies

Ham and Celery Pie* is made with layered ham, braised celery, and mushrooms in a cheese pastry pie crust.

Garnish the aspic with artichoke hearts, raw apple, a *few* sliced raw mushrooms, and sliced avocado or, if desired, heart of palm. Serve green goddess dressing with it.

Spritz cookies are very thin butter cookies.

MENU NO. 19

*Lobster Capon Madeira**
Baked Tomatoes with Saffron Rice
Finger Sandwiches
Watercress Rolled Sandwiches
Grapefruit and Avocado Salad
Linzer Tortes

Bake halves of little tomatoes with saffron rice on top.

Finger sandwiches might include shredded iceberg lettuce with mustard mayonnaise, and crumbled Roquefort or thinly sliced Swiss cheese on cracked wheat bread.

Make the salad with ruby leaf lettuce if possible. A lemon and oil dressing is best for this kind of salad, or use Paprika Dressing*.

MENU NO. 20

Small Freshly Broiled Top Sirloin Hamburgers
Bread and Butter Pickles
Shoestring Potatoes or Potato Chips
Vegetable Platter
Ice Cream Cones

Hamburgers should be pink in center. Serve with Artichoke Mustard Relish*, Old Plantation relish, sliced onions, catsup, and regular mustard on 2½-inch sandwich buns.

On vegetable platter are cauliflowerets, carrots, celery, Belgian endive, cucumber sticks, cherry tomatoes, green and red sweet pepper rings.

Have various flavors of ice cream for the small-sized cones.

MENU NO. 21

*Lasagna Ercole**
Hot Buttered Sesame Bread
Cheese Tray with Crackers
Combination Turkey, Ham, and Swiss Cheese Layered Sandwiches
Grape Juice Aspic Mold
Puffed Rice Candy
Divinity Fudge

Mold seedless green grapes, halves of blue Italian grapes, Tokay grapes, and, if you wish, a few Bing cherries in the aspic. Garnish with a few small clusters of fresh grapes. Serve with whipped cream and toasted pecan salad dressing.

MENU NO. 22

*Ham Pineapple Cocktail Mousse Mold**
Thin Spaghetti with Oysters and Mushrooms in Cream Sauce
Pineapple and Tomato Slices
Chocolate-filled Finger Macaroons
Rum-filled Macaroons
Orange-filled Macaroons

MENU NO. 23

Chicken in Spinach Crêpes
Dry Melba Toast Points
Broccoli Salad
Platter of Fresh Fruit
Chocolate Turtle Cookies
Minted Fondant-covered Marshmallows

Add fresh spinach to your pancake batter for the crêpes. Fill with chopped creamed chicken. Serve with mushroom sauce or thin cheese rarebit sauce.

For the salad, toss Bibb lettuce and broccoli buds with a lemon and oil dressing.

The fruit platter can be made up of whatever is in season.

MENU NO. 24

Curried Lamb Balls
Individual Crab Meat Tarts
Lima Bean Salad
Parmesan Melba Toast*
Brie Cheese and Crackers
Caraway Sugar Cookies
Tiny Oatmeal Cookies

The tarts are thin pastry shells filled with crab meat and whole seedless grapes in a white wine sauce. Or you can use a crab Dewey mixture with green pepper.

Make the salad with cold cooked Fordhook lima beans and sliced olives in a sesame vinaigrette dressing. Garnish with tomato wedges or cherry tomatoes.

MENU NO. 25

Glazed Ham Balls* with Raspberry Apples
Oysters in Cream Sauce
Molded Fruit Salad
English Muffins with Parsley Butter
Praline Cookies
Macaroons

To prepare the apples, defrost red raspberries, slice apples, and add therein the raspberries. Bake in 325° F. oven for 20 to 25 minutes.

Make a delicate Roquefort cream sauce for the oysters and serve them on seashells on a bed of rock salt. If you wish, crisp bacon can be sprinkled on top.

The salad is made in a ring mold with mandarin oranges and halves of canned apricots in orange gelatin, with grated fresh orange rind added. A few sliced kumquats would add tang. Surround with giant spiced prunes stuffed with soft cream cheese and chopped walnuts. Arrange on romaine leaves and place a large bouquet of watercress in the center of the ring.

MENU NO. 26

Deviled Eggs with Mushroom Sauce
Thuringer Cornucopias
Open Cold Filet of Beef Sandwiches
Coca-Cola Aspic Ring

Arrange ice-cold deviled egg halves on Melba toast and cover with piping-hot mushroom sauce.

For the sausage cornucopias, slice summer sausage very thin. Fill with a mixture of mashed avocado, lemon rind, and chopped watercress.

Slice the beef thin and layer with a horseradish spread on thin slices of round dill party bread.

In the Coca-Cola Aspic Ring are diced apple, canned pineapple, and Bing cherries or white pitted Queen Anne cherries. To serve, fill the center of the ring with fresh blueberries and arrange tiny clusters of seedless grapes around the outside. Add grated orange rind to mayonnaise for the dressing. (See recipe for Coca-Cola Salad* for further hints on how to make this aspic ring.)

CHAPTER 8

THE WEE HOURS BREAKFAST

About twice a year parents have to be concerned with serving early morning meals, anywhere from 2 A.M. to 5 A.M., as their children enter the graduation period, either their own or their friends'. This is not to say that the parents themselves may not come home from a very late party and find themselves hungry—although not if they've been to one we've catered!

For the youngsters, however, I have learned that they do not eat too heartily at this hour because most of them have had some kind of food around 11 P.M. or midnight, even if it was only a hamburger. Nevertheless, these occasions *do* occur, and they are complicated by the fact that the young are unpredictable. If you plan on a lot of food, you may have a great deal left over. If you don't put much out, you may just as likely be deluged and embarrassed.

I recommend having a kind of emergency supply on hand. Don't be in too much of a hurry to set it out. Wait and see how the crowd develops. If the first arrivals dig into the food with real enthusiasm, chances are the others will follow suit. If the first ones just "pick," the others may do likewise. In any case, I hope you have a freezer to take care of anything that's left.

MENU NO. 1

Scrambled Eggs
Little Link Sausages
Spiced Crab Apples
Thin Sliced Canadian Bacon
Party Bread
Tiny Sweet Rolls

It doesn't take long to scramble eggs, so keep making them in batches as you go. Don't let them get too hard. Add a little milk to stretch them further.

Provide milk and orange juice as well as coffee for beverages.

MENU NO. 2

Creamed Ham on Melba Toast
Eggs Sunny Side Up
Applesauce
Fried Cakes

To prepare the eggs, melt butter in foil tart pans arranged on cookie sheets. You can bake about 50 on two cookie sheets at one time. Drop an egg in each pan and bake at 300° F. for about 10 to 12 minutes. These look much like poached eggs and are delicious.

Have a variety of fried cakes—plain, powdered sugar, cinnamon sugar. (In the East, you know these as doughnuts.)

MENU NO. 3

Little Glazed Ham Balls*
Tiny Blueberry Pancakes
Fried Apples
White Bread
Tiny Pecan Rolls

Bread should be fresh and sliced thin, served with whipped salted butter.

MENU NO. 4

Eggs Goldenrod
Frizzled Shaved Ham in Brown Butter
Melba Toast and Soft Fresh Bread
Small Danish Pastries

MENU NO. 5

Little Rolled or Flat Pancakes
Brown Sugar Syrup
Little Link Sausages
Tiny Sweet Rolls
Tiny Blueberry Muffins

If the pancakes are rolled, you can start to make them ahead of time. They're especially good outdoors, cooked on a potbellied coal or wood stove.

MENU NO. 6

Hot Ham Loaf
Corn or Apple Fritters
Maple Syrup
Fried Tomatoes
Cinnamon Rolls

Fry the fritters early and reheat on a cooky sheet.

MENU NO. 7

Scrambled Eggs
Fresh Fruit Cups
Buttered Toast or English Muffins
Glazed Doughnuts

Sprinkle crisp crinkled bacon over the top of the eggs. Cut up the fruit and arrange in little paper soufflé cups.

MENU NO. 8

Quiches Lorraine
Fresh Fruit Cups
Sesame Melba Toast* or Toasted Scones
Fried Cakes and Sugared Doughnuts

Quiches Lorraine (Swiss cheese and bacon custard pies) are cut in wedges and are easy to serve.

Cut up the fruit and put it in paper soufflé cups.

MENU NO. 9

Thin Wedges of Cantaloupe
Creamed Dried Beef on Toast
Bakery Coffee Cakes

Add a little melted cheese to the dried beef. Heat the coffee cakes.

MENU NO. 10

French Toast
Shaved Frizzled Ham in Butter
Pastries

Bake the French toast on a big flat griddle. Serve with it an array of cinnamon and powdered sugar, syrup, currant jelly, and honey.

Pastries should include a variety of cherry, blueberry, apricot, prune, and cream cheese fillings.

MENU NO. 11

Cereal with Fruit
Peanut Butter Toast

Purchase a number of plastic cereal bowls and a collection of individual boxes of cold dry cereal. Have strawberries, bananas, and blueberries (or whatever fruit is in season) with brown and white sugar and plenty of milk. Let the guests fix their own cereal to taste.

Serve with peanut butter toast sprinkled generously with crisp, crumbled bacon tidbits.

Part Three

The Four Seasons

CHAPTER 1

SPRING

June in January Party

June and January have little in common except that both are graduation months. The snow may be a foot deep outside the house, but somehow people have more time to entertain in the first month of the year than the sixth, so why not have a "June in January" party? You could put on the invitations "Come dressed in June attire." What follows should make several conversation pieces.

Lemonade and iced tea should be in evidence as the guests arrive.

The table should have a summery look, perhaps an organdy or a pastel-colored cloth with a bowl of roses for the centerpiece. An electric fan in one corner of the buffet will add to the atmosphere.

For this party, here are three menu ideas.

MENU NO. 1

Spanish or Mexican Melons
Boston Strip Steaks
Mashed Potato Balls Rolled in Cornflakes
Individual Broccoli or Asparagus Timbales
Individual Roquefort Cream Aspic Molds with Fresh Fruits
Crusty Hard Rolls
Strawberry Ice Cream
Party Cupcakes
Rosebud Mints

An alternative to the melons suggested would be Cranshaw melon with prosciutto.

Charcoal-broil the strip steaks. We have a chef who does this even in zero weather; he comes dressed in ski boots and warm clothes. As many as 60 to 70 guests can be served this way.

A subtle whisper of peanut butter can be added to the potato balls.

Bake the timbales in Pyrex custard cups.

Grill the hard rolls ahead of time, then reheat.

Garnish the ice cream with fresh strawberries.

Put an icing rose on each cupcake.

This, it may go without saying, is a sit-down dinner.

MENU NO. 2

Avocado Crab Meat Salad
Cheese Pastry Straws
Charcoal-broiled Individual Filets Mignon
Braised Celery Virginia*
Stuffed Mushroom Caps
Caesar Salad with Croutons
Red Raspberry Bavarian
Tart Red Raspberry Sauce*
Assorted Miniature Cookies
Rosebud Mints

The first salad is made with diced avocado, diced celery, crab meat, and Pink Remoulade*. Garnish with crisp bacon or julienne ham.

Don't serve bacon with the filets mignon.

Add a few peas to the Braised Celery Virginia*.

Partially cook the mushroom caps, then fill with mashed potatoes spiraled into the cap with a pastry tube and finish cooking in the oven.

This, too, is a sit-down dinner.

BUFFET DINNER

Flaked Fresh Salmon in Aspic*
Creamed Chicken, Sweetbreads, and Mushrooms in Pie Pastry
   Shells
Swedish Meatballs in Brown Gravy
Peas with Slivered Almonds
Cucumber Sour Cream Aspic Mold
Bowl of Salad Greens with Avocado
Rose Toth Dressing*
Blueberry Muffins   Tiny Parkerhouse Rolls
Meringue Shells with Ice Cream

Cut chicken breasts in large pieces, add to sweetbreads and mushrooms in cream sauce. Put this in deep pie pastry shells.

Fill the center of the aspic mold with pickled cherry beets.

Cut the avocado for the salad bowl in slivers.

Fill tiny fresh pink meringue shells with strawberry or vanilla ice cream and serve with strawberry sauce.

The Hard Times Party

Invitations should read: "Come in old clothes to our Hard Times Party." A good time to have this party is after the holidays, or after April 15, when everyone is feeling broke. People seem to enjoy wearing patched trousers, old shoes, old felt hats, calicos and ginghams. You can be sure your guests will demonstrate imagination and ingenuity.

Use your oldest tablecloth or bright oilcloth on the buffet table. If guests are to sit at tables, use blue denim or oilcloth and plain, cheap wooden chairs. The centerpiece could be cans (leave the labels on or wash them off), and the flowers would be skimpy— use some carrot tops in place of ferns.

Guests should eat off pie tins. You can buy foil pie pans very reasonably. Be sure to use your old silver, and if need be, borrow some rather than use sterling. It's more effective if knives and forks don't match. Use various kinds of jelly glasses for the water glasses. Paper napkins are appropriate.

A buffet is best for this kind of party. Here are some samples:

MENU NO. 1

Bean Soup
Beef Stew with Vegetables
Cole Slaw
Crusty French Bread
Old-fashioned Cinnamon Bread Pudding

If you omit potatoes from the stew, serve mashed potatoes.
Add diced raw red apple to the cole slaw.
Rice pudding may be substituted for bread pudding. In either case, serve with a thin custard sauce.

MENU NO. 2

Split Pea Soup
Meat Loaf
Scalloped Potatoes
Carrots and Peas
Perfection Salad
Celery Seed Dressing
Rye, Whole Wheat, and White Bread
Apple Pie with Longhorn Cheese
Peanuts   Mints

Make the pea soup with a ham bone.
Add a dash of onion to the scalloped potatoes.
Be sure the salad has lots of flavor.
Mints should be the little white kind called after-dinner mints.

MENU NO. 3

Old-fashioned Vegetable Soup
Stuffed Veal Breasts
French-fried Brussels Sprouts
Tomato Aspic with Chive Cottage Cheese
Tossed Green Salad
Banana Cream Pie with Meringue

Include lentils or barley in the soup.

Instead of veal breasts, you might prefer individual veal birds with stuffing. Serve veal birds with brown beef stock gravy.

Dip the Brussels sprouts in egg and bread crumbs before frying. If possible, get a few dandelion greens for the salad.

MENU NO. 4

Split Pea and Tomato Bouillon
Breaded City Chickens
Macaroni and Cheese with Croutons
Boiled Small Whole Onions
Green Beans
Molded Apple Mincemeat Waldorf Salad
Dark Pumpernickel Bread
Meringue-topped Tapioca Pudding

Pour brown butter over the onions just before serving.

Use long, whole green beans, and serve sweet-sour German style.

To regular Waldorf salad, add a little mincemeat, mold in lemon gelatin.

Maple Syrup Party

If you had a country childhood, you remember that late February or March is the maple syrup season. Use a beige and brown or brown and white color scheme for your party. The centerpiece can be white narcissus, tulips, or hayacinths, with pussywillows. Those thoughtful enough to plan the party during the previous fall can use a few pressed maple leaves; otherwise you can cut some out of brown paper. Use a band of dark brown velvet around the buffet table. Here's a chance to use that brown burlap cloth and caramel, brown, and white candles.

This party seems to go best in a suburban home. One thing to remember about the menu is that, when you serve food with a maple flavor, there should be a salty, counteracting food to cut the sweetness.

Here are a few menu ideas for large and small groups:

MENU NO. 1

Hot Rolled Crêpes Suzette*
Warm Maple Syrup
Salted Filbert Nuts and Salted Cashews

This is suitable for a small group. The crêpes can be made a day ahead, lightly dusted with powdered sugar, then put in foil pans or cookie sheets and reheated.

MENU NO. 2

Spicy Canadian Bacon or Ham
Corn Fritters with Hot Maple Syrup
Tiny Maple-iced Chocolate and Spice Cupcakes
Pecans and Almonds

This would be a good menu for a large open house, as would Menu No. 3 following.

Slice the bacon or ham thin and serve hot.

Dip the ends of the pecans and almonds in maple fondant.

MENU NO. 3

Glazed Ham Balls*
Apple Beignets
Hot Maple Syrup
Tiny Maple- and Chocolate-Iced Eclairs
Maple Puff Kisses with Toasted Pecans

Apple Beignets are small fritters made with sliced apples dipped in batter and French-fried. Dust with powdered sugar.

Cream puffs may be substituted for the eclairs.

MENU NO. 4

For a simple dessert to be served with coffee, make individual Maple Syrup Velvet Mousses* with ladyfingers lining the dishes. Garnish with walnut or pecan halves, and serve with maple syrup.

MENU NO. 5

For a late snack to be served with coffee or decaffeinated coffee, try tiny raisin cinnamon rolls with maple icing, and tiny pecan or poppy seed butterfly rolls with maple icing. Crystallized maple sugar candy in maple leaf shapes may also be served, along with macadamia nuts.

Black Velvet Party

"Come to a Black Velvet party!" That's the kind of invitation calculated to arouse some excited anticipation, since no one is likely to know what it means. Should the ladies wear black velvet gowns? The more the grapevine buzzes, the better it will be. I don't suppose everyone will be so thorough as the hostess I know who had her own kind of "black velvet" party because her husband always thought she was most chic when she wore black. On his sixtieth birthday she planned a huge party and had the ceiling of the club canopied in stunning black and white chiffon. She ordered a white chiffon birthday cake with really dark semi-sweet chocolate fudge icing, and the cake was decorated in white.

"Black velvet," of course, is actually the name of a wicked English drink, combining Guinness stout and champagne (rum, in some versions). This blend produces a drink that is nearly black and as lethal as it looks. We recommend a blackberry cordial with Coca-Cola and soda added, but I leave it to you to concoct your own version.

But yes, the hostess *can* wear her best black velvet gown, and it won't matter at this party if a few ladies show up wearing the same fabric. The tablecloth can be white with a wide band of black velvet down the center, or it can be a tailored white satin or net cloth with a narrow band of black velvet ribbon. Use black candles, or all white. The floral centerpiece can be white flowers with a few black velvet leaves pasted on the real leaves. If you have black wrought-iron candelabra, by all means use these, although silver candlesticks will gleam very strikingly on the black background.

This party is usually a reception or an open house. The cocktail napkins can have monograms or initials in black printing. Here is the menu:

Ripe Olives   Porcupine Celery*
Caviar in Cucumber Boats*
Deviled Eggs
Filled Prunes
Lobster and King Crab Chunks with Cocktail Sauce
Chicken Breast Pinover Sandwiches*
Open Ripe Olive Cream Cheese Canapés
Hot Shaved Ham Toasted Sandwiches
Mushroom Sandwiches
Black Licorice and White Mint Wafers
Dainty Sliced Licorice Pectin Jellies

Olives and celery should be served on shaved ice.

Place black Danish or Russian caviar in the Cucumber Boats* and arrange on a platter like the petals of a daisy, alternating with chopped hard-boiled egg, chopped parsley, green onion tops, and sour cream. Be generous with the parsley garnish and lemon wedges. Serve small white crackers or toasted Melba medallions on a separate tray. Don't use saltines; they're too salty.

Deviled eggs should be pullet-sized. Cut them off at the bottom so they can be made to stand up vertically, remove the tops and the egg yolks, then refill with your favorite egg yolk mixture, and recap with a ripe olive garnish.

Use firm medium black prunes, seeded, and fill them with green pepper cream cheese and toasted pecans.

Put the crab and lobster chunks in a black (or silver) bowl, over ice snow. Use black toothpicks. Serve the cocktail sauce in very dark eggplant shells.

The chicken breast sandwiches are calla-lily shaped, in cornucopia style, with anchovy cream cheese and an anchovy filet for the stamen.

Edge the open canapés with dark toasted pecans.

Brush the tops of the toasted sandwiches with butter and dust them heavily with poppy seeds.

For the Mushroom Sandwiches, use thin dark buttered bread,

cut out the top slice of bread to make a hole like a doughnut, and insert a tiny mushroom cap. Toast in oven.

If you want this party to be a buffet supper, repeat some of the items in the above menu and add Whitefish à la Rhine*, with a lemon sauce remoulade, a light shake of coarse black pepper, and a sprinkling of capers. Also serve charcoal-broiled 2-ounce beef filets in flat poppy seed buns. If licorice ice cream is obtainable in your city, serve it in angel food Mary Ann shells.

Bread and Butter Party

This is a really novel idea. Set up your table as for a smorgasbord. The waiter could wear a big baker's hat. There should be some bread boards and bread knives, an electric toaster, and an electric grill—more of these, of course, if the party is large.

On the table place a great variety of breads: fresh, crusty Jewish rye; pumpernickel or sesame Italian; Holland with a rice-flour topping; Vienna; potato poppy seed; French; dill; Swedish limpa; whole wheat oatmeal.

As a dessert item, arrange on one side these dessert breads: raisin; cinnamon; Boston brown; date nut; banana; cranberry; pecan orange.

There should be plenty of butter of various kinds: regular salt butter, sweet butter, honey butter, lemon butter, date butter, herb parsley butter, toasted sesame butter, peanut butter, and apple butter.

The butter can be arranged in fancy shapes, some molded like bars of soap, some in little brown jugs or crocks. If you have butter paddles, you can make butter balls to put in shaved ice. Our cake decorators have even made butter roses, using soft butter put through a regular rose petal metal tube; calla lilies and tulips are other possibilities.

A Fan Collector's Party

A Cleveland lady had a daughter who realized how much her mother's hobby of collecting fans meant to her, so she made it the theme of a party for a seventieth birthday. Perhaps you will want to adapt this idea to your own uses and have a fan party.

In a novelty shop or a Japanese store it's easy to buy inexpensive fans for decorations. A florist has fan-shaped vases for flowers, and a fan-shaped birthday cake is not difficult to design. The color scheme could be pink, aqua (or turquoise), and lavender.

For an afternoon tea, you might have both open and closed sandwiches. Use a large round cookie cutter and cut circle into three parts to make fan-shaped sandwiches out of thin sliced white and whole wheat bread after spreading on the filling.

MENU

Sandwiches
Canapés
Orange Cinnamon Pastry Fans
Fan-shaped Frosted Cakes
Wafer Mints

Sandwiches could be both open and closed. In the latter category, try mashed avocado with grated lemon rind, a small amount of cream cheese and fresh chopped mint or watercress. Also a minced chicken salad sandwich, with a dash of curry if you like. For an open sandwich, pimiento cream cheese with pistachio nuts.

The canapés are crab meat salad with just a little grated lemon rind added; and tomato on cucumber spread.

The pastry fans are made of puff pastry, fan-shaped, half of them plain and half dipped in dark chocolate and decorated.

Make the frosted cakes tiny, and again decorate them in pink, aqua, and lavender.

For the Cleveland lady's birthday, her daughter had a third of the wafer mints decorated with "70," a third with the honored guest's initials, and a third with fans.

To add one more idea: It would be entertaining if the invitations could be sent with an inexpensive fan attached, and a request to each guest to write a message for the honored one, either prose or poetry.

Jack Spratt Party

Here's a party I've imagined for a long time but never had an opportunity to give. But I could almost guarantee it would be a lot of fun.

Invitations should be in the shape of an oval platter. If the hostess is particularly slender, she might add a lot of padding to her dress for that evening.

The buffet table should be quite long. Get an artist friend to make two comical silhouettes—one a tall, skinny man broken almost in two, the other a plump lady of considerable proportions. Prop them up with a simple wooden "scaffolding" in the middle of the table, and place a toy wooden fence between. On the fat lady's side, put all the fattening, calorie-filled items, with the low-calorie foods on the skinny man's side. Let people line up for one or both.

Since the menu amounts to a smorgasbord, you may as well invite a large group of your friends. Use your imagination about the menu, but here are some lean and fat suggestions that may help:

Lean: Cold lean roast beef (filet preferred); cold breast of turkey; salmon in aspic; tossed green salad with vinegar and oil dressing; raw vegetable platter; asparagus vinaigrette; sliced tomatoes with parsley; thin sliced plain bread without butter; braised celery in consommé; platter of grapefruit and fresh unsweetened pineapple; unfrosted angel food cake; oatmeal cookies; macaroons; plain mints.

Fat: Sliced corned beef; baked ham or cold crown roast of pork with dressing; potato salad; baked beans with plenty of salt pork; creamed potatoes au gratin; corn on the cob; cucumbers in sour cream or cucumber sour cream aspic; buttered bread; herring in sour cream; seafood Newburg; lima bean salad with mayonnaise and Swiss cheese; miniature cream puffs or Charlottes Russe; chocolate eclairs; chocolate cake; chocolate candy.

Friday the 13th

In the center of your table have a black china cat (or else a black cardboard silhouette), a broken small mirror, and a doll walking under a ladder. As an antidote, the invitations can be cut out of colored paper in the shape of horseshoes. If you have a seated dinner, be sure to put thirteen guests to a table.

MENU

Cream of Asparagus Soup
Triscuits
Stuffed Baked Whitefish with Lemon Wedges
Tartar Sauce
French-fried Parsley*
Stuffed Tomatoes
Salad
Rose Toth Dressing
Lemon Soufflé

Bake the tomatoes, scoop out, and fill with lima bean or green pea purée.

The salad is made with Belgian endive, chopped Bibb lettuce, and chopped hard-boiled eggs.

Lemon snow pudding may be substituted for the soufflé. Serve it with tart lemon custard sauce.

The Bonnet Party

For an early spring sales meeting of about two hundred sales-ladies, we thought up the idea of adding interest to the occasion by offering prizes for the oldest hat worn, the prettiest hat, the most unusual hat, and the biggest hat. Such creations! It was a good thing we had an impartial group of judges.

Not to be outdone by the ladies, I bought a dime-store peaked cap and then had the cake decorators fashion a small beehive out of hard icing. They also made a half-dozen bees on thin wires, which wiggled back and forth while I talked, along with a few loose bees placed in my hair. I made a speech to the ladies that day, titled

"Bees in My Bonnet," and whenever I made a new point, I tipped my hat to the ladies and pulled a bee out of my bonnet.

Behind all this nonsense, I was trying to emphasize for the personnel of the store their forthcoming effort to sell bonnet cakes and bonnet petits fours for an Easter promotion. We have made these cakes for years and they please women of all ages, from grandmothers to the young and smart set. They are fashioned in the shape of a sailor-type hat, with a thin, single 9-inch layer for the brim, topped with a low 6-inch cake crown. A band of real ribbon (easily pulled off), a pretty bow, and a gay perky flower are the finishing touches. They're easier to make at home than the individual petits fours hats, and they provide an edible center-piece which can be used for almost any occasion. We have also used them at parties for ladies who are retiring from the millinery section of a department store—or who are merely having a birth-day party.

CHAPTER 2

SUMMER

Summer is a delightful time to entertain. There are many people whose homes are comparatively small—too small to have in a large group for a buffet supper—but the optimists are always hopeful that the guests can be outdoors for at least part of the evening. Daylight saving time helps, if your state observes it; twilight lasts until nine or ten o'clock. Only teeming rain or cold can really spoil things, but guests will usually understand if they're forced inside by the weather, since we all have to share it.

One of the nicest summer party ideas I know is the one that follows:

The Oldest Friends on the Longest Day of the Year

Usually summer begins on June 21. What better way to start the season than by inviting your oldest friends for dinner? If you have time, get out old snapshots and mount them on a couple of large pieces of cardboard. If you have childhood pictures, so much the better. Number the photos and offer a prize for the guest who gets the most names right.

Be sure to limit the number of guests to those you're able to seat at dinner. Most people over fifty prefer being seated to eat, rather than balancing a tray or plate on their laps. It can be buffet or a served meal. You'll find menus here for both.

June is the month for roses and daisies. If you use roses, maybe you'll want to have an old-rose pink tablecloth and green napkins. If you're using daisies, select yellow cloths with green napkins, or vice versa. In summer, dispense with plastic floral centerpieces entirely and use fresh flowers, no matter how simple the arrangement may be.

Let's begin with two buffet menus:

BUFFET NO. 1

Poached Cold Salmon
Coq Au Vin
Orange Rice Balls*
Zucchini Squash Casserole*
Fresh Fruit Platter
Tiny Pecan Rolls and Tiny Rolls or Muffins
Ice Rings with Ice Cream
Ladyfingers   Mints   Florence Cake

With the salmon serve watercress dill sauce, mustard caper sauce, or cucumber sour cream sauce. You can use scooped-out eggplant shells for these (see front cover jacket) or else cut glass or slim Revere bowls. Garnish with parsley and daisies or roses.

Coq au vin is, of course, chicken in wine sauce, but you may serve instead, if you like, breast of chicken with Currant Wine Sauce*. Garnish with fresh currants, if they're obtainable.

For the fruit platter, keep the fruits separate by using large scooped-out fresh pineapple shells with a different kind of fruit in each. Serve Poppy Seed* or Paprika Dressing* with the fruit.

Pass the dessert. It consists of rings of lime or mint ice with balls of strawberry ice cream in the center. Pound cake may substitute for the Florence cake.

BUFFET NO. 2

Lobster Salad
Canadian Bacon
Zucchini Squash Boats
Vegetable Wheel Vinaigrette*
Hominy Watercress Muffins
Fruited Cantaloupe Rings
Pastel Mints

Instead of lobster, you might have a shrimp salad, or a seafood salad with a combination of crab, lobster, and shrimp.

Serve the Canadian bacon piping hot, carved at the buffet, with a thin brown mustard sauce.

Cut medium-sized squash into 4-inch lengths. Scoop out and fill with chopped onion, bread crumbs, mushrooms, and herbs.

Dessert consists of individual rings of cantaloupe filled with fresh fruits and topped with a small scoop of lime or pineapple sherbet. Garnish with fresh mint.

The pastel mints should be in the shape of roses or daisies.

SIT-DOWN DINNER NO. 1

*Flaked Fresh Salmon in Aspic**
Boned Chicken Breasts
*Grape Sauce**
Noodle Croquettes
Stuffed Tomatoes
Yellow Salad
*Ruth Just's Roman Dressing**
*Poppy Seed and Sesame Melba Sticks**
Fruit and Sherbet
Pastel Mints

Serve the salmon with dill watercress mayonnaise, top with capers, and garnish with lemon wedges. Pass your favorite tiny crackers.

With the chicken breasts, serve Grape Sauce* made with both seedless grapes and seeded Tokay grapes. Add a little wine if you wish.

Roll the noodle croquettes in Rice Krispies. They can be served either plain or with mushrooms added to the noodles.

Scoop out small peeled tomatoes and fill with a mixture of grated carrots, diced celery, and new cabbage.

For the salad, use yellow wax beans, water chestnuts, and loads of chive parsley butter. You can also add artichoke hearts (use the frozen ones), if you wish.

For dessert, serve ¼ of a fresh pineapple, with the pineapple sliced through and away from the shell. Top with mint or lime sherbet. Serve large chewy almond macaroons with this. Or arrange wedges of honeydew melon on geranium leaves with two small scoops of watermelon sherbet.

SIT-DOWN DINNER NO. 2

Vichyssoise
Tiny Crab Meat Canapés
Spring Broilers
Yellow Country Chicken Gravy
Stuffed Spinach Blintzes*
Minted Fresh Peas
Tiny Orange Rolls
Individual Bing Cherry Salad Molds*
Sherbet and Melon Balls
Angel Food Cake
Mints

Be sure the vichyssoise is ice cold.

Brush the spring broiler with butter and bake it well. Serve ½ broiler per person.

Sauté the peas with fresh chopped mint and lots of butter or margarine.

The salad molds are tiny and individual, and lavishly garnished with fresh pitted Bing cherries. You can stuff a few with pink-tinted cream cheese balls or leave them plain.

For dessert, serve rings of watermelon sherbet filled with honey-dew melon balls, or wedges of cantaloupe with vanilla ice cream, on fresh leaves.

The angel food (or chiffon if you prefer) cake should be cut in dainty wedges.

The Strawberry Tea

A very gracious hostess I know had a passionate love for strawberries. Friends and family often remembered her with gifts of linen, china, and ornaments decorated with strawberries. It was especially appropriate, then, when she decided to give her grand-daughter a coming-out tea with a strawberry motif. It could not have taken place at a better time—the middle of June, just at the height of the home-grown strawberry season.

Two large straw rugs were specially painted with huge strawberries for use on the terrace where the receiving line was to be. We found pretty paper cocktail napkins with a border of strawberries to be used outdoors. Her embroidered linen ones were used at the tea table in the house. Little café tables had strawberry-embroidered organdy cloths over pink, and were decorated with strawberry ornaments, both metallic and porcelain.

Wild fresh strawberry leaves were gathered from nearby fields, along with fresh mint. On these were placed handsome fresh giant berries, arranged with a bowl of powdered sugar dip in the middle.

Candies were strawberry pectin jellies and fresh strawberries dipped in melted pastel pink chocolate.

A fresh strawberry punch was made with frozen lemonade, fresh cranberry juice, strawberry extract, and sparkling soda water, with diced strawberries added.

Since men were also invited to the reception, we agreed that we should have other things than simply the featured strawberry items. Happily, our hostess had two very attractive brass Turkish barbecue sets, so we had a chef, dressed in pink satin pantaloons and turban, broiling tiny sausages and miniature shish kebabs.

Shaved pinkish roast beef sandwiches on paper-thin bread, with horseradish mayonnaise, and turkey breast fingers were served, along with Open Strawberry Canapés* on whole wheat bread spread with pineapple cream cheese; Fresh Chopped Mint Sandwiches*; and fresh glazed strawberry tarts and strawberry petits fours were also served.

Still another idea, one we didn't use: It would be effective, and admittedly a lot of work, to string strawberries (firm ones) and have a garland of them around the top of a carrousel table.

The Butterfly Tea (PLATE III)

I was preparing to leave on a trip to South America when an advance reservation came to us for a large coming-out reception at a country estate. The theme was to be butterflies. When I got to

South America, I discovered, by a happy coincidence, that butter-fly motifs were plentiful all over the continent—on ashtrays in Brazil, embroidery in Paraguay, interesting bone work in Chile. The local display company at home also had a fine selection of colorful plastic butterflies, and we used these on bushes, trees, and evergreens. It was a delightful change to depart from a theme color; the effect of multicolored decorations was especially gay.

Yellow and black are the first colors most people think of when they hear the word "butterfly." So we put a yellow ruffled organdy skirt on the main buffet table, with a black linen runner over the top, beautifully embroidered with bright multicolored butterflies. The effect was stunning, particularly when we added a narrow black velvet ribbon along the edge. Black rickrack tape could be used instead of the ribbon.

For this kind of party, café tables can be covered in aqua, deep turquoise, yellow, and apricot. The ashtrays we had were mainly in turquoise. Our maintenance department had to make us a butterfly cookie cutter when we discovered we didn't have one.

These were the main things we served:

Butterfly-shaped Shaved Ham Sandwiches on rye or whole wheat, and Turkey Sandwiches. The bread was sliced very thin and then cut with a cookie cutter.

Butterfly Cucumber Open Sandwiches. These were made with cucumbers cut with a crinkled round cutter; then the slices were cut in half and turned back to back.

Butterfly Shrimp Canapés, with two shrimp forming the butter-fly.

Roquefort Cream Cheese Canapés with walnut halves quartered and used for the wings. A wedge of orange rind served for the body.

Butterfly-type Waffles, made with a special die and lightly sprinkled with powdered sugar.

Very thin hand-cut butter cookies in the shape of a butterfly, decorated in very thin bright icing that outlined the edge of each cookie with red and orange, yellow and apricot, aqua and lavender —all as gay as possible.

Butterfly-shaped Mints. If your candy store doesn't have them, the thing to do is to order flat yellow, aqua, and apricot heart-shaped mints, cut them in half while they're fresh, then reverse them and stick them together with melted semi-sweet chocolate. Almonds, both blanched and with skins.

A Dinner of Herbs

When I think of an herb dinner, I think of those wise words of Solomon: "Better is a dinner of herbs where love is than a stalled ox and hatred therewith." Hostesses might remember the principle suggested by the proverb—no matter how simple the meal or refreshments, the most successful entertaining comes when the guests get from their host and hostess the feeling of friendly affection and respect. Occasionally I have attended parties which seemed to have been given merely to impress friends and to "outdo" neighbors, with a consequent lack of warm sincerity. Sometimes, too, a hostess gets so wrought up over the details of a party that she is too tense and nervous to have any interest in the people she invites. I've seen the mother of the bride leave the receiving line to check on some homemade floral arrangements at the last minute.

In arranging herb dinners, I have always been much indebted to the Cleveland Herb Society for many wonderful suggestions, and I heartily recommend their cookbooks. Once the society entertained their Ohio chapter at a lovely estate. There the centerpieces were tall wrought-iron hurricane lamps, with a topiary effect of spicy red carnations combined with beautiful bright green fresh mint. Tablecloths were an antique Chinese red with green napkins.

We sometimes use a Shrimp Tree (PLATE V), which is made with six disks of various sizes. In between are generous clumps of curly washed parsley over crushed ice, with a ball of parsley at the top. The fresh shrimp are buried ahead of time in crushed ice, with fresh lemon squeezed over them to deodorize. Then the shrimp are hung on the disks, thick side at the top. After all the disks are filled, we stick toothpicks (red, yellow, green, or blue) in all of them at the same angle. We also scoop out honeydew melon shells and make a scalloped top to hold the shrimp sauce. Eggplant shells or summer squash can also be used in this way instead of glass or silver dishes.

Here are the menus—two buffets and a dinner:

HERB DINNER BUFFET

Cold Ham Mousse with Spiced Crab Apples
Hot Country Fried Cut-up Chicken
Currant Wine Sauce*
Herb Rice Ring
Sliced Tomatoes
Wilted Sesame Spinach Salad
Herb-buttered French Bread
Minted Fresh Pineapple
Caraway Sugar Cookies

Dip the chicken in beaten eggs, then in chopped cashew nuts before frying.

Marinate the sliced tomatoes in French dressing. Arrange on a platter and cover generously with chopped green onion and watercress.

Serve the pineapple in a ring of mint ice, garnished with fresh sprigs of mint. An alternate dessert would be mint parfaits with chocolate ice cream, pistachio ice cream, and mint ice. Skip the whipped cream topping but use a green cherry and a sprig of mint.

HERB BUFFET

Snow Pea Pods, Stuffed with Crab Meat*
Standing Ribs of Beef
Horseradish Mousse*
French-fried Parsley*
Hot Glazed Mushroom Caps
Dill Bread
Stuffed Tomatoes
Cauliflower Salad
Silver Chiffon Cake
Benne Seed Cookies
Licorice Mints

Garnish the aspic mold with tufts of watercress.

Serve the mushroom caps with chestnuts in sherry consommé sauce.

Scoop out the tomatoes and fill them with a mixture of cottage cheese, grated Roquefort cheese, and chives. Arrange on Bibb lettuce.

The salad is cold cooked cauliflower smothered with dill, dressed with a watercress remoulade, and surrounded with asparagus vinaigrette.

Cake can be spicy or plain, with a Root Beer Icing*.

SIT-DOWN HERB DINNER

*Spiced Meat Wedges**
Fresh Figs and Prosciutto
Vichyssoise
Herb-buttered Melba Medallions
Boned Chicken Breasts
Poppy Seed Noodle Casserole
Tiny Glazed Silver Onions
Peas with Fresh Chopped Mint Butter
Fresh Melon Ball Salad
Curried Vinaigrette Dressing
Miniature Herb Baking Powder Biscuits
Honey Butter
Lemon Sherbet with Blueberry Sauce
Wintergreen Mints

Spiced Meat Wedges* are served as appetizers with cocktails. Cut the fresh figs in quarters and wrap them in prosciutto ham.

Remember to have the vichyssoise ice cold. An ice-cold cucumber soup may be substituted.

With the boned chicken breasts serve a thin, hot watercress gravy—*no* cream.

The onions are glazed in currant jelly.

In angel food Mary Ann cake shells, put lemon sherbet with blueberry sauce to which a dash of ground cloves has been added.

The Garden Party

One of the loveliest garden dinner parties we ever catered was on the shores of Lake Erie at a dignified Italian villa. Tables were arranged along garden walks around the lily pools at various angles, with a second setting inside the house to be used if it rained. And the rains did come. Fortunately the sun came out again about five o'clock and a beautiful, balmy June evening began. Because the area was so heavily shrubbed, it was necessary to use two huge bug bombs to dispel the mosquitoes. We always think it important to take precautions against insects. A party can be ruined if flies or mosquitoes are too much in evidence.

For the table, garlands of pachysandra cleverly strung together by ardent garden club members enhanced the old-rose pink cloths. Here and there were artistic clusters and arrangements of pink garden flowers in white, pink, and American Beauty. Deep pink napkins were used.

Here is the menu for that occasion:

*Avocado in the Snow**
Lobster Thermidor
*French-fried Parsley**
Peas with Fresh Chopped Mint and Water Chestnuts
Green Salad
*Ruth Just's Roman Dressing**
French Croissant Rolls
Fruit and Sherbet Flower Pots
Macaroons

The salad was Bibb lettuce and French endive tossed with the dressing.

Dessert was spectacular. We had red clay flower pots, lined with foil, and filled with ice-cold summer fruits, covered with pineapple sherbet and dusted with cinnamon sugar and cocoa, to look like dirt, with assorted fresh flowers inserted.

Remembering the garden parties we have catered, two luncheons in particular stand out. One was in an arboretum under a huge tent. Tables were covered with green burlap. Miniature bushel baskets, half of them green and half rustic brown, were lined with a pretty lavender print and a cluster of plastic violets on the side. Lunch was served in these baskets.

It included: crisp French hard rolls, freshly baked, but extra thin. These were split, spread with sweet butter, chopped watercress, layered breast of turkey, and thin slices of prosciutto ham. A thin coating of mayonnaise had Dijon mustard added. For vegetables, raw cauliflowerets, cherry tomatoes, and Porcupine Celery*, with celery salt dip in a little flowered paper cup. There were also wedges of Ohio Swiss cheese and two small cakes of Geauga County maple sugar. Dessert was a small paper soufflé cup of lemon orange Bavarian cream, topped with crystallized violet blossoms. A small bottle of white wine, complete with wineglass, was included in each basket.

Another garden luncheon long to be remembered was held in a big white tent. The theme was old-fashioned anemones. Huge colorful paper anemones were fastened to each tent pole on graceful strong wires so they bobbed back and forth in the breeze. Round tables were covered in the bright anemone colors with napkins in a different shade on each table. Fresh anemones, which happened to be scarce, were arranged on each table, and the florist filled in with white daisies to supplement the supply. Around the tent were placed old-fashioned big-wheel bicycles and straw baskets of daisies.

The food was arranged on plates and set in place before the ladies sat down because they were on a rigid schedule. This is what we served:

*Flaked Fresh Salmon in Aspic**
*Dill Watercress Remoulade Dressing**
Artichokes Vinaigrette on Bibb Lettuce
Cucumber Slices
Flaky Croissants
Fresh Pineapple
Tiny Macaroons and Thin Butter Cookies

The cucumber slices had scalloped edges.

We used quarters of fresh pineapple, with the pineapple loosened into wedges and garnished with fresh mint.

Many receptions are held in gardens, but these are described in the chapters on "Debutante Parties" and "The Wedding."

Orange Blossom Tree

Relish Tree

PLATE V

Four Trees

Strawberry Tree

Shrimp Tree

PLATE VI

Luncheon

Ham Cornucopias with Saffron Rice
Tomatoes Stuffed with Seedless Grapes Vinaigrette
Pencil Cheese Sesame Melba Sticks

Rainbows

The "pot of gold at the end of the rainbow" theme is especially appropriate if the occasion has to do with fund-raising.

For one such party I found in the home where it was to be given a large antique brass candelabrum with eight holders. We had pink, red, orange, yellow, green, blue, light violet, and purple candles inserted, and placed it on one end of the buffet. In the center our artists made a huge cardboard rainbow, and at the end, opposite the candelabrum, I made a large "pot of gold" by using two extra-large yellow summer squash. One was inverted to make an impressive stand, and the other was well scooped out; both were brushed with streaks of gilt paint. Around the base I had chocolate coins covered with gold foil (many candy stores have these imported goodies), and the *pièce dé resistance* was the gold pot temptingly filled with lobster salad, dressed with a yellowish curried mayonnaise, and heavily dusted with grated egg yolk.

The buffet table was covered with rainbow-shaded cloths, and the round tables scattered on the lawn each had a cloth in a different color of the rainbow. The centerpieces were simple: hurricane lamps surrounded with pachysandra and bright glamellias (plucked gladioli). We could have used instead six small altar candles in red, orange, yellow, green, blue, and violet around a regular flower piece.

Almost any menu can be used for this party, but a huge Vegetable Wheel Vinaigrette* should occupy a prominent spot. I like a platter or chop plate at least two feet in diameter.

Here is one way to arrange the wheel, each item or set of items to be arranged in a pie-shaped wedge: beets or tomatoes; carrots; bright yellow wax beans combined with a little cooked, diced yellow summer squash or whole-kernel corn; green peas or bright green broccoli; fluffy rice with blueberries or with tinted blue coconut; or braised hearts of celery with capers dyed blue; and purple cabbage slaw, grated very finely.

Care should be taken not to marinate the yellow wax beans or broccoli too far in advance, because the vinaigrette dressing tends to discolor the vegetables and they lose their attractiveness. Swathe the whole dramatic platter with watercress. If you don't have a round platter, arrange the vegetables in rows, diagonally across the platter.

Most popular main entrée would probably be sliced ham and turkey, the platters surrounded by turnip roses dipped in pastel rainbow colors. (This idea could also be used at a party honoring anyone identified with the Rainbow Eastern Star groups.)

Crescent-shaped petits fours, iced with thin piping lines of rainbow colors, can be used for dessert. Round, flat white mints can have a dainty rainbow on them. You might also serve, in low silver bowls, various colored ice creams and sherbets, piled to make a colorful effect.

I have to admit that the whole idea of the rainbow party may flounder if the sunshine doesn't appear through the raindrops. And I don't suppose I will ever again see the remarkable coincidence that occurred when one hostess left the entire garden supper in my hands and I decided to use the rainbow motif. You can imagine my surprise when the lady came to her party attired in a rainbow chiffon party dress bought for the event weeks ahead.

Watermelons Are Ripe!

If you can make a bargain with your fruit man, this has delightful possibilities. For a small party, attractive watermelon mats are available. For a larger group, use watermelon-pink organdy or nylon net over white cloths. Dark emerald-green napkins make a nice contrast. Deep pink gladioli or roses, asters, or zinnias can be used for flowers—but be sure they're deep pink. Mints on each table can be tinted the same deep shade.

This would be the menu for a seated dinner:

Cold Crab Meat Salad
Shish Kebabs
Tiny Parsley Potatoes
Pickled Watermelon and Cantaloupe Rind
Hot Rolls
Dessert

A simple menu, but it requires a good deal of explanation. First, the crab meat salad is served in individual deep pink madrilene aspic rings. To get that color, use a little pink vegetable color in the madrilene. Add several grapes jubilee, if you wish; they're rosy pink canned seedless grapes in a maraschino syrup.

Ordinarily, the shish kebabs, which are the main course, would be simple, but these should be done with showmanship. First, make inverted watermelon bells, using about one third of a watermelon turned over on a light tray. In the top of the bell, scoop out a small hole, insert a big half of an egg shell, fill with large loaf sugar and saturate at the last minute with lemon extract. Punch holes with an ice pick around the entire melon—six, eight, or ten, depending on how many guests there are at each table, plus an extra, so no one takes the last. Shish kebabs on long skewers are taken from the oven or charcoal broiler and stuck into the holes in the melon bell. Just as the waiter or waitress gets near the table, touch a match to the saturated loaf sugar and carry the platter in flaming. You could use a sparkler in the middle, but it's harder to serve and someone might get burned, so we prefer the extract. Occasionally we insert an altar candle.

Now to the shish kebabs themselves. There are three or four kinds I would recommend for this party. One is lamb with 1 kumquat, 2 mushroom caps, 1 small whole onion, and 1 small wedge of green pepper. Another would be Hawaiian: large chunks of chicken breast, 2 large jumbo shrimp, green pepper, a small whole onion, and, at the top, a pink watermelon ball for looks. Still another: mushroom caps, whole onion, cherry tomato, and wedges of tenderloin tips of beef. Finally, a double-decker: Arrange the long skewers around the lower level of the melon ball. Then at the top have fruit shish kebabs on short skewers with kumquats, watermelon rind, red cherries, banana, or what have you.

In any case, it would be wise to make a test run before the actual event. You'll find several ways to get the various items to remain on the skewers. Remember, you'll have to be well organized to get these attractive entrees to the guests piping hot. There must be no delay once they come out of the oven.

Instead of the tiny parsley potatoes, you might prefer to bring to the table a small casserole of Hashed in Cream Potatoes*, or an au gratin casserole of vegetables.

The rolls should be piping hot and buttered in advance.

Dessert might be watermelon wedges with three huge strawberries speared with toothpicks. Or it might be a cone of watermelon, made by twisting a narrow tablespoon into the meaty part of the melon, and enhanced with lime or mint sherbet. Or perhaps a ring of watermelon sherbet, surrounded by watermelon balls on a sheaf of fresh mint in the center, one for each table.

With any of these, serve South Carolina benne seed cookies, and watermelon coconut candy, if it's obtainable.

If you want an appetizer with cocktails before dinner, a watermelon basket filled with shaved ice and raw vegetables is effective. With this you can have some kind of onion soup dip and dry celery salt for a "dry" dip.

The Basket Supper

From the standpoint of less fuss and muss, less help and more fun, basket suppers are the answer out of doors. They are also fun if you suddenly have to make a dash for shelter from an unexpected shower. If the night is cool, serve a hot soup to start. There are two ways to handle the serving: Have all the items piled on a buffet and let each guest collect his meal, or fix the baskets in the kitchen and put them completed in a handy location.

Here are the four menus to put in the baskets:

MENU NO. 1

Cut-up Baked Chicken
Hot Baked Beans in Pot
Cold Potato Salad
Pickle Cup
Fruit Cup
Brownies or Cupcakes

Put two pieces of the baked chicken, wrapped in foil, in each basket. Save extras to be passed later.

Instead of potato salad, you might possibly serve macaroni salad, with lots of celery and chopped hard-boiled eggs added.

Make the fruit cup of fresh, cut-up fruit.

MENU NO. 2

Individual Meat Pies
Vegetable Cup
Small Whole Tomatoes
Potato Chips
Large Buttered Parkerhouse Rolls
Plain Baked Custard

The meat pies could be beef or chicken.

Cooked vegetables vinaigrette make the vegetable cup.

Instead of a small whole tomato, perhaps you'd prefer three or four small cherry tomatoes.

Make the custard in a foil cup. Or, instead, serve any kind of Bavarian cream, with ladyfingers.

MENU NO. 3

Swedish Meatballs
Rice Pilaf, Macaroni, or Creamed Potatoes
Three-bean Salad Vinaigrette
. *Melba Sesame Sticks**
Deep Blueberry Tarts

The meatballs should be in individual casseroles or foil cups, and so should the rice, macaroni, or potatoes.

MENU NO. 4

Chicken Mexican*
Cottage Cheese Noodles
Stuffed Tomatoes
Italian Bread Sticks
Peach Shortcake

Chicken paprikash would be an alternate for the Chicken Mexican*.

The noodles are in foil cups.

Scoop out the tomatoes and fill with seedless grapes, finely diced celery, and Italian dressing.

Put fresh cut-up peaches on small shortcake biscuits.

Old Plantation

Some homes and yards lend themselves as perfect settings for a bit of ante-bellum Deep South. I recall one such outdoor supper where we were prepared to serve either in a tent or in the formal garden area. As it turned out, the weather was so cold the supper had to be held in the tent.

We used 8-foot-long tables with light green and avocado-green striped cloths. Black wrought-iron hurricane lamps centered each table. Strewn over the iron were lacy bits of old Spanish moss, in this case sent by a friend from northern Florida.

Around the hurricane lamps also were strands of mountain laurel, which blended with the green and white color scheme.

A long barbecue pit was made on a barren stretch of lawn, with a few loose cement blocks. It takes two men to handle these barbecues, because it's necessary to keep turning the grilled items so they don't get too charred. And here is the menu:

Peanut Soup
*Shrimp Biscuits**
Barbecued Ham Steaks
*Red Eye Country Gravy**
Small Whole Silver Onions
Fresh Pineapple Spears
"Green" Hominy Casseroles
Corn Sticks
Watermelon Wedges
Praline Cookies

With the Shrimp Biscuits*, serve Artichoke Mustard Relish*.
Wrap the onions in foil, with two butter pats in each, and bake.
Rub the pineapple spears with melted butter and grill them.
Mix chopped parsley, chives, and watercress in the hominy to make it green. An alternative to hominy is corn pudding.
Deck the watermelon wedges with huge strawberries on picks.

Lavender and Old Lace

I know an eighty-year-old lady who has lived a long and color-ful life, and now in her twilight years enjoys having one big party a year, on her June birthday. Since the same guests return year after year, she has had to use various themes to keep the parties from becoming monotonous.

One of her ideas was a "lavender and old lace" party. I visited a nearby department store and bought some pretty lavender cur-tains with a crocheted edge, and some soft, frilly lavender boudoir lampshades. The curtains were converted into tea aprons for the waitresses, and the lampshades made quaint poke bonnet hats for them.

The buffet table was covered in lavender Indian head and pleated lavender nylon net with a band of lace along the top edge. At the dime store I found a number of plastic lace doilies and these were used as "place mats." On the center of each round table we had a glass cake stand with a hurricane lamp in the middle. Around this were corsage-shaped petits fours in paper lace-frilled doilies, each with lavender ribbon streamers. The guests were invited to eat the petits fours with dessert or take them home as favors.

This is one menu for the "lavender and old lace" party:

Standing Ribs of Beef
Lobster Newburg
Stuffed Turkey
Bing Cherry Salad Mold*
Assorted Rolls
Ice Cream and Birthday Cake
Lavender Mints   Salted Nuts

Serve the beef very rare.

Have plenty of gravy with the big turkey.

At this particular party we made the salad mold with grape juice and garnished it with fresh fruit.

Here is another suggestion for a seated dinner:

Individual Shrimp Mousse
Dijon Mustard Remoulade
*Sesame Melba Toast**
Crisp Boned Breast of Duckling
*Currant Wine Sauce**
Rice Croquettes
Green Garden Peas
Tiny Parkerhouse Rolls
Celery   Olives
Ice Cream
Petits Fours
Lavender and White Mints

Serve each mousse in a purple cabbage leaf, lined with shredded endive and surrounded with ½-inch cubes of tomato aspic. Garnish the top with purple Greek olives.

Arrange the duckling on platters, and surround it with the soft, golden-brown rice croquettes. Serve the sauce in eggplant shells.

Cook the peas French style with purple Italian onion and lettuce.

Butter the rolls ahead of time.

The ice cream is in melon molds of vanilla ice cream and blueberry sherbet, with strained Tart Red Raspberry Sauce*.

Little petits fours can be iced with violet trim.

The Purple Dinner

An aunt of mine in Brooklyn years ago knit me a beautiful purple bedspread. It was done in three or four shades of purple and orchid, with a contrasting stripe of bright green. This gave me the idea of decorating the bedroom in shades of purple, with purple grass cloth walls and multicolored drapes of purple, mauve, and blue. I found it necessary to have strong white lighting in the room to keep it bright.

When the room was completed, I decided it would be fun to show off the new room by having friends over and giving them a purple dinner. Before I could carry out this plan, two women came into my office and requested an unusual party. They had no actual event to celebrate—just wanted to entertain their mutual friends with a big August dinner party, but they wanted it to be unusual and different. "Would you like a purple dinner?" I asked them. They were puzzled at first, but game, and after I explained it to them, they agreed to let me do it.

This dinner was held at a private club rented for the evening. By an odd coincidence, the room had cove lighting and every fourth light bulb was lavender. We made purple tablecloths and used pink napkins. Centerpieces were pink, lavender, mauve, and purple asters. Each table had a candy dish with pink, white, and lavender mints. We had pink matchbooks with metallic purple monograms.

The buffet was two-tone pink and lavender with orchid net. Purple candles were used, and the huge floral centerpiece was made of delphinium in blues, orchids, and deep purples.

For cocktail appetizers, we had generous chunks of lobster arranged on a large silver platter of ice snow, held in place by purple cabbage leaves. Toothpicks had been dyed purple and left in the sun for a good week to dry, so the dye wouldn't run. A huge fresh lobster, arranged on one side of the platter, was painted purple—and that was the most difficult chore of the whole party. It was surrounded by a cluster of white gardenias. The two sauce dips (regular cocktail sauce and Pink Remoulade*) were put in scooped-out eggplant shells (rubbed inside with lemon juice). They were on a bed of parsley, surrounded with purple asters.

The buffet table was a thing of splendor. This was what we put on it:

Standing Ribs of Beef
Zucchini Squash Boats
Tossed Greek Salad
*Bing Cherry Salad Mold**
Tiny Assorted Rolls
Blueberry Mary Anns

We carved the beef at the table. The platter was garnished with purple and white Turnip Roses*. A horseradish sour cream sauce, in eggplant shells, was served with the beef.

For the Squash Boats, use medium zucchini about the size of small Idaho potatoes, scooped out and stuffed with a mixture of purple cabbage, caraway seeds, and raw apple.

The tossed Greek salad was arranged on a huge round platter edged with large whole purple cabbage leaves, with Bibb and iceberg lettuce, fresh spinach, romaine, and escarole tossed together with lemon vinegar and oil dressing. This was generously sprinkled with pitted purple Greek olives, shaved purple Italian onion, and white goat's milk (feta) cheese.

The salad mold was made with grape juice instead of the regular cherry juice, and it was embellished with tiny pink cream cheese balls.

Dessert was individual angel food Mary Ann shells, pink meringue shells could have been used instead, with vanilla ice cream and fresh blueberry sauce.

Throughout the meal, the abundance of lavender and purple was the subject of conversation. With the exception of the painted lobster, however, all were natural foods. It was so successful a party that we have repeated it many times in different parts of the state and before different groups. But before *you* try it, better be sure your husband likes purple well enough to pay the bill.

CHAPTER 3

FALL

The White Elephant Tea

Many cities have white elephant sales to raise money for worthy projects. In Cleveland, where this event is a biennial affair, it is traditional to bring the many committee members together for tea in a private home, for discussion, refreshments, and final planning.

For these parties we make a white cardboard elephant, and every year we try to give him a different amusing pose. (You can also use this animal for a Republican party.) We coat ours with a hard royal white icing that almost looks like plaster of Paris. We also have an elephant-shaped cookie cutter, so at least one kind of sandwich is cut out of thin white bread in that shape.

But the event that guests look forward to every two years is the cutting of two fabulous dark chocolate ribbon layer cakes—moist thin layers of chocolate cake with chocolate mocha filling and dark chocolate fudge icing. Our decorators make an elephant stencil out of cardboard. This is laid on top of the fudge cake after the frosting has dried, and then white buttercream icing is brushed over this and smoothed with a spatula, making a clean-cut silhouette of a white elephant.

Forks have to be served at this tea, so plates and cups without saucers are provided. The cake is rich but terribly good, and now and then it's different to go to a tea where forks are used.

Often when we cater big dinner parties for public affairs, we use an idea that is both effective and economical. We keep a number of glass cake stands, and a 7-inch layer cake with moist filling becomes not only a very pretty centerpiece, but an edible one. Usually one person at each table, often a man, volunteers to slice and serve the cake. It saves time when there is a full program following the dinner. By using a stencil, an organization insignia can be put on top of the cakes in frosting. This is quite effective.

Once, at a university alumni dinner where the speaker was a Navy submarine commander who had served in the Arctic, we used delicious layer cakes in the shape of igloos with toy sailors standing outside. These in the center of blue tablecloths made an impressive appearance.

Once in a Blue Moon

In a card shop one day I found a rather unusual anniversary card. It said, "Once in a blue moon we meet a couple as nice as you." I decided that would make a nice theme, even for a birthday party.

We fashioned a large first-quarter moon out of styrofoam and spread it with blue hard icing. This was hung from the dining room chandelier with a mobile galaxy of paper stars. The tablecloth was blue net over blue and fastened with royal blue velvet ribbon. In the center of the table we had a crescent-shaped moon made of aluminum foil, edged in pachysandra and filled with dark blue bachelor buttons.

Another foil moon with built-up sides, filled with ice snow, became a shrimp bowl. We used dark blue toothpicks for the shrimp.

We concocted a moon-shaped small cream cheese mold made of blue cheese, and around this had crescent Melba toast.

On the sideboard at this party we had a man's birthday cake with 70 blue candles, and "Happy 70th, Dad," written at the top of the cake. At the bottom was, "Once in a blue moon we meet a fellow as nice as you." The artist depicted a man in the moon with blue and white striped shirt and a cocky straw hat.

Dad was certainly pleased. This is the kind of party that elevates a man's ego.

Beehives and Honey

There's something fascinating about bees, but they *can* be obnoxious. A few years ago we catered a fashion benefit garden party in September. The committee planned a stunning dessert to be served in clay flower pots. To enhance the fruit, they requested a thin Kirsch syrup. We never realized there were so many bees in September—even on a cloudy afternoon. There were at least three hundred guests, but the bees outnumbered them and nearly ruined the party, even though we had sprayed for flies and insects in advance. Fortunately a fairly strong wind that day saved us, but this is a word of caution to givers of garden parties: take bees into account if you're serving a sweet, syrupy dessert outdoors.

A "beehive and honey" party, however, can be nice. It's especially appropriate for busy bee ladies whom you might want to invite in, for example, to greet a popular friend who is in town for a short time. Since the ladies usually *are* so busy, the best time is probably a 9:30 or 10 A.M. coffee hour.

Keep the flowers casual and simple. Chrysanthemums are plentiful in the fall. If you were to do this in the spring, honeysuckle with a few garden flowers or forsythia would be fine. To be really creative, fashion a small paper beehive for a centerpiece on your table.

Refreshments can be very easy at that hour. You might begin with hot baking powder biscuits, English muffins, crumpets, toast, or scones. Whichever one you have, the important thing is to serve them piping hot and have jars of honey and combs ready at hand.

With the hot breads serve crisp Caramelized Bacon*. It's a perfect item to offer; ladies love it. But be sure it's slow-baked and crisp. And, of course, plenty of steaming hot coffee.

There's an added reward for the guests at the end. The thoughtful hostess lifts up the beehive and discloses a small jar of honey for each guest, a graceful compensation for the time they've taken to come over.

Oodles of Noodles

In our town there was a jovial, husky gentleman who simply *loved* noodles. Nothing made him happier than a good beef pot roast with lots of gravy over a big plateful of noodles. When his friends decided to give him a party on his sixtieth birthday, they called the bakery and ordered a large layer cake, on the top of which our artist was to depict a fat man with beaming face, sitting at a table with a huge plate of noodles. The border of this cake had fine scroll lines, looking for all the world like noodles.

The invitations conveyed the idea of "Oodles of Noodles," and the theme was carried out quite literally. Long dried noodles were draped around the dining room chandelier, held in place with cellophane tape. The menu, of course, was even more literal:

French-fried Mushroom Noodle Croquettes
Chicken Paprikash
Beef Stroganoff
Green Beans with Macadamia Nuts
Cucumber, Orange, and Onion Salad
Tiny Cheese Rolls
Noodle Crêpes Suzette

Accompanying the paprikash and Stroganoff were noodles, tossed with cracker crumbs fried in butter.

The crêpes were made of regular crêpe batter, with a few cooked fine noodles added, and were served with a Tart Red Raspberry Sauce*.

We used a similar menu for the fiftieth birthday of the president of the largest noodle company in Ohio. This one began with chopped chicken livers and medium noodles made into small croquettes, rolled in Rice Krispies and French-fried ahead of time, then reheated. This was followed by lasagna made with green spinach noodles. Then came a chicken noodle casserole made with artichoke hearts and water chestnuts added. Sauerbraten would have been an acceptable substitute. Finally there was a Hungarian poppy seed noodle "pudding" made with cottage cheese, sour cream sauce, and finely ground poppy seeds.

CHAPTER 4

WINTER

Fisherman's Wharf

What's your favorite seacoast spot? Well, it doesn't matter, because it won't take much effort to transform your home into one of these charming resorts. Travel posters help. Fishnets and boat lights and all such nautical gear can be rented easily from a display house.

Rig up a small oyster bar, covered with burlap. Fill a huge washtub or metal container with ice snow and order a couple of bushels of oysters in the shell. Find some ambitious man with lots of strength in his hands to crack open the oysters, unless you have one of those newfangled oyster shuckers. Plenty of zippy catsup horseradish cocktail sauce should be available.

For people who don't like oysters—and there are quite a few in that class—have a shrimp bowl and more of the same sauce.

For the buffet, have generous quantities of French-fried scallops. They're quite popular everywhere. You may offer two or three kinds of fish, but try not to have the kinds that are too smelly. If you have Swedish guests, you might be adventuresome with smoked eel or pickled herring. A big poached salmon, served hot with egg sauce, is nice but has more fish smell than when it's served cold. Some items, like codfish balls or crab meat croquettes, can be made ahead of time and just reheated for the chafing dishes at the last minute. A good tartar sauce is a must, and it's easier to handle if it's put in little paper soufflé cups.

If you want the British touch with fish and chips, plan on either potato chips or French-fried potatoes, which can be the frozen kind, heated.

Peas with little silver onions would be my choice of vegetable—juicy with brown butter.

A big bowl of fresh new cabbage slaw and sliced tomatoes will round out the menu.

After a meal like this, I prefer lemon meringue pie or lemon chiffon. New Englanders may want pumpkin pie instead.

Old King Cole

A Cleveland family used this theme for a pre-Christmas toast. Our artist made a freehand drawing of King Cole with his pipe, wassail bowl, and the three fiddlers. Nobody listens to music at an open house, but it's a nice touch to add a string trio.

There was a bowl of wassail at this party, although I must confess that I find few people who like this hot spiced drink. I'm sure hot spiced tomato bouillon or hot Watercress Soup* would have been more popular. The decorations were crowns and violins.

To garnish the canapé platters, we had crowns made out of fresh grapefruit and jeweled with candied cherries, arranged on clusters of parsley. At this particular party, only hors d'oeuvres were served, but if one wanted a buffet, it would be easy enough to think of a menu fit for Old King Cole himself, perhaps like this:

*Hot Lobster Capon Madeira**
Large Cold Turkey
Hot Chestnut Stuffing and Artichoke Hearts
Tomato and Cauliflower Aspic
Tiny Buttered Hot Parkerhouse Rolls
*Sesame Melba Toast**
Finger French Pastries

Bake the chestnut stuffing in well-greased ring molds and serve hot with artichoke hearts sautéed in chive butter in the center.

Make salad in bombe molds of two-tone tomato and cauliflower aspic.

Make the Melba toast violin-shaped.

Sleigh Party

The sleigh is still a symbol of Christmas nostalgia, although it has almost disappeared from the American landscape. I remember one party we did, however, with sleighs all over the place.

Graceful sleighs were lined with foil for shrimp bowls. The cocktail sauce was put in ceramic florist's sleigh-shaped planters.

We baked a huge bread sleigh and arranged it full of sandwiches.

There was a sleigh made out of cake on the sweet table, with a Santa up front.

The florist designed a beautiful centerpiece for the main table, again using an ornamental light metal sleigh.

The waiters wore red vests, and the waitresses had Christmasy aprons with little bells sewed on so that they tinkled and jingled as they walked.

Partridge in a Pear Tree

I always get ideas for parties from Christmas cards. One year I got several cards with the partridge in a pear tree as the design, and I saved these in the pile of notes I have labeled "future inspiration."

For this party, the florist took a four- to five-foot bare tree and wired it with lemon leaves and plastic pears. We couldn't find a real partridge, but we did get a stuffed pheasant, which proved to be a little bigger bird than we wanted. We had to hide him partially under the lemon leaves.

The host for this party was an avid hunter, and his freezer was full of both pheasant and partridge. We cooked these and made delectable finger sandwiches from them, arranging them on platters and surrounding them with tiny pickled Seckel pears.

A huge cake in the shape of a pear had a sketch of a modern partridge in a pear tree. This was centered on the tea table where we had the desserts, which included pear-shaped petits fours and pectin pear jellies.

Through the evening the record player kept playing "The Twelve Days of Christmas," and I think our help got pretty tired of it, but the guests, as I've said, seldom are aware of the background music.

Fire Department Party

One of our clients is always in search of colorful ideas for his parties, and every year we try to dream up something especially lively for his holiday open house. This is always a little complicated because guests are received in the big house and transported to the guest house for supper. One year we rented an antique fire engine to provide the transportation, discovering that there was plenty of room on the running boards and rear step to move ten or twelve guests at a time.

The host borrowed the local fire chief's official helmet, and as each guest arrived, he was given a plastic fire helmet of his own. When supper was ready, they had the thrill of a short ride, with the bell clanging and the siren shrieking as they were whisked away.

Our theme, naturally, was fire. The buffet table was covered in flame-colored cloths—red, orange, and yellow. A styrofoam apartment building was placed on it, with pixie dolls being rescued by brave firemen, and other dolls hanging out windows waiting to be saved. Holly-red carnations and pine made a colorful over-all picture. Candles were red, yellow, and orange.

This was the menu:

> *Corned Beef Sandwiches*
> *Lobster Thermidor*
> *Grilled Steak Sandwiches*
> *Eggplant Casserole*
> *Fruit Platter*
> *Pastries and Cookies*

The sandwiches were the open, Danish-type variety, on rye bread.

The servings of lobster thermidor were small, of course, and served in lobster tail shells.

In the center of the room there was a huge, built-in barbecue, where twelve or sixteen guests at a time could gather around and grill their own small filet steaks to order. We bought little ceramic antique fire-engine planters from the local florist and filled these with horseradish and barbecue sauces, and had several trays of dill bread nearby to make sandwiches.

The casserole was made with eggplant, tomatoes, water chestnuts, mushrooms, and Parmesan cheese.

For the fruit platter—in this case, a 30-inch round one—we had molded fresh fruits in raspberry, lemon, and orange gelatin, generously sprinkled with fresh strawberries and surrounded with a row of alternating spiced peaches and crab apples.

On the dessert table we had Santa climbing up a hook and ladder and more red carnations. There were cream cheese pastries with cherry, apricot, lemon, and cheese fillings; little hatchet cookies with thin piping of red, yellow, and orange, and mints with the same three colors.

A *Seventeenth-century Dinner*

Not everyone likes to dress up in period costumes, but once in a while it can be exciting. One of our clients gave a seventeenth-century dinner during the Christmas holiday season, at which the costumes included wigs, knee breeches, and buckled shoes for the men, and floor-length hoop skirts, leg-of-mutton sleeves, and frilly collars for the ladies.

In the spacious dining room we stretched the table as long as it would go and covered it with red felt, trimmed in white and gold. Two five-foot topiary trees gave importance and height to the buffet. They were made with red carnations, white mums, and gold-painted mountain laurel.

The *pièce de résistance* was three huge suckling pigs. When dinner was announced, we had a Scots Highlander dressed in full regalia, stepping high, playing his bagpipes, and followed by three waiters, each holding a pig beautifully garnished. The waitresses were in country peasant costumes.

This was our seventeenth-century menu:

Roast Suckling Pig
Halves of Stuffed Pigeon
Cranberry Jelly Molds
*Kumquat Orange Molded Salad**
Beef and Kidney Pie
Escalloped Oysters in Sherry
Tiered Spiced Fruit Compotes
Small Hot Scones
Dessert

The pigs were stuffed with apple and celery bread stuffing, and brown thin onion gravy was passed.

We used halves of small Rock Cornish game hens and pretended they were pigeon. Chestnut dressing was served with them.

Our tall, fancy cranberry jelly molds were surrounded by tart cranberry sauce.

The Kumquat Orange Molded Salads* were garnished with halves of kumquats. The beef and kidney pie was covered with puff pastry crust. Gooseberry chutney accompanied the oysters.

If you really want to go all out, curried lamb might follow the oysters.

In the fruit compotes, the emphasis was on prunes, red apples, and pears.

A feast for dessert: plain or sultana butter pound cake, marzipan pastries, mincemeat tarts, currant drop cookies, tiny plum puddings with hard sauce, red and white fleur-de-lis-shaped mints, and chocolate-covered orange peel.

Both host and hostess took a bow for this one. Even the cooks were beaming.

The Mushroom Tree—and Trees in General

A pretty little hors d'oeuvre tray once attracted my attention. It wasn't the canapés I noticed so much as an interesting mushroom-shaped candle, surrounded by curly parsley, a couple of red carnations, and a cluster of white button mushrooms that had been dipped in salad oil to prevent them from turning brown. Tray garnishes are important, especially when you're serving sandwiches that are not too colorful in themselves.

The tray gave me an idea. It was amplified further when I visited a park and saw there large three-foot mushrooms made of cement or a kind of glazed pottery, and painted with red and white polka dots. They were quite decorative in the green foliage of the park, and I never knew why they were placed there. I just assumed that someone was fond of mushrooms, as so many people are and as I am, which you probably have guessed from reading my menus.

In Germany the mushroom is a symbol of good luck, and you'll often find Christmas tree ornaments in mushroom shape, with little elves or dwarfs reclining under them.

All these chance encounters with mushrooms came to mind one year when I undertook, as we do annually, to cater a huge Christmas party for a large hospital. Everyone in the place is invited, and the attendance is usually about a thousand people. Every year the refreshments have a certain tradition, and many items, such as a shrimp bowl, are repeated, but the decorations have to be varied to delight and surprise the same personnel.

Remembering the mushroom garnish on the hors d'oeuvre tray, I ordered three dozen mushroom-shaped candles from Dallas. The whole top of the mushroom glows when it has been lit for a while.

Two tall, tiered dummy cake centerpieces graced the two long buffets. We were able to get some large toadstools at a display store, and two 10-inch dwarfs reclined under them. Around the base of the dummies, we had a wide bed of very curly parsley, fresh red carnations and mushrooms, dipped in salad oil.

Naturally, the menu consisted of many mushroom items, along with the usual shrimp bowl, canapés and sandwiches, deviled eggs, and sweets. By ordering in advance, we bought several thousand uniform small mushroom caps. There were washed and the stems pulled out. In my opinion there's no comparison between fresh and canned mushrooms, although I realize that fresh ones aren't obtainable everywhere.

There's one thing about a mushroom: you can stuff it with almost anything. Here are some suggestions:

Chopped stems, bread crumbs, chopped celery, parsley,
   and butter.
Ground beef.
Crab meat in white sauce.
Chopped shrimp.
Minced chicken livers.
Ground sausage.
Chopped ham or ham salad.
Bread and chopped crinkled bacon.
Cheese puff mixture.
Chopped artichoke hearts and chives.
Minced kosher corned beef with mustard or horseradish.

I don't recommend you use so large a variety for one party.
Pick out the four or five that appeal to you most. They don't need
to be baked too long, especially when you're eating them with your
fingers. The cookie sheet should be lightly greased or the mushrooms may stick.

The most popular single hot canapé we make is the Hot Toasted
Mushroom Sandwich*. We sell thousands of them all the year
round, and people never seem to get tired of them. A slightly
different version is a tiny cheese biscuit, split and filled with the
same mushroom spread.

On the sweet table we had mushrooms in another form. Short
thick stems were made of shortbread cookie dough. After these
were baked, we topped the stems with a very stiff apricot jam and
then capped them with a small fresh macaroon. To make them
more decorative, our cake artists made dots of chocolate, vanilla,
and avocado-green icing, making them look like fairy-tale toadstools. We made some mint meringue toadstools as well.

The hospital party was so successful that we decided to repeat
the mushroom theme in several other parts of the city, making
sure the guests at each one would be different. For these parties
we decided to make a mushroom tree.

A large four-foot bare tree sapling was put into a pot. In the
forks of the larger branches we secured wet oasis wrapped in thin
green foil. Graceful stems of springerii fern and lovely red carnations were fastened into the oasis. On the tip of every twig we
put a fresh white mushroom cap, dipped in salad oil, and of course

at the base of the tree we had the mushroom candles glowing and the grinning dwarf.

Many men, who normally don't take notice of a floral center-piece, went out of their way to inspect this one.

It isn't necessary to wait for Christmas to use trees at a party.

At a large evening reception in the Cleveland Public Library, with 2,000 in attendance, we needed height for the table, as is always the case with such a large crowd, so we ordered two pairs of five-foot-high topiary trees, made of pink and lavender and purple asters. Against the white and black marble walls, this color was most effective. One table was covered with pink Indian head with lavender net, the other had a purple cloth with pink net. Refreshments were limited to a sweets table—pastries, little cakes and cookies, mints and nuts, with punch and coffee, but the tables were impressive and brought scores of compliments.

On another occasion, a hostess was asked to give a reception for the National Garden Club convention. Her own greenhouses and gardens were quite a distance from the main house, so she decided to have her trees at home. All were live young trees in pots—about 8- to 10-foot saplings. At the entrance portico were two pink and white carnation trees. In the front foyer were two yellow and white daisy trees. In the big east room, the library, she had a pair of Happiness dark red rose trees, and on the sun porch two laven-der and white aster trees. But the most unusual were by a large fireplace—a pair of graceful baby's-breath trees, made entirely of baby's breath. I couldn't help thinking what a perfect background they would have made for a home wedding.

I was still thinking about the baby's-breath trees when I was asked to make a fruit tree for a coming-out party. The mother of the deb had picked the same date as her own coming-out party twenty-five years before, when her caterer had made a pretty fruit tree and served fresh fruits on picks all around the base of the tree.

This time I began with a bare tree, about five feet tall, potted. In the forks of the branches we put oasis wrapped in green foil. Then we used graceful long stems of white baby's breath, and on the branches were stuck and wired Bing cherries, giant strawber-ries, nectarines, plums, clusters of grapes. At the base were large silver bowls of melon balls, strawberries, pitted Bing cherries, seedless grape clusters, etc. Colors for the party were quite neutral, with blues and greens, so this colorful tree was a particularly attractive background for picture-taking.

If you should use Orange Blossom Trees* in June, instead of bothering with the pulled green sugar leaves, you might wire mock orange blossoms onto several branches. Do it just before serving, because they wilt very quickly.

We've often used a pickle tree at holiday time instead of the usual floral centerpiece. The only drawback is that they're so breathtakingly beautiful the guests act as though we had placed a "Do Not Disturb" sign on them, and waitresses have to assure them that it is an edible tree, not merely decorative. We do them with pickles of every description, and sometimes with pickles and spiced fruit. Recently we had a request for an olive tree, and did it entirely of olives, the giant queen variety—stuffed, stone, and ripe, with a few Greek olives added for their unusual color.

Last New Year's I was shown through a home at an open-house party, and found that the family had made a striking pyramid or cone-shaped tree of Scotch pine and hard bright red apples. That gave me another idea. Next Christmas I'll try an apple tree!

The Cheese Board

If you want to keep your refreshments simple, why not copy the British, who often confine themselves to selecting eighteen or twenty kinds of cheese, complement it with an array of crackers and several varieties of bread, and red and white wine? They come in all shapes and flavors and sizes, as you know; cheese in crocks, cheese in blocks, wedges, slices, soft spreads or dips. There should be at least one kind of mild cheese, like Swiss, and perhaps a medium snappy York State Cheddar. Others might include smoked Herkimer, imported Roquefort (or domestic), a small amount of Liederkranz, and by all means Brie, which must be taken out of the refrigerator twelve to twenty-four hours in advance so it will be of the right consistency.

Have a cheese board or two in plain sight, so the guests can hack away without scratching silver trays. Use butter spreaders for the soft ones. To expedite serving groups, it's nice to have some cheese cubes on picks, stuck into an apple, grapefruit, orange, melon, or pineapple. Whatever you do, be sure to get height to the table; don't keep everything flat.

Most stores have an array of crackers, and it's a pleasure to select them. Be sure they're not all salty. As for bread in addition, try Jewish rye, pumpernickel, whole wheat, or crusty Italian bread to provide greater variety.

The Topsy-turvy Party

Some of our clients are really adventurous. At one party we did, nothing matched. The hostess had a huge butler's pantry filled with various sets of china, so she took a place setting from each set. As the table was quite long, she used two different cloths that didn't match. There were different kinds of napkins, colored, small and large. Cups did not match saucers and the silver didn't match either. The floral centerpiece was made up of wild colors that fought with each other. But what fun it turned out to be!

I've also heard about, but not attended, the party at which everything is done backward—the dessert and coffee served, then the salad, the main course and finally hot soup. Silver flatware is put on the opposite side of what would be normal, and both the water glass and the cup and saucer are on the left. A sample menu:

Fresh Fruit and Sherbet in Cantaloupe Rings
Thin Butter Cookies and Coffee
Small Caesar Salads
Crusty Hard Rolls
Ragout of Beef with Fresh Vegetables and Mushrooms
Hot Mushroom Tomato Bouillon

Roman Bath Party

A few years ago several girls went to Italy for their summer vacation and fell in love with it, as so many girls do. When they came home, they persuaded one of the parents to underwrite a "Roman Bath" party with a real Italian atmosphere, centered around the indoor swimming pool of a private home.

A special 18-inch-high table was constructed around the edge of the pool and braced so it wouldn't move. We rented pillows from the local stadium so that sixty guests could be seated around the pool. A huge cornucopia was made to appear as though it were coming out of the diving board; it was garnished with leaves and ferns. We bought bushels of fruits, especially grapes. The table was covered in pink, lavender, purple, green, and blue nylon taffeta, and these exquisite colors were reflected in the water. Water-lily candles floated in the pool, setting off Cleopatra—a mannequin borrowed from a department store—on her royal barge. She was dressed in a toga and held a large bunch of grapes in her hand.

Laurel roping entwined around several pillars at one end of the pool added to the Italian setting.

Guests were asked to come dressed as Romans. Many wore sandals and togas. A few had real metal armor costumes with shiny shields and swords.

Salami cornucopias and pizza were served as cocktail appetizers. By candlelight, we served the following dinner:

Prosciutto
Spaghetti with Meat Sauce
Wide Italian Green Beans with Almonds
Italian Bread
Ripe, Stuffed, and Green Stone Olives
Green Salad
Bisque Tortoni
Fresh Fruit
Italian Cheese

Meatballs were served with the spaghetti.
There were bottles of Italian wine on the table.

A Night at the Beach

Since indoor pools are becoming more numerous, people are beginning to plan more parties around them, winter and summer. At one party in Cleveland, a six-piece orchestra floated on a sturdy raft to provide music for dancing and listening. The musicians wore officers' hats and blue coats to look like a real Navy band. Fishnets and anchors decorated the walls.

Peanuts, popcorn, Cracker Jack, and Fritos were put around the terrace in little sand pails. Hors d'oeuvres were served from an aqua-covered table in the dining room.

At about eleven o'clock a big built-in charcoal grill was put to use, with a chef barbecuing 2½-ounce filet mignon steaks as well as medium-sized frankfurters.

Part Four

Holidays and Nationality Menus

CHAPTER 1

HOLIDAYS

Twelfth Night

If you've had the common experience of not being able to find a convenient date during the holidays that won't conflict with other parties, the sixth of January (Twelfth Night) can be just the time to have your friends in, either for supper or for a late evening simple buffet. In England, Twelfth Night is the traditional time for the burning of the Christmas evergreens. Your table centerpiece could be a small bonfire with orange, yellow, and red crepe paper flames. Altar candles can be used on twigs and evergreens. At one party we had a small live Christmas tree with red, orange, and yellow crepe paper streamers. At the back of the buffet table we had a small electric fan to blow the streamers and give a flamelike effect.

After the rich food of the holidays, most guests will prefer something simple. Usually we serve a huge platter of fresh grapefruit, sliced oranges, avocado sections, and a few seeded Tokay grapes. Almost always, we use a Twelfth Night cake—plain white or yellow butter cake or spice cake, which traditionally has three tokens, wrapped in wax paper, inserted in it. A dime, a dried pea, and a bean are old-fashioned fortune-telling symbols.

Here are three Twelfth Night menus:

MENU NO. 1

Dried Beef Casserole
Melba Toast   Toasted Scones
Fresh Fruit Platter
Twelfth Night Cake

Make the casserole with artichoke hearts, chopped dried beef, mushrooms, and water chestnuts in cream sauce, with a bowl of grated Parmesan cheese alongside.

MENU NO. 2

Hot Corned Beef
Thin Rye and White Party Breads
Mustard Sauce
Hot Seafood Casserole
Toasted English Muffins
Spiced Fruit Compote
Twelfth Night Cake

Slice the corned beef on a board at the table.

MENU NO. 3

Hot Tomato and Split Pea Bouillon
Filets Mignon
Dill Party Bread
Horseradish Sour Cream Sauce
Artichoke Relish Sauce
Fruit Platter
Twelfth Night Cake

The steaks should weigh 2 or 2½ ounces each, with bacon omitted. They can be broiled on an electric broiler at the dining room table, in five or six minutes.

Lincoln's Birthday

Make a log cabin for the centerpiece. Use a burlap tablecloth for the buffet. And here are three menus to honor Honest Abe:

MENU NO. 1

Hot Ham Loaf
Spinach Sauce*
Corn Fritters with Maple Syrup
Spiced Broiled Peaches
Wilted Lettuce
Lincoln Log Cake

Flavor the Spinach Sauce* delicately with mustard for the ham loaf.

Add melted butter to the wilted lettuce.

Lincoln Log Cake is white cake with chocolate icing, rolled like a jelly roll.

MENU NO. 2

Corn Sticks   Bread Sticks
Little Broiled Sausages
Baked Chicken Livers
Parslied Hominy
Raw Vegetable Platter
Hot Gingerbread
Chocolate Whipped Cream Log

Garnish the log with hickory nuts or walnuts.

MENU NO. 3

Baked Pork Loin Roast
Succotash
Fried Apples
Corn Muffins
Molded Broccoli Aspic
Celery Seed Mayonnaise
Individual Lincoln Logs

Season the roast with mustard and rosemary.

Baked beans might replace the succotash.

Apples baked with red raspberries are an alternate to fried apples.

Corn sticks, perhaps, might substitute for corn muffins.

The logs are nut sponge cake with mocha cream filling and icing, and Mr. Arthur's Butterscotch Sauce* is passed with it.

Valentine's Day

Red and white are always popular, but deep pink and light pink or pink and American Beauty can be used effectively. Flowers and candles should be in the same colors as tablecloth and napkins. Here are some menu ideas for both dinner and buffet:

RED AND WHITE DINNER

Tomato Juice
*Parmesan Melba Toast**
Hot Ham Mousse
Harvard Cherry Beets
Hot Corn Soufflé
Perfection Salad
Watercress Mayonnaise or Green Goddess Dressing
Tiny Cinnamon Rolls
Tiny Bran Muffins
Deep Cherry Tarts à la Mode
Red and White Heart-shaped Mints

Instead of tomato juice, you may prefer Tomato Orange Bouillon*.

The Melba toast is heart-shaped and buttered, sprinkled with red paprika just as it comes from the oven.

Bake the mousse in a heart-shaped buttered cake pan.

Cut out tiny pimiento hearts, and garnish the loaf after unmolding.

Add grated orange rind to the beets.

The salads, individual ring molds, have cottage cheese in the center, garnished with cherry tomatoes.

RED AND PINK DINNER

Eggs à la Russe*
Baked Ham
Red Eye Country Gravy*
Mashed Sweet Potato Casserole
Lima Beans
Baking Powder Biscuits
Strawberry Bavarian Cream
Heart-shaped Butter Cookies
Red and White Mints

Use heart-shaped Melba toast for the Eggs à la Russe*.

Cherry sauce might be served with the ham instead of the gravy.

On the casserole place marshmallows tinted pink with beet juice or left plain.

Into the lima beans put a dash of sour cream, chopped pimiento, and water chestnuts.

Cut out the biscuits with a heart-shaped cooky cutter.

Garnish the Bavarian cream with fresh or frozen whole strawberries.

Heart-shaped petits fours may be substituted for the cookies.

RED AND PINK BUFFET

Crab Bisque
Cold Pinkish Roast Beef
Cold Ham Mousse
Chicken Liver Mold
Heart-shaped Caraway Rye Melba Toast
Egg Salad Mold
Potato Flake Crackers
Bing Cherry Salad Mold*
Asparagus Vinaigrette
Cranberry Orange Muffins
Strawberry Chiffon Pie
Pink and Red Mints

Lobster bisque may be substituted for crab bisque.

Slice the roast beef paper thin.

Make the mousse in a heart-shaped mold and garnish with pimiento hearts.

Make chicken liver mold and egg salad mold in heart-shaped pan. Cover the center of the egg salad mold with red caviar. On the outside edge put a thin piping of pink onion-flavored cream cheese.

Make the Bing Cherry Salad Mold* in a ring mold. Fill the center with pink cottage cheese. With it, serve sweet cherry mayonnaise made with grated lemon rind.

The strawberry chiffon pie is made in a graham cracker crust. Tiny strawberry tarts might be an alternate dessert.

The mints may be moonbeam or sandwich mints.

Washington's Birthday

Make a miniature cherry tree for the centerpiece. Cut a small live branch of a tree, put it in a pot or stand, and wire a few fresh green leaves on it. Stick red maraschino cherries on the end of every twig. You can use a white tablecloth with bands of red, white, and blue ribbon or tiny American flags down the center. If you are serving as many as 24 people, use one table with red cloth, white and blue napkins; one table with white cloth, red and blue napkins; one table with blue cloth, white and red napkins. It will liven up the whole room.

MENU NO. 1—BUFFET

*Patriotic Fruit Plate**
Tiny Ham and Shrimp Shish Kebabs
Stuffed Giant Mushroom Caps
Chicken Salad
Stuffed Cherry Tomatoes
Tiny Hominy Muffins
Finger Desserts
Red, White, and Blue Wafer Mints
Chocolate-covered Cherry Cordials

Broil the shish kebabs in butter with a red candied cherry on each.

Stuff the mushroom caps with minced kosher corned beef and a little mustard sauce.

Garnish the chicken salad with tomato wedges or radish roses.

Stuff the cherry tomatoes with a dab of sour cream and caviar.

Add chopped parsley, chopped chives, and chopped watercress to the hominy muffin batter.

Finger desserts would include tiny cherry pastry turnovers or tiny cherry tarts, hatchet-shaped butter cookies with a candied cherry, and little white frosted cakes with paper or silk flags.

MENU NO. 2

Oyster Bisque
Sesame Bread Sticks
Chicken Maryland
Crisp French-fried Cauliflower*
Peas with Diced Zucchini
Tiny Corn Sticks or Muffins
Martha Washington Pie
Red, White, and Blue Mints
Divinity Fudge   Candied Cherries

A fair-sized log with sprigs of boxwood, and a toy hatchet sticking up in the log, would make a good centerpiece.

Add sherry to the oyster bisque.

The bread sticks should be pencil slim.

For the Chicken Maryland, place boned breast of chicken over thin slices of country ham. Serve with a thin brown mushroom sauce.

Martha Washington Pie is like Boston Cream pie. Whipped cream may be used instead of custard for the filling.

Put a candied cherry on top of each piece of fudge.

St. Patrick's Day

You'll want emerald-green tablecloths, of course, and on them live shamrock plants in pots, or tinted carnations, or Bells of Ireland. Naturally, the color scheme should be green and white.

The following menus ought to please any Irishman:

MENU NO. 1

Cream of Split Pea Soup
Buttered Shamrock-shaped Melba Toast
Boned Leg of Lamb
Mint Jelly
Parsley-buttered New Potatoes
Spinach Croquettes*
Three-bean Salad Vinaigrette
Tiny Cloverleaf Rolls
Lime Sherbet and Pistachio Ice Cream Parfaits
Shamrock Butter Cookies

Sprinkle chopped watercress on top of the pea soup just before serving.

Spread the Melba toast generously with chopped parsley just as it comes from the oven.

Broiled lamb chops may be substituted for the leg of lamb.

The croquettes are rolled in cornflakes. A substitute would be peas with toasted croutons.

Instead of the salad vinaigrette, you might want minted pears with cottage cheese.

Top each parfait with a green cherry.

MENU NO. 2

Irish Beef Stew with Vegetables
Tossed Green Salad
Irish Soda Bread
Apple Pie with Cheese
Green and White Shamrock Mints

A centerpiece might be a green foil paper derby and a cane with emerald-green bow.

Be sure to put chunks of potato in the stew.

Put a swathe of watercress all around the salad bowl.

MENU NO. 3

This one is a light buffet supper.

Lemon Lime Cocktail
Open Shamrock Sandwiches
Mr. Jiggs's Brussels Sprouts*
Miniature Stuffed Cabbages
Ivy League Triangles*
Toasted Ham and Cheese Sandwiches
Salad
Petits Fours   Marzipan "Potatoes"
Tiny Chocolate Tarts

Make the Lemon Lime Cocktails with bottled lime juice, to which these ingredients are added: a little vegetable coloring, frozen lemonade, fresh sliced limes, and the juice from a few limes, plus soda.

Open Shamrock Sandwiches are made of cucumber cream cheese, some edged in chopped parsley, some in chopped pistachio nuts.

Stuff miniature cabbages with a chopped ham mixture.

For the toasted ham and cheese sandwiches I like to use miniature scones, if possible. Garnish with French-fried Parlsey*.

For salad, raw green pepper rings, cucumber sticks, and green stone olives arranged in a green glass bowl or platter with shaved ice. Garnish with stuffed celery—half with mashed avocado, to which is added a little cream cheese, lemon rind, and crisp crinkled bacon; the other half with Roquefort cream cheese and toasted pecans.

Tiny petits fours may be garnished with bright green frosting; marzipan "potatoes" dusted with cinnamon sugar; and tiny chocolate-filled tarts with a thin coating of green mint fondant.

MENU NO. 4

Corned beef and cabbage are virtually unknown in Ireland as a combination, but Americans think of it as *the* typically Irish dish. The Irish do, however, serve boiled bacon (ham) and cabbage. And they do serve corned beef, too, so here is a menu on which it is the principal feature.

Hot Corned Beef Brisket
Stewed Cut-up Chicken
Baked Potatoes Colcannon
Lime Gelatin Salad
Irish Soda Bread and Butter
Decorated Cake
Pistachio Ice Cream

Make the brisket with a Chili Sauce Glaze: blend 2 parts chili sauce with 1 part corn syrup, and bake 20 to 30 minutes after pouring on the glaze.

Serve lemon butter sauce with the chicken, and lots of chopped parsley.

To make Baked Potatoes Colcannon, blend mashed baked potatoes with some boiled cabbage and put back into the potato jackets. Brush with butter and run under the broiler.

Make the salad with apple and celery, with cottage cheese in the center.

Easter

Your Easter table can have lavender or purple Indian head cloth, or a runner of purple nylon net over a white cloth. A potted Easter lily, hyacinths, or a pot of tulips will always look springlike and festive.

MENU NO. 1

Crab Meat in Madrilene Aspic Rings
Baked Ham
Gingersnap Gravy*
Spinach Soufflé Ring
Tiny Hot Cross Buns
Spiced Fruit Platter
Sherbets
Easter Petits Fours

The crab meat is molded in individual rings of madrilene aspic. Fill the centers with tiny grapes on top of a generous tablespoon of Pink Remoulade*. Arrange on curly endive and add a wedge of fresh lemon. (Note on grapes: There's a new, colorful "Grape Jubilee" seedless grape that is quite delicious if you zip it up with grated lemon or orange rind.)

The spinach soufflé ring is surrounded with glazed baby carrots. Serve relish dishes instead of the fruit platter, if you like.

Put pastel sherbets in tiny flower pots and dust them with cinnamon sugar, with a fresh flower sticking out of the top.

Instead of petits fours, you may prefer the traditional coconut-iced lamb cake.

MENU NO. 2

Eggs à la Russe* on Melba Toast
Boned Chicken Breasts
Orange Rice Balls*
Asparagus
Broiled Peaches
Tiny Blueberry Muffins
Tiny Baking Powder Biscuits
Lime Ice and Strawberry Sherbet in Pastel Meringue Shells
Strawberry Sauce

Garnish the Eggs à la Russe* with cherry tomatoes or sliced stuffed olives.

The chicken breasts are large halves or small whole ones. With them serve watercress gravy, made with chicken stock and julienne ham added.

Serve the cut-up asparagus with sesame butter, grated lemon rind, and a few buttered toasted crumbs.

Sprinkle red raspberries lightly on the broiled peaches just before serving.

Add poultry seasoning to the baking powder biscuits.

MENU NO. 3—BUFFET FOR A BIG FAMILY GROUP

Chilled Grape Juice Shrub
*Chicken Mandarin**
Parslied Rice Ring
Broccoli Croquettes
Avocado Aspic Ring
Tiny Butterscotch Rolls
Tiny Parkerhouse Rolls
*Lemon Sherbet Baskets**
Daffodil Cake

Add mayonnaise and cottage cheese to the aspic. Fill the ring with fresh fruits of the season—but no oranges.

Orange sherbet may be substituted for lemon sherbet.

MENU NO. 4—EASTER NIGHT SUPPER

Mild Lamb Curry
Fluffy Rice
Lime Cucumber Molded Salad Ring
Toasted English Muffins
Daffodil Cake

Arrange the condiments in large purple cabbage leaves around a silver Revere bowl of chutney. Among the condiments should be chopped egg yolk, chopped egg white, chopped green pepper, chopped walnuts or peanuts, grated fresh or frozen coconut, crisp crinkled bacon, grated orange rind, Sultana raisins.

Surround the salad ring with pink and green spiced pear halves. Have scones, if you like, instead of English muffins.

Lemon ribbon cake might replace the daffodil cake.

MENU NO. 5—EASTER SUPPER

Chicken Breasts
Large Noodle Ring
Molded Fruit Salads
Tiny Buttered Rolls
*Caramelized Cornflake Ring**

Serve broiled grapefruit sections to garnish the chicken breasts.

Fill the noodle ring with creamed braised celery topped with toasted pecans.

Garnish the individual multicolored salads with fresh strawberries.

Tiny hot cross buns, if you can get them, would be nice instead of the rolls. Or perhaps Dresden fruited stollen.

Assorted ice cream balls fill the center of the Caramelized Cornflake Ring*.

Mother's Day

It's popular these days to take Mother out to a restaurant on "her" day, but maybe she doesn't like crowds, and at the best places you may have to wait an hour or so even if you have a reservation. Maybe Mother would appreciate it more if she were taken out to eat on her birthday or wedding anniversary, or both.

Most mothers, I think, would consider it the best celebration to be queen for a day in their own homes, beginning with breakfast in bed, and with the knowledge that they won't have to do a dish or make a bed all day. Dad and the children can plan the main dinner, do the shopping, and surprise Mother with the menu.

There may be two or three mothers present; grandmas and grandpas should be invited, if it's possible. Each lady can have a nice big pink carnation pinned on her dress, and have a bowl of pink carnations on the table. That's the traditional flower for the day.

If Dad has a hand in the meal, it might be an outdoor barbecue, either steak or chicken, so I'll give you two menus built around those entrees.

Mother's likes and dislikes should get first consideration. If she's very fond of crab meat or lobster, she should have it. If she likes caviar, buy her a small jar.

MENU NO. 1

Molded Crab Meat Salad
Porterhouse or T-Bone Steak
Noodles with Fried Buttered Cracker Crumbs
Fresh Green Beans with Toasted Almonds
Hot Rolls
Mother's Day Cake
Ice Cream

The crab meat salad is in lemon gelatin on a thin slice of tomato, with lemon wedge and Pink Remoulade*.

Broil or barbecue the steak.

Remember, green beans taste better if you buy them fresh and cut them in ½-inch lengths.

Make the cake in the shape of a bonnet or heart. Serve Mother's favorite ice cream and a fresh fruit sauce with it.

MENU NO. 2

California Antipasto Plates
Barbecued Cut-up Chicken
Mushroom Chicken Gravy
Parslied Rice
Corn and Peas
Hot Rolls
Mother's Day Cake
Sherbet with Fresh Fruit Sauces

For the antipasto plates: fresh spears of pineapple; fresh avocado slices, dipped in lemon; chunks of fresh lobster meat; a ripe olive garnish.

Be sure the chicken is golden brown and crisp.

For the vegetable, combine whole-kernel corn, peas, and sliced water chestnuts.

The cake should be her favorite—possibly angel food or chocolate fudge layer, with a special decoration. Serve a heaping bowl of two kinds of sherbet and the fresh fruit sauces.

MENU NO. 3

Fresh Fruit Cup
Broiled Double Loin Lamb Chops
Large Glazed Mushroom Caps
Crisp Strips of Bacon
Broiled Tomato Halves
Creamed Peas and Zucchini
Pickled Watermelon Rind
Giant Queen Stuffed Olives
Ice Cream and Cake

Use all fresh fruit in the fruit cup; *don't* use canned.

Sprinkle herbs and mustard bread crumbs over the tomato halves.

Slice the zucchini and add a dash of Cheddar cheese. Combine with the peas.

Skip the potatoes—Mother won't mind a bit!

Make a personalized decorated cake to go with the ice cream (or junket or sherbet). For instance, have a picture of a throne and Mother with a crown on her head, and an inscription reading: "We love you, Mother! Our Queen for the Day!" Maybe the children could make a paper crown and color it with crayons and write on it "Mother is our Queen!" for her to wear during dinner.

Father's Day

Every dad likes to be fussed over a little, and here's your opportunity to show him a little special attention.

On this day *his* likes and dislikes should be considered first. If it's steak he loves, give him his favorite. If he likes standing ribs or pork chops, that's what he should have.

Dad, of course, is "King for a Day," and the youngsters could make him a paper crown. For one day, too, maybe he should be spared the job of carving the roast, unless that's something he likes to do. If he likes to eat outdoors or on the porch, by all means do that, if it's warm enough.

MENU NO. 1

Shrimp Cocktail
Boston Strip Steaks
Baked Potatoes
Yellow Wax Beans and Corn
Stuffed Tomatoes
Hot Hard Crusty Rolls
Sheet Cake
Chocolate Chip Ice Cream with Chocolate Sauce

Have parsley chive butter for the potatoes.

Combine whole-kernel corn and watercress butter with wax beans for the vegetable dish.

Stuff the tomatoes with seedless grapes and diced celery vinaigrette.

On the cake, letter "Dad." It can be chocolate or white.

MENU NO. 2

Fresh Fruit Cup
Standing Ribs of Beef
Au Gratin Potatoes
Pickled Beets   *Mustard Pickles*
Fresh Frenched Green Beans
Iceberg Lettuce with Russian Dressing
Garlic French Bread
Pie

Serve the fruit cup in half or third of a pineapple shell.

Make the potatoes with Cheddar cheese.

Serve the green beans with brown butter.

Whatever his favorite pie is, serve it. Coconut Cream is my choice for this menu.

MENU NO. 3

Clam Chowder
Golden-brown Baked Pork Chops with Apple Celery Stuffing
Noodle Pudding
Peas
Watermelon and Cantaloupe Rind Pickle
Salad
Dessert

Noodle croquettes may be substituted for the noodle pudding.
You might find out if Dad likes the small French variety of canned peas instead of fresh ones. Some men do.

Salad could be wilted lettuce or tossed greens, with whatever Dad's favorite dressing may be.

Serve his favorite dessert, whatever it is.

MENU NO. 4

Cold Lobster Chunks
Chicken Paprikash
Noodles
Succotash
Hot Popovers
Strawberry Biscuit Shortcake

Serve the lobster chunks on a bed of endive with a mustard remoulade sauce to which capers have been added.

Be sure to have lots of gravy for the paprikash.

Top the noodles with buttered cracker crumbs and macadamia nuts.

Make the succotash with brown butter only, not with cream sauce.

Be sure the biscuits are piping hot and fresh for the shortcake, and be generous with the berries. Serve the whipped cream separately, or else use a vanilla ice cream topping.

Decoration Day

The theme can be based on red, white, and blue or on geraniums. As a change, set the table in wicker if the party is informal. Have a large wicker basket full of red Irene geraniums in the center on a royal blue cloth, a red and white checked cloth, or a blue and white checked gingham cloth.

Following are a few menus to match the decor.

MENU NO. 1

Flower Pot Fruit Cup
Charcoal-broiled Boston Strip Steaks
Individual Spinach Pies*
Hot Cherry Tomatoes Basil*
Sesame-buttered French Bread
Raw Vegetable Salad Tray
Angel Food Crème Brûlée*
Tart Red Raspberry Sauce*
Macaroons

Use ordinary red clay flower pots for the fruit cup. Line each one with a foil cup or paper drinking cup. Use fresh fruits, add a tablespoonful of pineapple sherbet, and dust the top with cinnamon sugar. Insert a blue bachelor button, red carnation, or geranium in each pot.

Have broiled tomatoes instead of the cherry tomatoes, if you like. Herb bread may be substituted for French bread.

MENU NO. 2

Patriotic Fruit Platter*
Poppy Seed Dressing*
Barbecued Spareribs
Mushroom Pie*
Green Beans
Two-tone Tomato and Cucumber Aspic Molds
Watercress Mayonnaise
Tiny Grilled Hard Rolls
Cherry Vanilla Mary Anns

Alongside the Fruit Platter* put tiny soufflé cups of dressing.

Supplement the spareribs, if you like, with small 2-ounce individual filets or cubed steaks.

The green beans should be the long whole ones. Serve with grated lemon rind and bread crumbs and chopped hard-boiled egg.

Tomato and asparagus aspic molds may be substituted for the tomato and cucumber.

For the dessert, put vanilla ice cream in individual angel food cake shells and cover with red sour cherry sauce.

MENU NO. 3

Warm Canadian Bacon
Hashed Brown Potatoes with Onion
Stuffed Tomatoes
Scrambled Eggs with Chopped Chives
Hot Buttered Crusty Italian Bread
Angel Food Cake Ring with Sherbet

This is a brunch menu.

Rub the bacon with brown sugar and cloves and bake in spiced crab apple juice.

Fry the potatoes outdoors if the weather permits.

Skin the tomatoes ahead of time, scoop them out, and fill with seedless grapes, diced celery, and sour cream dressing.

Heat the bread in foil, then allow it to crisp after unwrapping.

Fill the center of the angel food cake ring with strawberry sherbet and swirl blueberry whipped cream around the outside. Sprinkle with fresh blueberries and top with giant strawberries.

July 4th

It would be hard to avoid red, white, and blue, if you're entertaining at home, but at this time of year picnics are the order of the day in many places, and that's what I'm suggesting in these menus. Since it's impossible to tell in advance whether it will be hot or cool, it's a good idea to have one or two hot dishes regardless.

MENU NO. 1

Fried Cut-up Chicken
Wieners
New England Style Baked Beans
Stuffed Tomatoes
Relish Tray
Watermelon Sherbet
Assorted Large Cookies

Dip the chicken in beaten whole eggs and sesame seeds before frying.

Split the wieners in half lengthwise and fill with American or Cheddar cheese, wrap them in bacon, and bake or broil. Serve in wiener rolls, toasted if possible.

Have succotash, if you don't care for baked beans.

Scoop out medium-sized tomatoes and fill with potato salad, diced very small.

If you have time, make a pickle tree instead of a relish tray.

Mix the sherbet with chunks of watermelon and put it into a scooped-out melon. Blueberries may be added if desired.

We make shield-shaped butter cookies with red and blue sugar sprinkled on them.

MENU NO. 2

Shrimp on Shaved Ice
Individual Ham Loaves
Hashed in Cream Potatoes*
Cole Slaw
Dill and Sweet Pickles
Buttered Parkerhouse Rolls
Eskimo Pies

With the shrimp, use red, white, and blue toothpicks, and put the sauce in a blue glass bowl.

You may want Glazed Ham Balls* instead of ham loaves. In either case, serve with a thin mustard sauce.

Serve the cole slaw in a scooped-out huge head of green cabbage.

MENU NO. 3—BASKET SUPPER

Cut-up Crisp Fried Chicken
Hot Mushroom Tetrazzini
Carrot Sticks, Celery, and Olives
Fresh Fruit Cups
Potato Chips
Tiny Spice Cupcakes
Brownies

Line generous-sized miniature "bushel" baskets with cloth or paper napkins. Put the relishes and fruit cups in first. At the last minute, add the hot food.

Put two pieces of chicken per person in each basket, and have a few extras available, to be passed for second helpings.

Mushroom Tetrazzini is thin spaghetti tossed with mushrooms in a cream sauce to which has been added port wine. Serve hot in medium foil cups with grated Parmesan cheese.

Put the potato chips in little cellophane bags.

Individual coconut snowballs may be subsituted for the brownies, if you like.

MENU NO. 4—BASKET SUPPER

Individual Hot Ham Loaves
Old-fashioned Creamed Potatoes
Pickles
Melon Ball Fruit Cups
Tiny Blueberry Muffins
Tiny Pecan Rolls
Macaroons
Ice Cream

Hot meat loaves could be a substitute for the ham loaves.

Cook the potatoes in individual foil pans, and they'll be all ready to pop in the baskets.

Macaroni and cheese would be a possible substitute for the potatoes.

Put pickles in individual cups.

Macaroons should be big and chewy.

Dixie cups of ice cream can be passed at the end of the meal.

Labor Day

This is the last holiday of the summer, and it's likely to be quite warm. People have been having a lot of outdoor barbecues all summer, and going on quite a few picnics too, so this could be the time to do something a little startling or different.

For this party, the brighter colors of late summer will be very attractive—yellow, apricot, and orange, or red and orange, or six shades of green, with lots of avocado and olive. Brown tones are interesting when mixed with earth colors.

MENU NO. 1

Jellied Beet Borsch
Cheese Pastry Straws
Standing Ribs of Beef
Stuffed Giant Mushroom Caps
Corn on the Cob
Stuffed Tomatoes
Celery Seed Bread
Broiled Fresh Peaches

This is a menu for a sit-down dinner.

Add beef consommé to the borsch and serve with lemon wedges.

Stuff the mushroom caps with broccoli or zucchini.

If corn on the cob is not available, serve whole-kernel corn with plain butter.

Peel medium whole tomatoes, yellow if possible, and stuff with diced celery, avocado, crisp bacon, and zippy mustard mayonnaise.

Sour cream and brown sugar are thinly spread on the peaches. Then broil and lift them onto Swedish Gaufrettes (Wafers)* or lace cookies.

MENU NO. 2

Avocado in the Snow*
Baked Chicken Breasts with Orange Pecan Stuffing
Country Chicken Gravy
Zucchini Squash Casserole*
Broiled Tomatoes
Tiny Croissants with Currant Jelly
Peach Mary Anns

Add crisp bacon to the squash and zucchini.

Instead of broiled tomatoes, you might have sliced cold tomatoes with pineapple.

For dessert, fill angel food cake shells with peach or vanilla ice cream and top with fresh peach sauce.

MENU NO. 3—PICNIC SUPPER

French-fried Frogs' Legs
Tartar Sauce
Arabian Nights Eggplant*
French-fried Cauliflower
Fruit Salad
Orange Whipped Cream Dressing
Cheese Rolls
Orange Sherbet Baskets
French Twirls*

Quickly French fry the frogs' legs ahead of time, then reheat in oven under broiler. Serve with the tartar sauce and lemon wedges. Substitute chicken legs, if you don't like frogs' legs.

For the salad, use yellow and green fruits only; omit watermelon. Fresh peaches, fresh pineapple, green grapes, honeydew melon, and cantaloupe make a nice combination. Add grated orange to whipped cream dressing.

For the Sherbet Baskets, use half peach or vanilla ice cream and half orange sherbet to fill baskets made of scooped-out orange shells. Be sure to grate fresh orange rind over the tops.

Instead of French Twirls* you might have benne seed cookies.

Halloween

A bright pumpkin-colored cloth, an orange one, or even black will make a striking background for your Halloween buffet. Burlap is also appropriate for this informal season. Black candles can be put in fresh oranges (leveled off at the bottom) instead of regular candlesticks. Many homes have black wrought-iron candelabra. These are perfect with orange candles.

For a modern setting, take unusual shaped twigs that have bewitching gaunt lines and spray them black. Wire a few orange glamellias (plucked gladioli) to the twigs or use dried seed pods painted orange. Milkweed pods can look quite weird when painted orange and yellow.

MENU NO. 1

Beef Stew
Rice Ring
*Apple Mincemeat Waldorf Salad**
Hot Gingerbread
Bread Sticks
Marble Sheet Cake
Caramel Corn   Peanuts   Molasses Candy

The beef stew is a real production—it's served in a big pumpkin tureen. Scoop out your pumpkin but keep the top part for a lid. Line the pumpkin with foil, and then, half an hour before serving time, fill with boiling-hot water. Prepare a regular beef stew with vegetables (with or without potatoes) and you might also toss in a handful of raisins, a few prunes or dried apricots that have been soaked for several hours. Any kind of stew or beef bourguignon can be used. Garnish the pumpkin with fall oak leaves, marigolds, and parsley. This can be used as a centerpiece right in the middle of the table if you wish. If you like symmetry, put the stew at one end and use a similar-sized pumpkin with scalloped edge at the other end. Fill it with shaved ice snow and arrange raw vegetable relishes, especially carrot sticks and Porcupine Celery*, at the top.

The rice ring (or perhaps a noodle ring) would be served only if no potatoes are used in the stew.

The salad can be either loosely arranged or molded in lemon aspic.

Cut the hot gingerbread in wedges.

Be sure to have Halloween decorations on the cake.

MENU NO. 2

Broiled Wieners
Carrot Soufflé*
Mandarin Orange Molded Salad
Corn Sticks
Assorted Doughnuts

Split the wieners lengthwise and put a thin slice of American cheese in the center. Broil them either plain or wrapped in bacon, and serve on toasted wiener buns.

Have carrot pudding instead of the Carrot Soufflé*, if you choose.

Make the salad in a round dish, with no hole. When it's unmolded, use ripe olives to make eyes, nose, and mouth.

MENU NO. 3

Grilled Little Sausages
Canadian Bacon
Broiled Peaches
New England Baked Beans
Boston Brown Bread Crescents
Moon-shaped Sandwiches
Orange Sherbet
Butter Cookies

Serve the broiled peaches round side up, with cloves for eyes and nose, and a slice of red apple for mouth, to make a Halloween face.

Add dark molasses to baked beans.

Make the brown bread sandwiches with pimiento or olive cheese.

Scoop out orange halves and fill with orange sherbet.

Make the butter cookies in some traditional Halloween shapes, or serve decorated petits fours instead.

MENU NO. 4

Ham Crêpes
Hot Corn Fritters
Spiced Prunes   Spiced Cantaloupe Rind
Long Melba Toast Sticks
Sliced Orange and Cucumber Salad
Chive or Green Onion Transparent Dressing
Tiny Apricot and Blackberry Tarts

For the crêpes, large thin slices of boiled or baked ham are rolled up with saffron rice, mushrooms, and grated carrots as filling.

Serve dark brown sugar syrup or maple syrup with the corn fritters.

The prunes are the big, black kind.

Prepare the toast sticks with melted American cheese.

Arrange alternating rows of the apricot and blackberry (or perhaps black raspberry) tarts on the serving tray.

MENU NO. 5

Open Apricot Canapés*
Boneless Pork Loin Roast
Escalloped Apples
Butternut Squash Ring
Carrot Sticks   Ripe Olives
Pumpkin Chiffon Pie

A small amount of chutney may be added to the apricot canapés.

Serve traditional bread dressing with the well-cooked roast.

Surround the squash ring with whole glazed mushrooms.

Put the carrot sticks and olives in shaved ice and arrange in a pumpkin shell.

When making the pie, substitute gingersnap crumbs for half the amount of graham crackers called for in a graham cracker crust recipe.

MENU NO. 6

Fresh Flaked Salmon in Aspic*
Dill Dressing with Capers
Chicken Mexican*
Glazed Carrots in Orange Sauce
Green Salad with Artichoke Hearts
Tiny Gingerbread Muffins   Salt Caraway Sticks
Pumpkin Tarts

Columbus Day

See the Spanish menus in the "Nationality Menus" chapter. Note: the centerpiece for this party could be a cardboard silhouette of an old Spanish ship.

Thanksgiving

On the Wednesday evening before the big feast day, some families have to entertain part of the family who have arrived to visit. Since most people eat turkey on the day itself, we suggest roast beef, filet, or roast pork the evening before.

The traditional holiday dinner menu, with a few new embellishments, is obviously in order, since we have such a rich heritage of tradition for this meal.

MENU NO. 1

Apricot Nectar
Roast Turkey with Chestnut Dressing
Broccoli Croquettes
Creamed Onions
Candied Sweet Potatoes or Yams
Cranberry Jelly and Sauce
Olives   Porcupine Celery*
Pumpkin Pie   Mince Pie
Almonds and Pecans   Mints

Add ⅓ unsweetened pineapple juice to the apricot nectar.

Surround the turkey with broiled peach halves topped with currant jelly.

You may make the sauce for the onions with or without cheese.

Serve the olives and celery in shaved ice. Skip salad with this hearty meal.

For the children, you might have ice cream and petits fours, for most children, I've found, don't care for the traditional pies.

MENU NO. 2

Shrimp Cocktail
Roast Turkey
French-fried Brussels Sprouts
Cranberry Jelly and Sauce
Bunch of Grapes Salad*
Tiny Assorted Rolls
Pumpkin Chiffon Pie
Salted Mixed Nuts   Wafer Mints

Instead of the usual shrimp cocktail, you might have individual shrimp plates arranged with paper soufflé cups of sauce in the middle. Be sure to serve lemon wedges, in either case.

Make a traditional bread stuffing for the turkey.

Dip the Brussels sprouts in Rice Krispies before cooking. French-fried Parsnips* would be an alternative.

Make the pie with a graham cracker crust. Pumpkin ice cream may be substituted.

Dip one end of the wafers in chocolate.

MENU NO. 3

Apricot Gold Shrub
Melba Toast
Roast Turkey
Butternut Squash
Yellow Wax Beans
Apple Mincemeat Waldorf Salad*
Poppy Seed Dressing*
Porcupine Celery*   Olives
Assorted Tiny Rolls
Pumpkin Pie   Mince Pie
Vanilla Ice Cream with Peach Sauce
Salted Nuts   Mints

To make Apricot Gold Shrub, add lemon or pineapple sherbet to apricot nectar. Serve fresh lemon wedges with this.

Garnish the turkey with broiled halves of pear topped with butter, brown sugar, and a pinch of red sugar to make them blush.

Serve the squash with a whisper of onion juice, brown sugar, and sprinkle with crisp crinkled bacon tidbits and toasted pecans.

Add parsley butter and green onion tops to the wax beans. Or serve them with sliced stuffed olives and a dash of sour cream. Or add water chestnuts, mushrooms, and chopped watercress butter.

Order both sweet and plain tiny rolls from your baker.

Pumpkin chiffon pie may be substituted for the traditional kind.

MENU NO. 4

This is a Thanksgiving supper for a family who has had a big dinner at one or two o'clock away from home.

Stuffed Giant Mushroom Caps
Sesame Melba Toast*
Kumquat Orange Molded Salad*
Fruit Cake

Stuff the mushroom caps with chopped ham and serve with Spinach Sauce*.

Scones or toasted English muffins may be substituted for the Melba toast.

Lace cookies or brandy snaps are alternatives for the fruit cake.

MENU NO. 5

This is another Thanksgiving supper.

*Mushroom Fritters**
*Julienne Ham in Spinach Sauce**
*Bing Cherry Salad Mold**
Herb-buttered Melba Toast
Little White Cupcakes with Sherbet

Dried beef may be served instead of the ham.

Instead of the cherry salad, you might like a molded Apple Mincemeat Waldorf Salad*.

Make the Melba toast long, pencil-slim sticks.

Scoop out the cupcakes and put in a teaspoon of apricot sherbet.

Christmas

Everyone has lots to do, everyone is in a hurry, people coming home from out of town, decorations still to be done, presents unwrapped—so the night-before meal should be very simple.

MENU NO. 1—CHRISTMAS EVE DINNER

Stuffed Celery
English Meat Pie with Vegetables
*Christmas Salad**
Celery Seed or Watercress Mayonnaise
Toasted English Muffins
Fruited Dresden Stollen

Stuff the celery with chopped shrimp or crab meat salad.

Instead of meat pie, you might have beef stew with a biscuit topping.

Make parsley butter for the muffins.

MENU NO. 2

Green Noodle Ring
Swedish Meatballs in Brown Gravy
Two-tone Tomato and Asparagus Aspic
Hot Poppy Seed Rolls
*Peppermint Stick Mousse**
Chocolate Sauce
Christmas Cookies

Parslied rice ring may be substituted for the noodle ring.

If you don't want to bother with meatballs, just brown ground beef with onions and serve in gravy.

Fold an extra can of asparagus tips into the mayonnaise for the aspic, and serve separately.

Split and butter the rolls ahead of time.

Make the mousse in individual dessert cups. Or serve peppermint stick ice cream with hot chocolate sauce.

MENU NO. 3

Hot Ham Loaf
Red Sour Cherry Sauce
Creamed Peas and Braised Diced Celery
Christmas Finger Sweets

Gingersnap Gravy* may be substituted for the cherry sauce.

Sprinkle the peas and celery with really brown toasted pecans, and serve on Holland rusks.

The Christmas Dinner

Most of us have family traditions when it comes to Christmas dinner. Younger couples may introduce embellishments, but most families hesitate to change much. Since help is scarce, the fewer courses the better.

MENU NO. 1

Roast Turkey
Cranberry Sauce or Gooseberry Chutney
Creamed Peas and Onions
Candied Sweet Potatoes or Yams
Celery and Olives in Shaved Ice
Mince Pie
Steamed Plum Pudding with Tart Lemon Foam Sauce
Ice Cream Molds
Cookies
Mints   Salted Nuts

Make a traditional stuffing for the turkey. If you have a large family or many guests and cook two birds, fill one with chestnut stuffing and one with a little sausage added to your regular stuffing. Garnish the platter with stars of cranberry jelly on orange slices.

Leave out the peas if you'd rather have plain creamed onions. You won't need a salad with this meal.

The ice cream molds are for the young people.

MENU NO. 2

Tomato Aspic Bells
Roast Turkey
*Plain Gravy   Giblet Gravy   Currant Wine Sauce**
Cranberry Jelly
*Broccoli Croquettes**
Spiced Fruit Tray
Tiny Butterscotch Rolls
Tiny Sesame Croissants
Nesselrode Chiffon Pie
Eggnog Chiffon Pie
Mints   Nuts

Make a clear tomato aspic ½-inch thick in a flat cookie sheet. Cut out in bell shapes. Put on shredded iceberg lettuce and garnish with soft cream cheese squeezed through a pastry tube. Green pepper and sliced olives can be used to make bells Christmasy. These can be served as a first-course salad or in the usual order, after the main course.

Make the Nesselrode pie with a graham cracker crust.

The eggnog pie is in a crushed Hydrox cookie crust, topped with shaved semi-sweet chocolate curls. A strawberry Bavarian cream mold, garnished with fresh strawberries, may be substituted for the eggnog pie.

MENU NO. 3

Chilled Cranberry Cocktail
Bell-shaped Sesame Melba Toast*
Roast Turkey
Grape Sauce*   *Cranberry Jelly*
Herb and Egg Creamed Spinach Casserole
Harvard Beets
Sautéed Vegetables
Cucumber Sour Cream Aspic
Tiny Rolls
Mince Pie   Plum Pudding
Bavarian Cream with Cherry Sauce
Peppermint Stick Mousse* with Chocolate Sauce
Salted Nuts   Mints

Blend cranberry juice with frozen lemonade and frozen crushed strawberries to make the cocktail.

Make the Grape Sauce* with Tokay grapes.

Add grated orange rind and a whisper of horseradish to the beets.

The vegetables are green beans, water chestnuts, mushrooms, and artichoke hearts, sautéed in watercress butter.

Serve the aspic on thin slices of tomato. You may substitute Christmas Salad* for the cucumber aspic.

MENU NO. 4—CHRISTMAS SUPPER

Cold Leftover Turkey
Hot Cheese Rarebit with Crisp Crumbled Bacon
Dry Melba Toast
Raisin Bread Toast
Rhubarb Strawberry Mold*
Fruit Cake and Cookies

Sprinkle toasted almonds over the rarebit.

Baked Ham
Leftover Cold White Meat of Turkey
Thin Sliced Party White and Rye Bread
Artichoke Mustard Relish*
Brown Mustard Sauce
Celery Seed Mayonnaise
Hot Scalloped Oysters
Fruit Cake and Cookies

Garnish the ham with spiced crab apples.

If you don't like oysters, medium seashells filled with crab Dewey topped with buttered, toasted bread crumbs would be nice.

New Year's Eve

Thrifty people will probably still be using Christmas decorations, but I'm all for getting rid of red and green in the dining room. Use pink or lavender and aqua, or brown and white, or black and white. A big old-fashioned clock, with the hands pointing to 12 and with a spray of tiny orchids across it, would make a good centerpiece. Father Time and a baby doll may be a little more work, but certainly apropos.

Oysters Rockefeller
Lasagna Ercole*
Cold Sliced Rare Filet of Beef
Dill Party Bread
Horseradish Mousse*
Platter of Grapefruit Sections and Grapes
Paprika Dressing*
Tiny Cream Cheese Pastries
Finger Bavarian Pastries

Bring the oysters right in on cookie sheets that have been spread with rock salt. Put plenty of parsley around the edges of the cookie sheet and rest it on a large silver platter.

The dill party bread should be thinly sliced, and half of it lightly buttered.

Surround the mousse mold with white asparagus vinaigrette and diagonally sliced Belgian endive.

Sprinkle the grapefruit sections with pitted Tokay grapes and a few reddish Grapes Jubilee*. Garnish with fresh strawberries, if obtainable.

The cream cheese pastries are variously filled with apricot, prune, nut, and cheese.

MENU NO. 2—BUFFET

Creamed Dried Beef
Bell-shaped Melba Toast
Broiled Miniature Beef Shish Kebabs
French-fried Frogs' Legs
Tartar Sauce
*Tiered Pickle Tree**
Orange Molded Salad
*Cheese Blintzes**
*Tart Red Raspberry Sauce**

Mix water chestnuts, artichoke hearts, and mushrooms with the dried beef. Serve on large pieces of dry bell-shaped Melba toast, with a bowl of grated Parmesan cheese alongside.

Serve lemon wedges with the tartar sauce for the frogs' legs.

For the Tiered Pickle Tree*, get every kind of pickle you can lay hands on.

The salad consists of diced celery, sliced oranges, diced green pepper, and chives molded in orange gelatin.

Roll medium blintzes with a mixture of cottage cheese, cream cheese, and sour cream that is not runny. Alternate sauces would be blueberry, lingonberry, or tart orange.

Beef and Kidney Pie
Shrimp Creole with Rice Ring
Pâté Maison*
Bell-shaped Melba Toast
Bunch of Grapes Salad*
Tiny Cucumber Sandwiches with Watercress
Bell-shaped Petits Fours
Round Petits Fours

Instead of the pie, you might have beef puff pastry turnovers.

As a substitute for shrimp creole, serve Hot Lobster Capon Madeira* and the rice ring.

Mold the pâté in a bell shape. Make it of ⅓ chopped chicken liver, ⅓ goose liver, ⅓ finely ground ham.

Put the year date on the small bell-shaped petits fours. On the round petits fours, have the face of a clock with the hands pointing to 12 o'clock.

Hot Soup Bar
Corned Beef Hash
Pepper Relish
Thin Sliced Roast Beef and Cold Turkey
Green and White Vegetable Salad*
Herb Baking Powder Biscuits
Large Chewy Macaroons
Thin French Chocolate Leaves

On the hot soup bar, have a choice of crab bisque, tomato chicken bouillon, and asparagus or Watercress Soup*. Serve old-fashioned saltines with the soups.

Blend a little catsup into the pepper relish.

Surround the salad platter with a wreath of watercress.

MENU NO. 5

Mushroom Bouillon
Bell-shaped Pie Pastry
Boston Strip Roast
Artichoke Bottoms with Pea Purée
Broiled Tomato Halves
Green Salad
Rose Toth Dressing*
Butter Rolls
Coffee Baked Alaska*
Mr. Arthur's Butterscotch Sauce* or Crème de Cacao

The bouillon should be boiling hot and delicate. Add sherry at the last minute if desired. With it serve *thin* pie pastry cut in bell shapes and made with Parmesan cheese and herbs in the dough.

Garnish the roast with small broiled dried apricots, chutney, and bacon.

Fill the Artichoke Bottoms with a delicately curried Pea Purée and small croutons.

Butter the tomato halves and sprinkle with basil before broiling.

Make the salad with Belgian endive and Bibb lettuce.

The butter rolls should be tiny, 1 inch by 1 inch.

Make a large Coffee Baked Alaska* and bring it to the table flaming. Insert half of an empty egg shell in the top of the meringue. At the last minute fill with 3 or 4 sugar cubes dipped in lemon extract. Light with a match just as you enter the dining room.

MENU NO. 6

Avocado in the Snow*
Standing Ribs of Beef
Mushroom Pie*
Rice and Green Bean Casserole
Broccoli with Braised Diced Celery Butter
Tossed Greek Salad
Lemon and Oil Dressing
Herb or Sesame French Bread
Chocolate Whipped Cream Roll
Bell-shaped Mints

For the casserole, combine green beans with rice cooked in consommé, mushrooms, and grated American cheese.

To make the Braised Diced Celery Butter, put diced celery through a food chopper and then sauté in butter. Instead of the broccoli, you might serve Fordhook lima beans sprinkled with crisp bacon and croutons.

Arrange the salad on purple cabbage leaves.

Grapefruit Cake* or Coffee Baked Alaska* with chocolate sauce may be substituted for the chocolate roll.

MENU NO. 7

This is for a New Year's early morning breakfast.

Eggs Benedict on Melba Toast
Browned Little Link Sausages
Tiny Blueberry Muffins
Tiny Pecan Rolls
Tiny Danish Raisin Snails

Sprinkle crisp crinkled bacon on the sausages.

MENU NO. 8—NEW YEAR'S DAY BRUNCH

Hot Miniature Crêpes with Tart Orange Sauce
Baked Stuffed Tomatoes
*Baked Bananas**
Stuffed Prunes
Fresh Baked Kuchen

Use skinned tomatoes and stuff with chopped ham and a mustard sauce.

Stuff the prunes with cream cheese.

CHAPTER 2

NATIONALITY MENUS

Every year more people travel to Europe, South America, Hawaii, everywhere on the globe, as jet travel brings the world to everyone's doorstep.

When people come back from a trip, many want to share their experiences—and their Kodachrome slides—with family and friends. Why not invite your friends for a buffet dinner and serve them a meal similar to the kind of food you had wherever you've been?

The foreign menu idea can also be used at farewell and bon voyage parties. It enlivens the partings and sometimes keeps them from being too sentimental and sad.

If you have several waitresses, it would be interesting to dress them in native costumes and thus add a little more color. Air travel agencies and steamship lines are always helpful about furnishing colorful travel posters to provide additional atmosphere. We often use the colors found in a country's flag for a theme, and place small silk flags in the table centerpiece.

The importance of nationality dinners has been impressed upon us over the past six or seven years because our company has catered the suppers at an improvised pavilion set up in the basement beneath Cleveland's famous Public Hall, where a week of Metropolitan Opera performances includes a series of buffet dinners. Usually menus are planned so that the dinner takes on the nationality of the opera. For example, before the curtain rises on

Aida, the guarantors and their friends have dined on Egyptian dishes. As a prelude to *Faust,* the menu features German cooking, and so on.

Hawaiian

The centerpiece may be orchids on driftwood—plastic, or fresh with ferns. Crepe paper leis are colorful; the extravagant host orders flower leis from Hawaii. Anthurium in plastic are available, and when they're put with fresh green foliage, it's hard to tell the difference. Little hula dolls are helpful if you can find them. Occasionally we rent palm trees from a local display house.

For this party, one usually thinks in bold colors. It can be held any time of year, but hot August nights seem ideal. Wherever it's possible, get many pillows and mats and let peoole sit at low tables with legs crossed, as for Chinese or Japanese parties.

We like to cover the tables with burlap, either green or brown, and if they're obtainable from your florist, get large ti leaves to spread here and there at angles. Pastel teardrop lights, altar candles, or regular candles may be used. Tables should be approximately 18 inches from the floor. The buffet table can be standard height; make it as colorful as possible.

MENU NO. 1—BUFFET

Hawaiian-style Suckling Pig
Apple Bread Dressing
Hawaiian Chicken
Fluffy White Rice
Hot French-fried Bananas
Green Salad
Crusty Hearth Bread
Fruits
Fresh Coconut Snowballs

Bake cut-up pieces of chicken in pineapple onion sauce.

Make the salad with spinach and avocado, or grapefruit if desired, and serve it in individual bowls.

Half a pineapple shell filled with fresh fruits and garnished with fresh strawberries makes a pretty dessert.

MENU NO. 2

Hawaiian Chicken Livers
Shrimp in Avocado
Baked Fresh Ham
Brown Rice
Peas with Macadamia Nuts
Bananas Fried in Olive Oil
Spinach Croquettes*
Fresh Fruits with Lime Sherbet
Peanut Butter Cookies

Insert a water chestnut in each chicken liver, wrap in bacon or pastrami, dip in brown sugar, and bake at 400° F. about 25 minutes, or broil. Serve with a sweet-sour soya sauce for dunking.

The shrimp are nestled in cocktail sauce in halves of ripe avocado. Garnish with lemon wedges.

Cook the ham very well, at least 5 hours. Score and rub with brown sugar.

Roll the Spinach Croquettes* in coconut.

Serve the fresh fruits in cantaloupe rings and top with a ball of sherbet.

MENU NO. 3

Hot Crab Meat and Avocado
Browned Beef Tenderloin Tips en Brochette
Candied Yams
Hot Creamed Spinach with Coconut
Peas with Chopped Shrimp
Cut-up Chicken
Barbecue Sauce
Little Rice Cakes
Fruit Salad
Apricot Dressing
Watermelon Dessert

Make a crab meat salad and toss with avocado slivers. Serve it hot on big seashells.

Cook the tenderloin tips on skewers with mushrooms and onions.

Serve chicken with a sweet-sour tomato barbecue sauce containing plenty of sliced ripe olives.

Make the salad with oranges, pineapple, and bananas.

For the dessert, place watermelon sherbet around cones of watermelon.

MENU NO. 4

Curried Beef
Fluffy Rice
Condiments
Green Beans with Macadamia Nuts
Chicken and Shrimp in Pineapple Onion Sauce
French-fried Eggplant
Spinach Pie*
Avocado Aspic Ring
Fresh Pineapple Dessert

With the beef, serve chutney with raw apple added, and other condiments as desired: peanuts, toasted coconut, raisins, chopped hard-boiled eggs, chopped green pepper, for instance.

Be sure the chicken and shrimp dish is not overly sweet. Add a little chopped crystallized ginger to the sauce.

Dust the eggplant lightly with cinnamon after frying.

Sprinkle coconut and chopped bacon on the Spinach Pie*.

Surround the aspic ring with tomato sections, green pepper sticks or rings, and fill the center with coleslaw to which you have added red apple or bananas.

For the dessert, serve quarters (or thirds) of fresh pineapple topped with pineapple sherbet and shredded pineapple.

MENU NO. 5

Shrimp and Chicken Salad
Roast Boneless Loin of Pork
Brown Rice
Green Beans
Avocado Aspic with Fresh Fruit
Hot Penny Buns
Banana Cream Pie or Tarts

PLATE VII

The Brown and White Tea

PLATE VIII

Dinner Menu #10:

Hot Deviled Crab Meat
Filet of Beef Tenderloin
Wild Rice and Mushroom Casserole
Horseradish Mousse
Caesar Salad with Croutons
Deep Blueberry Tarts à la Mode

Serve the shrimp and chicken salad in halves or thirds of scooped-out pineapple shells. Don't fill them until the last minute.

When you make the gravy for the pork, add ginger and chopped apples to it. It should be spicy.

Add braised onion slices to the brown rice.

To the green beans, add chopped hard-boiled egg and buttered bread crumbs.

Arrange any kind of fresh fruit in season around the avocado aspic.

Hot penny buns are small, raised yeast buns.

Make the pie with a meringue and sprinkle with toasted coconut.

MENU NO. 6

Barbecued Pineapple Spears
Barbecued Spareribs
Barbecued Halves of Chicken
Sweet Sour Sauce
Yams Baked with Apple Rings
Banana Fritters
Grilled Tomatoes
Heart of Palm Salad
Ripe Olive Dressing
Tossed Green Salad with Shrimp
Fresh Fruit in Watermelon Boat
Coconut Macaroons

Brush the pineapple spears with butter before broiling.

Dust the banana fritters with cinnamon and powdered sugar just before you serve them.

Sprinkle the tomatoes with chopped green onion and parsley.

Add grated orange rind to the heart of palm salad.

MENU NO. 7

Chilled Papaya Juice
Thin Ham Cornucopias
Broiled Sirloin Steak
Fluffy Rice with Peas
Giant Stuffed Mushrooms
Mango Chutney
Tomato Avocado Salad
Paprika Dressing*
Crusty Hearth Bread
Sliced Oranges and Bananas with Rum Syrup
Coconut Layer Cake

Fill the ham cornucopias with shrimp salad.

Cook the steak medium rare.

Stuff the mushrooms with spinach and sliced water chestnuts.

To make the salad, combine sliced tomatoes with strips of avocado. Garnish with fresh pineapple spears. Add chopped candied ginger to the Paprika Dressing*.

The bread should be dusted with rice flour on top.

English

Use the British Union Jack, with its red, white, and blue colors, for your theme. Set the table with snowy white linen, English Sheffield silver candelabra, and your best china—in brief, a formal table. Royal Doulton figurines may be used instead of fresh flowers. If you want to have flowers, I would suggest especially pansies, sweet William, and primroses in a colorful array. Waitresses should wear black uniforms to provide a formal atmosphere.

MENU NO. 1—BUFFET

Roast Sirloin of Beef
Mushroom Pie*
Brussels Sprouts
Tiny Peas
Molded Beets and Horseradish Salad
Small Bath Buns
Toasted Scones
Plunketts*

Carve the beef at the table.

Pressure-cook the Brussels sprouts to keep them bright green. Just before serving, toss in a few hot buttered prunes, pitted.

The tiny peas may be canned. Serve with plain butter.

MENU NO. 2

Standing Ribs of Beef
Yorkshire Pudding
Whole Browned Potatoes
French-fried Parsnips*
Hot Baked Tomatoes and Little White Onions
Toasted English Muffins
Little Mincemeat Tarts
Spiced Fruit Compote
Cheese and Cracker Tray

Sprinkle the parsnips with rosemary and dust them heavily with chopped parsley.

No salad is necessary with this dinner.

MENU NO. 3

Curried Lamb
Fluffy Rice
Gooseberry Chutney
Glazed Brown Mushrooms with Braised Celery
Cold New Cabbage Slaw
Hot Whole Wheat Biscuits with Cheese
Tapioca Pudding with Meringue

The potatoes should be finely diced.
Add a little diced raw apple to the slaw.
Garnish the pudding with fresh strawberries.

MENU NO. 4

Crab Meat in Sherry Cream Sauce
Eye of Beef with Horseradish
Browned Whole Potatoes
French-fried Brussels Sprouts*
Carrots Newburg
Whole Wheat Muffins
Celery and Peas in Aspic Rings
Tart Orange Charlotte Russe
Ladyfingers

Serve the crab meat in seashells.
Boil the potatoes in their jackets before browning.
Make the salad of little V-8 juice aspic rings filled with diagonally cut braised celery and canned peas. Serve a mustard dressing.
Garnish the Charlotte Russe with orange sections, strawberries, or blueberries.

MENU NO. 5

Beef Wellington
Mushroom Gravy
Baked Whole Tomatoes
Braised Celery
Kumquat Orange Molded Salad*
Paprika Dressing*
Fresh Fruit Trifle

Beef Wellington is a filet rubbed with chicken liver pâté and rolled in a pie pastry or puff pastry crust. Bake the filet 20 minutes in 350° F. oven before rolling in crust and 25 or 30 minutes after the crust is rolled at same temperature. Serve with a thin brown mushroom gravy.

Stuff the tomatoes with lima bean purée or with Fordhook lima beans and cover with a cheese sauce.

Add shaved water chestnuts and loads of chopped watercress to the celery.

Surround the salad with gherkins.

Make the trifle with a sherry-flavored custard, sponge cake, and whipped cream. Garnish with fresh fruits in season—strawberries, raspberries, peaches, or sliced bananas.

MENU NO. 6

Roast Leg of Lamb
Potato Turnip Ring with Peas
Spiced Beets
Whole Wheat Muffins
Hot Curried Pear Halves

Make the Potato Turnip Ring of creamy mashed potatoes, a small amount of mashed yellow turnips and a bit of melted Cheddar cheese. Fill the center of the ring with buttered peas.

Instead of pear halves, you might try French-fried pears dipped in almond macaroon crumbs. In either case pass brandied whipped cream.

MENU NO. 7

Broiled Rock Cornish Game Hens
*Currant Wine Sauce**
Chestnut Stuffing
Curried Carrots and Grapes
Mustard Pickles
Cranberry Salad Mold
Hot Bread
Tart Lemon Meringue Pie

Cook the game hens without stuffing, but make chestnut stuffing in a ring filled with browned mushrooms and serve it separately. The salad is made with cranberry juice and gelatin with chopped oranges and apples. Surround the mold with slices of orange, each topped with a little flower cut out of cranberry jelly.

Put little loaves of hot bread at each table on bread boards.

Instead of the pie, have individual rhubarb meringue tarts if you prefer.

MENU NO. 8

Beef and Oyster Pie
Baked Ham
Hot Turkey with Sage Dressing
Au Gratin Potatoes
Jellied Fruit Molds
London Sugar Buns with Sultana Raisins
Flaky Butter Rolls
Rhubarb Shortcake

The ham should be the kind with a bone.

Mold the fruit in tart raspberry gelatin.

Make the shortcake with rich biscuits, pink stewed rhubarb, and grated pineapple. Pass brandied whipped cream.

MENU NO. 9

Broiled Top Sirloin Steak
Butternut Squash Soufflé Ring Filled with Mushrooms
Creamed Peas and Celery in Tart Shells
Whole Wheat Fig Bran Muffins
Olives and Celery
Tossed Green Salad
Rice Pudding
*Tart Red Raspberry Sauce**

An alternative to the steak would be English-cut roast beef.

Sprinkle the peas and celery with grated cheese before serving.

Add chopped, unpeeled raw apple and a dash of green onion to the salad.

French

So many kinds of decoration suggest France. The red, white, and blue flag is obvious, and at French buffets we often have the flag somewhere in evidence. Cherub figurines may be used to suggest the art, fashion, and romance of Paris. In many homes we use small café tables seating a maximum of 4 for more intimate conversations.

MENU NO. 1

Filet of Beef Tenderloin
Brown Artichoke Pan Gravy
French-fried Parsley*
Spinach Soufflé Ring
Crusty French Bread
Sweet Butter Balls
Green Salad
Nut Sponge Cake Roll
Mr. Arthur's Butterscotch Sauce*

Thicken the gravy with a little cornstarch to keep it from being too runny.

Fill the center of the soufflé ring with mushrooms.

The salad is French endive with Bibb lettuce. For the dressing, blend ¾ Rose Toth Dressing* with ¼ Paprika Dressing*.

The cake roll is a nut sponge cake rolled up with whipped cream.

MENU NO. 2

Hot Lobster Capon Madeira*
Fluffy Rice
Filet Mignon
Yellow Wax Beans and Artichoke Hearts
Peas and Lettuce
Croissants
Asparagus Vinaigrette Salad
Assorted French Pastries
Crêpes Suzette*

The filets should weigh 2½ to 3 ounces apiece and be broiled quickly.

Saffron rice may be substituted for the fluffy rice.

French the wax beans and combine with slivered artichoke hearts and a little yellow summer squash, if obtainable. Toss in watercress butter.

Chop iceberg lettuce and combine with the peas. Add a little chervil at the last minute.

Serve an orange sauce with the Crêpes Suzette*.

MENU NO. 3

Boned Chicken Breasts
Orange Sauce
*Spinach Crêpes**
Tiny French Peas with Brown Butter
Chestnut Mousse
Crème de Cacao or Sherry Sauce

Wrap the crêpes around julienne cooked carrots, lightly curried if desired. Serve with a thin hot cheese rarebit sauce.

The peas are extra fancy canned ones.

MENU NO. 4

Eye of Beef
Mushroom Soufflé
*French-fried Cauliflower**
*Vegetable Wheel Vinaigrette**
French Bread
*Angel Food Crème Brûlée**
*Tart Red Raspberry Sauce**

An artichoke sauce with water chestnuts and lots of chopped cress should be passed with the soufflé.

For the Vegetable Wheel Vinaigrette*, use cooked carrots, corn, peas, lima beans, and beets.

The French bread should be torn apart, not cut.

MENU NO. 5

Filet of Beef Tenderloin
Glazed Whole Mushrooms
Potato Puffs
Baked Artichoke Bottoms, Carrots, and Onions
Chocolate Pot de Crème
Macaroons

The Potato Puffs are mashed potatoes blended with cream puff batter to make them extra light, then quickly French-fried.

Marinate the artichoke bottoms in a vinaigrette dressing, and bake with carrots and onions.

Serve the pot de crème in little china cups.

Italian

Your centerpiece may be the red, white, and green flag of Italy. Bowls of fresh fruit, Roman columns, and statuary suggest the romance of that lovely country.

MENU NO. 1

Ham Cornucopias
Chicken Tetrazzini
Italian Green Beans
*Spinach Croquettes**
Spiced Fruit
Green Salad
*Ruth Just's Roman Dressing**
Italian Crusty Bread
Bisque Tortoni

Fill the cornucopias with cottage cheese and finely chopped green onion tops.

The green beans are the wide variety. Mix them with water chestnuts and artichokes.

Bisque tortoni is a frozen mousse with crushed almond macaroons, lots of vanilla, and whipped cream. It is available in the frozen food departments in many places, or you may make your own.

MENU NO. 2

Veal Scaloppine in Wine
Lasagna Ercole*
Creamed Spinach
Broiled Tomatoes
Green Salad
Rose Toth Dressing*
Italian Bread with Sesame Seeds
Fresh Fruit Platter
Almond Macaroons

Add a dash of oregano or chervil to the spinach and garnish with chopped hard-boiled egg.

Sprinkle the tomatoes with grated Parmesan cheese.

Make the salad with romaine, escarole, endive, and artichoke hearts.

MENU NO. 3

Spaghetti with Meat Sauce
Roast Turkey Lombardy
Chestnut Stuffing
Porcupine Celery*   *Olives*
Lima Beans Viscania
Eggplant Sicilian
Molded Fresh Fruit Rings
Italian Bread Sticks
Vanilla Ice Cream
Mr. Arthur's Butterscotch Sauce*
Small Cookies

Don't serve meatballs with the spaghetti. It's never done in Italy.

Use ripe, stuffed, and stone olives.

To cooked lima beans add pimiento and chestnuts, and dress with butter and sour cream.

Garnish the fruit rings with fresh strawberries.

MENU NO. 4

Veal Scaloppine Milanese
Tower of Pisa Potatoes
French-fried Eggplant
Italian Green Beans
Caesar Salad
Hard and Poppy Seed Rolls
Peach Melba

Tower of Pisa Potatoes are mashed potatoes spiraled up into cone shape, so high they lean a little. Dust them with sesame seeds.

Mix the wide Italian beans with sliced stuffed olives and butter.

MENU NO. 5

Mushroom Tetrazzini*
Standing Ribs of Beef
Broiled Tomatoes
Broccoli Croquettes*
Grapefruit and Avocado Salad
Crusty Italian Bread
Fruit Canoli

Sirloin butt roast may be substituted for the standing ribs.
Sprinkle oregano and chopped parsley on the tomatoes.
Roll the Broccoli Croquettes* in Rice Krispies.
Canoli is a pastry dough filled with a mixture of whipped cream, sour cream, and candied fruit.
Serve spumoni ice cream instead of the fruit canoli, if you prefer.

MENU NO. 6

*Spaghetti alla Carbonara**
*Stuffed Artichoke Bottoms**
Zucchini
Tossed Green Salad
Oil, Vinegar, and Lemon Dressing
Little Round Flat Hard Rolls
Sweet Butter
Della Robbia Cake

Toss into the hot drained spaghetti chopped bacon and raw eggs (¾ egg per person). Garlic is optional with this dish.

Stuff the medium artichoke bottoms with shrimp in a wine-flavored cream sauce and Parmesan cheese.

Slice the zucchini thin, dress with green onion butter, and sprinkle with slivered toasted almonds.

To make the salad, add diced Italian sausage, croutons, and partly cooked firm julienne green beans to the greens.

Della Robbia Cake is a yellow butter cake covered with sherry-flavored whipped cream and surrounded with a wreath of grapes and a few cherries.

MENU NO. 7

*Spaghetti alla Carbonara**
Zucchini with Tomatoes
Orange, Onion, and Cucumber Salad
Coffee Ice Cream
Pistachio Nut Sauce

Sprinkle the zucchini and tomatoes with grated Parmesan cheese. Use romaine for a green with the salad.

Spanish

Have a centerpiece of old copper or brass, with red and yellow tablecloths and flowers. Antique brass or wrought-iron candelabra are nice touches.

MENU NO. 1

Scallops and Shrimp in White Wine Sauce
Spanish Dilled Beef
Saffron Rice Mold
Peas with Slivered Toasted Almonds
Baked Halves of Tomato
Green Salad
Ripe Olive Dressing
Ice Cream and Sponge Cake
Mandarin Orange Sauce*

Spanish dilled beef is similar to sauerbraten with fresh dill added.
Sprinkle chopped green onion over the tomato halves.
Sprinkle chopped hard-boiled egg on the salad.
Put vanilla ice cream and orange sherbet in layers over the
sponge cake, and pass the sauce separately.

MENU NO. 2

Small Spanish Artichokes Glazed in Wine Sauce
Paella
Tossed Green Salad
Rose Toth Dressing*
Hard Rolls
Fresh Fruit
Cheese

Paella, served in a big iron pot, is almost a one-dish meal.
Use many kinds of crisp greens for the salad.
The fruit may be either fresh fruit peeled and cut up (be sure to
include sections of Spanish melon) in a bowl or just a platter of
whole fresh fruit.

MENU NO. 3

Saffron Chicken and Ham
Spaghetti with Olive Sauce
French-fried Bananas
Tomato and Orange Salad
Spanish Custard

Use serving-sized pieces of chicken in a saffron-flavored chicken gravy to which small cubes of ham have been added.

Don't put any tomatoes in the spaghetti sauce.

Baked Bananas* may be substituted for French-fried bananas, if you prefer.

MENU NO. 4

Filet of Veal with Ham Stuffing
Fig Sauce*
French-fried Cucumbers*
Giant Stuffed Mushrooms
Tossed Green Salad
Olive Oil Dressing
Crusty Hearth Bread
Fresh Fruit Bowl
Cookies

Stuff the mushrooms with a mixture of rice and tomatoes. If the very large mushrooms are not obtainable, cook rice and tomatoes together, add mushrooms and chopped ripe olives, and serve in a casserole.

Add cooked whole-kernel corn and cooked green beans to the salad greens. A few artichoke hearts are optional.

Belgian—German

Both countries have red, gold, and black for their flag colors. Both have similar excellent cooking. Generally speaking, they like their meats cooked more than the average.

For a German party, beer steins depicting flowers or old castles on the Rhine are atmospheric. A few turrets and castle moats can be rigged up from loaf sugar or marshmallows, if you have the time.

When it comes to Beligum, one thinks of Brussels lace. Waitresses could have lace caps or bands in their hair or a little lace on their tea aprons. A lace cloth for the buffet is perfect, if you have one.

MENU NO. 1

Herring in Sour Cream
Sauerbraten
Butter Crumb Noodles
Sweet-Sour Green Beans
Plain Butternut Squash
Wilted Lettuce
Hot Yeast Rolls
German Sweet Chocolate Layer Cake

French the green beans lengthwise.
Be sure to have crumbled bacon with the wilted lettuce.

MENU NO. 2

Whitefish à la Rhine*
Roast Pork
Applesauce Horseradish Relish
Golden Farvel
Creamed Spinach
Brussels Sprouts
Cucumbers in Sour Cream
Dill Bread
Apfelstrudel

Serve the fish either hot or cold.
Mix diced celery and raisins with the relish.
Sautée cracker crumbs and onion in butter and add to the spinach.
The Brussels sprouts can be French-fried or done in brown butter.

MENU NO. 3

Sauerkraut and Spareribs
Mashed Potatoes
Peas Sautéed in Butter
Tomato and Lettuce Salad with Chive Cottage Cheese
Salt Caraway Rolls
Coconut Layer Cake

For those who don't like spareribs, serve baked chicken legs.
Make a lemon custard filling for the layer cake.

MENU NO. 4

Baked Ham
Platter of Assorted Cheeses
Chicken with Paprika Gravy
Hashed Brown Potatoes
Yellow Wax Beans
Icebox Pears   Spritz Cookies

Include Edam and Liederkranz with the cheeses.
Make the potatoes crispy and brown, with a little onion added.
Prepare the wax beans in a sweet-sour vinegar sauce.
Icebox Pears are halves of canned pears with 1 teaspoon dry
cocoa in each of the cavities. Chill 24 hours. Whipped cream may
be passed with these.

Hungarian

MENU NO. 1

Chicken Paprikash
Wide Noodles
Sweet-Sour Red Cabbage
Vegetable Wheel Vinaigrette*
Rich Butter Rolls
Bavarian Cream with Fresh Fruit

Put diced apple and caraway in the red cabbage.
Six kinds of vegetables make up the wheel: beets, peas, lima
beans, yellow beans with bacon, corn, broccoli or asparagus.

MENU NO. 2

Roast Loin of Pork
Stuffed Cabbage Rolls
Poppy Seed Noodle Pudding
Orange and Onion Salad
Crisp Hard Rolls with Sweet Butter
Hungarian Nut Strudel

Layer the noodles with sour cream and cottage cheese in the pudding.

Other possible strudels would be apple, cherry, cheese, and prune.

MENU NO. 3

Veal Paprikash
Buttered Noodles
Zucchini Squash Boats
Tomato Sauerkraut
Hot Buttered Vienna Bread
Hot Plum Kuchen

Toss buttered cracker crumbs with the noodles. Or substitute a noodle ring with sour cream.

Scoop out the zucchini and fill with red cabbage and caraway.

Combine fresh tomato, crisp bacon, and celery seeds with the sauerkraut.

Put cinnamon whipped cream on the plum kuchen. Or have upside-down plum cake with cinnamon whipped cream.

Egyptian

We once catered an important party to publicize some Egyptian art work being brought to Cleveland. On the tables we had gondolas floating down the Nile, pyramids, and palm trees.

MENU NO. 1

Stuffed Grape Leaves
Individual Ground Lamb Loaves
Rice Pilaf
Green Peas with Almonds
Orange and Cucumber Salad
Ruth Just's Roman Dressing*
Sesame Bread
Pyramid Nut Torte Cake

Stuff the grape leaves with a mixture of ground pork, rice, ripe olives, tomato paste, and green pepper. The pork may be omitted if you have Moslem guests.

A sauce flavored with rosemary should accompany the lamb loaves.

The bread is a crusty loaf baked on the hearth.

The cake is made of many layers, part chocolate and part white, with mocha filling and icing. It can be used as a centerpiece and then served with the coffee.

MENU NO. 2

Veal with Fig Sauce
Lamb and Mushroom Shish Kebabs
Cassava Croquettes
Eggplant Casserole
Cairo Salad
Apricot Dressing
Flat Syrian Bread
Individual Date Cakes

Put tomatoes and onions in the eggplant casserole.

Cairo Salad is made of sliced oranges and bananas with chopped romaine.

MENU NO. 3

Roast Leg of Lamb
Chutney
Saffron Rice
Eggplant Casserole
Carrots with Grapes
Tossed Greek Salad
Little Round Whole Wheat Rolls
Spice Roll

For easier carving, have the lamb leg boned by your butcher.

Add a few partially cooked prunes to the chutney.

Have French-fried eggplant instead of the casserole, if you like.

Add Feta cheese (made from goat's milk) and little hot peppers to the salad.

Spice Roll is a thin cake with a fig filling that looks like a jelly roll. Serve with a thin hot Lemon Sauce* or Mandarin Orange Sauce*.

MENU NO. 4

Chicken Kiev
Orange and Onion Brown Rice
Carrots, Celery, Figs, and Ham
*French-fried Cucumbers**
Hearts of Palm Salad
*Ruth Just's Roman Dressing**
Flat Monks Crackers
Old-fashioned Iced Sponge Cake

Cook brown rice in consommé and add grated orange rind and chopped onions.

Combine cooked carrots, diagonally cut braised celery, Kadota figs, and julienne ham and heat through.

Serve the hearts of palm with a few pimiento diamonds on romaine. Slice raw mushrooms into the dressing.

Substitute very flat crusty bread if you can't get monks crackers.

Ice the sponge cake with soft prune whip and garnish with grapes or bananas and toasted almonds.

Greek

The Greek flag is blue and white, reminding tourists of the beautiful blue Mediterranean along the coasts, so blue and white is an ideal color scheme. If they're available, make a centerpiece featuring grapes. If it's a garden party, have a few columns reminiscent of the Parthenon, or replicas of Greek statues. Wreaths of laurel or pachysandra would be nice.

Blue and white mints, candles, and bands of blue ribbon down a white cloth will provide an interesting background for your Grecian delicacies.

MENU NO. 1

Roast Leg of Lamb
Grecian Rice
Green Beans (optional)
Fried Eggplant with Minced Green Pepper
Tossed Greek Salad
Crusty Hearth Bread
Fresh Fruits
Honey Puffs

Cook the rice in consommé with apples, currants, and pine nuts.

Serve the salad on purple cabbage leaves. It is made of tossed greens, Feta (goat's milk) cheese, hot Greek peppers, and shaved Italian purple onions, pitted purple Greek olives and plenty of lemon in the oil dressing (PLATE IV).

French or Vienna bread can be substituted for the hearth bread.

Honey puffs are Profiteroles* drenched in Greek honey.

MENU NO. 2

Roast Suckling Pig
Stuffed Grape Leaves
Lamb Shish Kebabs
Paslicho
Hot Asparagus
Green Salad with Artichokes
Pineapple Athens

Stuff the grape leaves with ground lamb, chopped ripe olives, hot peppers, and tomato paste.

Paslicho is macaroni baked with cheese in a shallow pan or Pyrex dish.

Pineapple Athens is a slice of cored fresh pineapple with a ball of coconut sherbet in the center with Greek honey poured over it.

Scottish

Use bright plaid tablecloths; if your guest of honor is a Scot, try to find his clan plaid. American heather is a good substitute for Scottish heather; the thistle is another and very attractive symbol.

A bagpiper in kilts will add life to the party; and of course it would be fine if you had some Scottish waitresses.

MENU NO. 1

Rolled Sirloin of Beef
Browned Potatoes and Onions
Gooseberry Chutney
Curried Carrot Soufflé
Green Peas
Oatmeal Bread
Stuffed Tomatoes
Butterscotch Meringue Pie

Arrange the browned potatoes and onions around the roast.
Serve whole wheat muffins if you can't find oatmeal bread.
Skin small tomatoes and fill with coleslaw.
Pumpkin chiffon pie can be substituted for butterscotch. Make the pie with either a graham cracker or pastry crust.

MENU NO. 2

Baked Canadian Bacon or Ham
Curried Lamb
Condiments
Fluffy Rice
Diced Squash
Pea Soufflé
Hot Yeast Rolls
Pear Salad
Bowl of Fresh Fruit
Shortbread

Condiments with the curry should include grated orange rind, walnuts, coconut, and grated egg.

Cook the diced squash with onion sautéed in butter.

Add a few whole peas to the soufflé before baking.

To make the salad, dip canned pears in crushed macaroons and fill with cottage cheese and mint jelly. Serve on a bed of lettuce.

Mexican

Mexico is at our doorstep, so accessible that more tourists go there every year. Generally speaking, the native dishes are too spicy for many Americans, so the menus suggested here will be tempered more to the average taste.

Decorations might include sombreros, donkeys, or Mexican pottery vases. Again there's the chance to use plastic anthurium. Red, white, and green, plus a little goldy yellow, appear in the Mexican flag and make vivid decorative colors.

MENU NO. 1

Hot Tamales
Ragout of Lamb with Vegetables
Fluffy Rice
Asparagus Spears
Mexican Vegetable Salad Aspic*
Crusty Flat Hearth Bread
Melon and Ice Cream

Garnish the asparagus with grated lemon rind, bread crumbs, and chopped hard-boiled egg.

Garnish the aspic with avocado wedges.

Serve the melon in the skin, with a scoop of vanilla ice cream.

MENU NO. 2

Filet of Beef Tenderloin
Spanish Rice with Bacon and Green Pepper
Fried Zucchini
Corn Croquettes
Three-bean Salad
Garlic Dressing
Cut-up Fruit
Mexican Wedding Wafers

Fry the zucchini in olive oil with herbs, onions, and strong cheese.

Instead of corn croquettes, you might prefer buttered whole-kernel corn with chopped pimiento.

Add tomato, lettuce, and cucumber to the usual three-bean salad.

Mexican Wedding Wafers are flat nut shortbread cookies dusted with powdered sugar.

Dutch

Holland has a red, white, and blue flag. In the springtime, if you have a tulip garden, you'll want to share it with your friends, in the Dutch style. Holland is also the land of narcissus, hyacinths, and daffodils. If they're available, use these flowers for a centerpiece. A pair of souvenir wooden shoes or a little toy windmill add to the effect, and it's easy to make a silhouette windmill for background on your buffet.

MENU NO. 1—BUFFET

Herring in Sour Cream
Jellied Cold Veal and Pork
Tomatoes Stuffed with Potato Salad
Cauliflower Soufflé
White Asparagus Vinaigrette
Carrot and Celery Salad
Peach Kuchen

Smoked herring may be substituted for the herring in sour cream.

Dice the potatoes very finely for the salad and fill scooped-out tomatoes with it.

Cauliflower omelet may be substituted for the soufflé, if you wish.

The carrot and celery salad is made of finely diced celery and finely diced cooked carrots in a vinegar and cream dressing. New green cabbage may also be added.

Peach upside-down cake may be substituted for the kuchen.

MENU NO. 2

Thin Cauliflower Soup
Filet of Sole
Egg and Shrimp Sauce
Stuffed Veal Breast
Baked Turnips and Potatoes
Fresh Spinach
Edam Cheese
Pumpernickel Bread
Sweet Dutch Chocolate Cake

With the sole serve a cream sauce with chopped hard-boiled egg and shrimp added.

Make a bread and sausage dressing for the veal.

Blend mashed yellow turnips and mashed potatoes, bake on a greased cookie sheet, and sprinkle with chopped green onion.

Drain cooked fresh spinach and mash. Combine with fine cracker crumbs, raw egg, and sautéed onion.

Frost the cake with a milk chocolate icing.

Scandinavian

"Scandinavian" means smorgasbord to most people, gastronomically speaking. The blue and yellow smokestacks of Swedish liners are also readily identifiable to tourists. Norway's flag is red, white and blue, so there's a choice of colors. You may be fortunate enough to have one or two pieces of Royal Copenhagen to use for your centerpiece.

A smorgasbord is great fun to create, and it's beautiful to look at as well. Let your guests come back to the buffet two or three times so they won't miss any of the items.

Here are some ideas for the smorgasbord:

Smoked eel. Some guests may be startled by it, but those who know it understand what a great delicacy it is.

Whole salmon garnished with cucumber rings.

Herring in sour cream.

Smoked tongue. Slice it thinly, with pink cream cheese lacing it to look like an old-fashioned lady's high-topped shoe.

Baked ham, thinly sliced.

Sliced cold turkey or cold roast beef.

Chicken liver pâté. Serve it in a rooster mold, if possible, with deviled eggs as a garnish.

Pickled beets.

Bing Cherry Salad Mold.* Garnish with grapes in little clusters.

Chive cottage cheese in tomato aspic ring. Garnish with stuffed eggs.

Potato salad.

Hot macaroni with Cheddar cheese. Or hot au gratin potatoes, diced finely.

Grapefruit in little glass bowls or halves of grapefruit, with button anchovy or anchovy filet garnish.

Danish caviar in grapefruit halves or Cucumber Boats*.

Six or seven varieties of pickles, including pickled onions.

Celery stuffed with Roquefort cream cheese.

Sauerkraut balls.

Tiny corn or apple fritters with brown syrup.

Limpa bread with anise and orange peel.

Swedish hard tack.

Cardamon buns.

After all these hearty dishes, you probably won't want dessert, but if you do, I suggest a light chiffon cake with fluffy boiled icing, or Spritz cookies.

Israeli

Israel's colors are blue and white. A seven-branched candelabra would make an interesting centerpiece. Also appropriate is the Star of David, blue and white flowers.

MENU NO. 1

Baked Stuffed Whitefish
Dill Watercress Sauce
Pickled Herring in Sour Cream
Smoked Herring
Green Peas with Dill
Golden Farvel
Chicken Breasts
Rich Chicken Gravy with Mushrooms
Radishes   Porcupine Celery*
Cucumber, Orange, and Onion Salad
Poppy Seed and Dill Rolls
Sweet Butter
Cantaloupe Rings with Fresh Fruit

Poppy seed noodle pudding would be an alternate for the farvel.
Sprinkle the chicken breasts with sesame or cashew nuts.
Fill the cantaloupe rings with fresh fruit and top with sherbet.

MENU NO. 2

Green Lentil Soup
Standing Ribs of Beef
Potato Pancakes
French-fried Cucumbers*
Baked Stuffed Tomatoes
Horseradish Mousse*
Crusty Rye Rolls
Orange Charlotte Russe

Lentil soup would be an alternate for the cucumber soup.
Stuff the tomatoes with a mixture of bread, celery, and olives, and bake.

Fill the aspic mold with fresh fruits.

Sesame rolls may be substituted for the rye rolls, if you like.

Neither of the above menus is kosher since we've mixed dairy products and meat in each case. Menu No. 1 could be kosher if you delete the chicken breasts, gravy, and sweet butter.

Part Five

Recipes

HORS D'OEUVRES

Avocado Pinover Sandwiches

1½ avocados
1 cup (10 ounces) cream
   cheese, softened
Grated rind of ½ medium
   orange
Grated rind of lemon
½ teaspoon lemon juice
1 drop green food coloring

10 drops Worcestershire sauce
½ teaspoon salt
30 slices extra thinly sliced
   white bread
Butter Pecan halves
   (optional)
Chopped bacon (optional)

Put avocados through a food grinder, add cream cheese, grated orange, and lemon rind, lemon juice, food coloring, Worcestershire sauce, and salt. Beat until smooth.

Trim crusts off bread so that each slice is 2½ inches square. Butter two opposite corners of each square. Put about 1 teaspoonful of the spread diagonally on the bread, spreading it evenly up and down between the two points. Fold over the opposite points of the bread one on top of the other. The top point can be made to stick by spreading a little more mixture on the tip.

Put small toasted pecan halves on the exposed filling, or you may use crumbled bacon bits.

Makes 30 sandwiches.

Caramelized Bacon

½ pound bacon—cut ⅛-inch thick or thicker, if desired
2 tablespoons wet mustard
½ cup brown sugar

Cut bacon strips in half and lay on cookie sheet. Spread each slice with thin coating of mustard and cover generously with brown sugar. Bake in oven 20 minutes at 350° F. until crisp. Remove from pan while still hot and serve at once. It can be done early in day—then just reheat. Makes approximately 12 to 14 pieces.

Ham Pineapple Cocktail Mousse Mold

1 tablespoon gelatin
¼ cup cold water
1 pint finely chopped ham
2 hard-boiled eggs, diced
1 small onion, chopped
½ green pepper, chopped
2 tablespoons chopped
   parsley
½ teaspoon thyme, pulverized

½ cup grated pineapple
   (canned)
1 cup mayonnaise
1 teaspoon fresh lemon juice
Salt and pepper to taste
3 slices of lean baked ham
   —(for julienne strips)
Paprika
1 top of a fresh pineapple

Soften gelatin in cold water and dissolve over hot water. Add balance of ingredients except paprika, pineapple, and sliced ham, and pour into mold that has been dipped in cold water. An oblong bread pan is quite suitable. Chill.

After mixture is firm, remove and round into the shape of a fresh pineapple. Score diagonally with sharp knife and crisscross with slender julienne thin strips of ham. Generously dust with paprika. Fasten the pineapple top in one end—securing it with a wooden skewer (the type used for city chicken). Arrange on lettuce or ivy leaves. Serve as an appetizer with Melba toast points.

Serves 20 to 30 for appetizer or 8 to 10 for supper.

Mr. Jiggs's Brussels Sprouts

1 quart uniform fresh
  Brussels sprouts
1 pint boiling water
½ teaspoon salt
Lowry salt to taste

6 ounces lean kosher corned
  beef (cooked weight)
1½ tablespoons sour cream
1½ tablespoons mayonnaise

Parboil Brussels sprouts very quickly in boiling salted water. Drain and dry on paper towel. With sharp knife, cut off bottom cores and dig out the centers as deeply as you can. Sprinkle the cavities generously with Lowry salt.

Put corned beef through food grinder and add sour cream and mayonnaise. Stuff centers with corned beef mixture. Serve ice cold.

Yields 28 or 30 sprouts.

California Snow Pea Pods, Stuffed (PLATE I)

6 ounces fresh California snow pea pods (do not use frozen;
  they are too flabby)
1 quart boiling water
2 cups crab meat salad (chop crab meat finely)

Cut off both ends of each pea pod. Then toss them into boiling water for 45 seconds. Drain and slit the *long* side open with a thin, sharp paring knife but not clear to the ends. Open up the pod so it is canoe-shaped and stuff with crab meat salad.

Alternate fillings:
  Shrimp salad
  Deviled tongue spread
  Minced corned beef with sour cream
  Ham salad mixture
  Curried egg salad
  Minced ham
  Roquefort cream cheese
Makes approximately 55 hors d'oeuvres.

Hough's Blintzes

3 whole eggs, beaten slightly   1 cup bread flour
1 pint milk   ⅛ pound butter
½ teaspoon salt

Combine all ingredients together about 1 minute. Fry in a 5-inch frying pan (buttering only to start and then not again), or in a Griswold frying pan with 3-inch indentations.

Fill with Chicken and Mushroom Blintz Filling*, Sour Cream and Cream Cheese Blintz Filling*, or Smoked Sturgeon Filling for Blintzes*. Blintzes may also be filled with creamed cottage cheese and served with blueberry or strawberry sauce.

Makes approximately 24 blintzes 5 inches in diameter; 64 blintzes 3 inches in diameter.

Sour Cream and Cream Cheese Blintz Filling

¼ cup sour cream   6 drops Worcestershire sauce
¼ cup cream cheese   1 drop Tabasco
¼ teaspoon salt   2 teaspoons chopped chives

Combine all ingredients and mix well.
Makes ½ cup filling. Fills 16 miniature blintzes 3 inches in diameter or 2 blintzes 5 inches in diameter.

Chicken and Mushroom Blintz Filling

1 cup diced cooked chicken   ⅛ teaspoon pepper
¼ cup diced mushrooms   ¾ cup cream sauce (white
1 teaspoon sautéed onion   sauce)
¼ teaspoon salt

Combine all ingredients and mix well.
Serve with Watercress Sauce* as a luncheon dish (sauce to be passed separately).
Makes 2 cups filling. Fills 64 blintzes 3 inches in diameter or 8 blintzes 5 inches in diameter.

Smoked Sturgeon Filling for Blintzes

1½ pounds smoked sturgeon
½ cup mayonnaise

Chop sturgeon fairly fine and blend with mayonnaise as a binder. Put 1 teaspoonful fish on each blintz and roll up—not more than ¾-inch thick.
Fills 60 3-inch blintzes.

Stuffed Spinach Blintzes

½ cup frozen chopped spinach (thawed)
1 pint blintz batter
6 medium carrots, cooked

Onion salt
Celery salt
Curry (optional)
Thin cheese rarebit sauce

Blend spinach into the blintz batter. Fry blintzes a little longer than the cocktail size; they should be 5–6 inches.
Cut carrots in julienne strips 5 inches long.
Sprinkle carrots lightly with onion salt and celery salt after cutting. A pinch of curry may be added if desired. Stuff each blintz with 2 or 3 carrot strips—about ¼ of a whole carrot.
Heat at 325° F. for 20 minutes. Serve piping hot with rarebit sauce.
Makes 25 blintzes.

Pecan Croquettes

1 cup coarsely chopped toasted pecans
¼ cup thick cream sauce
½ teaspoon Worcestershire sauce

½ teaspoon sherry
¼ cup flour
1 whole egg, beaten
¼ cup bread crumbs

Mix pecans with cream sauce. Add Worcestershire sauce and sherry. Form into small croquettes the size of a pecan in shell. Roll in flour, then in the egg, and then in the bread crumbs.
Fry in deep fat heated to 375° F. until golden brown. These can

be frozen and reheated in oven at 300° F. for 20 minutes before serving.

Makes 12 to 14 croquettes.

Cheese Soufflé Dreams

10 ounces cream cheese
1 teaspoon baking powder
¼ teaspoon salt
Dash Tabasco
¼ teaspoon Worcestershire
   sauce
1 teaspoon onion juice
   (optional)

2 egg yolks
2 egg whites
36 round bread cups about 2
   inches in diameter, scooped
   out and brushed with melted
   butter
Paprika (optional)
Caraway seeds (optional)

Mix all ingredients except egg whites and bread cups for about 2 minutes, then add beaten egg whites. Fill the bread cups with this mixture—either with pastry bag or drop from a teaspoon. Dust with paprika or sprinkle with caraway seeds.

Bake at 350° F. for 15 to 20 minutes until golden brown, or they can be put under broiler. These can be frozen.

Makes 36.

Strawberry Tree (PLATE V)

Use a single 20-inch styrofoam cone or a pair of cones and cover them with generous sprigs of fresh mint. These are wired on with narrow green wire obtained from your florist.

Use the berries with hulls left on and fasten them into toothpicks that have already been "speared" into the cone. Use the smaller strawberries at the top of the tree, and the larger fruit toward the bottom.

A silver or glass dish of powdered sugar is placed next to the tree so guests may dip berries for extra sweetness.

Relish Tree (PLATE V)

Cover the sides of a 24-inch styrofoam cone with fresh greenery. You can use parsley or waxy green leaves fastened with short, slender wires. On toothpicks use cherry tomatoes, raw cauliflower, celery hearts, carrot sticks, radish roses, slivers of raw zucchini, and marinated artichoke hearts.

A dish of celery salt (blended with Lowry salt) is placed next to the tree to use as a dry dip.

Caviar in a "Daisy" of Cucumber Boats (PLATE I)

An attractive way to serve caviar is to put it in a small, scooped-out grapefruit shell.

The trimmings are arranged in hollowed-out cucumber "boats" placed on ivy leaves, to simulate the petals of a daisy. We suggest using minced onion, grated egg yolk, grated egg white, capers, plain sour cream, chive sour cream, chopped green pepper, and red caviar.

Have a tray of Melba toast rounds or crackers alongside.

Hot Toasted Mushroom Sandwiches

1 pint raw mushrooms, coarsely ground	Butter
	1 tablespoon flour
1 small onion, chopped very finely	1 cup thick cream sauce
	20 thin slices sandwich bread
¼ teaspoon salt	Melted butter
Dash of black pepper	

Sauté the mushrooms, onion, salt, and pepper in butter, until mushrooms are cooked. Add flour to thicken. Lastly, add the cup of thick cream sauce. Let cool.

Remove the bread crusts. Spread the paste on the thin slices of bread to make closed sandwiches. Cut into triangles. Brush tops with melted butter.

Toast these on one side ahead of time; just before serving, toast on the buttered side.

Makes 40 small triangles.

Ivy League Triangles
(Toasted Spinach Sandwiches)

1½ cups (1 package) frozen
  spinach, thawed
¼ cup water
¼ cup sautéed finely chopped
  onion

½ teaspoon salt
Dash white pepper
1 cup thick cream sauce
20 thin slices sandwich bread
Melted butter

Put spinach and water into saucepan and let come to a boil. Drain and squeeze dry. Add onion, salt, pepper, and cream sauce to make a pretty bright green paste.

Spread filling on thin bread to make closed sandwiches. Cut off crusts and brush tops with melted butter. Broil these on one side ahead of time. Just before serving, butter the unbroiled sides and broil until golden brown.

Makes 40 small triangles.

Pencil Cheese Sesame Melba Sticks (PLATE VI)

1 pound loaf cheese bread, sliced lengthwise
½ pound melted butter
1 cup toasted sesame seeds

Trim crusts off bread and cut each long slice lengthwise into approximately 7 strips. Brush generously on each side with melted butter. Dip in sesame seeds. Arrange on cookie sheets. Bake in 325° F. oven about 25 minutes.

Makes approximately 33 pieces.

FIRST COURSES

Avocado in the Snow

4 or 5 ripe ice-cold avocados
2 or 3 quarts shaved ice
1 large lemon
Salt (optional)
1 cup catsup
1 tablespoon butter

¼ cup brown sugar
1 tablespoon Kitchen Bouquet
1 tablespoon Worcestershire
  sauce
¼ teaspoon Tabasco

Cut the cold avocados in half lengthwise and place ½ in center of finger bowls or soup dishes that are ⅔ full of ice snow. Place a fresh lemon wedge alongside the avocado. Sprinkle with salt if desired.

Combine remaining ingredients and bring to a boil.

Just as guests are ready to be seated, fill the cavity of each avocado with the piping-hot sauce.

Makes 1½ cups sauce or 8 to 10 servings.

Caviar California

1 head Bibb lettuce
40 peeled cherry tomatoes
2 avocados cut into cubes
1 lemon
4 slices crisp fried bacon,
  crumbled

1 tablespoon minced green
  onion (or grated white
  onion)
1 cup mustard mayonnaise
2 ounces black Russian caviar
1 tablespoon chopped chives

Chop lettuce and sprinkle in bottom of 8 glass finger bowls. Arrange the cherry tomatoes on the lettuce. Dip avocado cubes in lemon juice and arrange in the bowls. Sprinkle the crisp bacon over avocado.

Stir the minced onion into the mustard mayonnaise and spoon it on top of the bacon. Then put a teaspoon of caviar in the center of each mound. Garnish with 2 pinches of chopped chives. Serve in ice bowls filled with ice snow.

You may omit bacon and use anchovies or crab meat instead of caviar.

Serves 8.

Flaked Fresh Salmon in Aspic

2¾ tablespoons lemon juice
2 teaspoons vinegar
1 quart water
1 tablespoon salt
1 bay leaf
2 peppercorns

1 small fine sliced onion
3 tablespoons gelatin
1 dill weed or 1 scant
   teaspoon dried dill
5½ cups fresh salmon, flaked

Boil all ingredients, except gelatin, dill weed and salmon, with 3 cups water and strain. Add gelatin dissolved in 1 cup of cold water. Add dill. Cool. Arrange individual paper cups or aluminum molds with flaked salmon and cover with gelatin mixture. Or mixture can be put in a 1½ quart fish mold. Serve with green goddess dressing or Dill Watercress Remoulade*.

Serves 6 to 8.

Whitefish à la Rhine

8 4-ounce pieces boned whitefish
1 cup Rhine or Sauternes wine
Salt and pepper to taste

Place whitefish on a sheet pan or drip pan. Season with salt and pepper. Pour the sauterne over and bake in 350° F. oven 20 minutes. Chill. Place on leaf lettuce or romaine and spread with special Lemon Sauce for Rhine Fish*. Finely grated egg yolk sprinkled on top will give color.

Serves 8.

Lemon Sauce for Rhine Fish

1 cup mayonnaise
¼ cup horseradish mayonnaise
¼ cup sour cream
¼ teaspoon salt
1 teaspoon wet mustard

1 tablespoon chopped chives
1 bunch watercress chopped
very finely
1 lemon—grated rind and the
juice also

Mix all ingredients together. Yields one pint.

Stuffed Eggs in Madrilene Aspic

1 short stalk of celery plus
leaves
1½ quarts water
5 tablespoons chicken base
Salt
Pepper

3½ tablespoons gelatin
3 cups tomato juice
½ cup consommé
1 teaspoon chopped parsley
9 *halves* deviled eggs

Boil celery until tender in 1 quart of water with the chicken base. Season with salt and pepper. Strain.

Dissolve gelatin in balance of water (2 cups). Add to hot chicken broth. Then add tomato juice and consommé. Strain all through cloth and add chopped parsley.

Let congeal slightly and fill 9 individual cups ½ full. Then invert deviled egg in cup with aspic. Fill cup. Let set. Allow ½ cup aspic per cup.

Makes 9 individual cups.

For crab aspic fill individual ring molds with aspic in bottom and then fill with flaked or chunks of crab.

Makes 15 to 16 individual ring molds.

Eggs à la Russe

6 large heart-shaped slices
  Melba toast
6 hard-boiled eggs
2 tablespoons chopped green
  onion tops or chives
1½ cups Thousand Island
  dressing

12 cherry tomatoes
6 dill blossoms or 6 sprigs
  parsley
6 radish roses (optional)

Cut the eggs in half lengthwise and put 2 halves (rounded side up) on each piece of Melba toast. Mix the green onion tops or chives with the salad dressing and spoon a generous amount of it over each rounded egg.

Cut the cherry tomatoes into flowers and garnish the eggs with these and the dill blossoms or parsley. If tomatoes are not available, use cutouts of pimiento. Add radish roses if desired.

Serves 6.

Patriotic Fruit Plate

8 large romaine leaves
2 pints fresh strawberries
2 cups frozen grapefruit
  sections or sections from 4
  fresh grapefruit

1 pint fresh blueberries or 1
  pint package frozen
  blueberries
½ cup Poppy Seed* or Paprika
  Dressing*

Arrange the romaine leaves on 8-inch glass plates. Put 5 or 6 strawberries at the left, 6 sections of grapefruit in the center, and 2 scant tablespoons of blueberries on the right. Put the dressing in small paper soufflé cups or ramekins below the grapefruit.

If you have to use frozen blueberries, be sure they are *barely* thawed at the last minute—they look much prettier and will "bleed" less.

Other fruits in season may be substituted: fresh pineapple slices, red raspberries, and dark blue Italian grapes with seeds removed. These require a little more work.

Serves 8.

Cranberry Raspberry Hallon Punch

½ gallon clear cranberry juice
1 cup concentrated lemonade
1 cup Hallon Juice (An extract of real raspberry)

Put ingredients in gallon jar and fill with water.
Place in punch bowl with 1 quart "Frozen Float"* and add
2 quarts soda. Yield is approximately 65 cups punch.

"Frozen Float"

1 6-ounce package frozen red raspberries (strawberries may be used
   instead)
½ cup Hallon concentrate
½ cup lemonade concentrate

Balance of quart container filled with water.
Freeze this solid.

Watercress Soup

2 tablespoons butter
2 tablespoons flour
1½ quarts chicken stock
Salt and pepper to taste

1 teaspoon sautéed onion
¾ cup finely chopped
   watercress
¼ cup cream (optional)

Melt butter, add flour, and let simmer 1 minute. Add the
chicken stock, salt, pepper, and onion and stir until it boils. Add
½ cup chopped watercress, and if you want soup a little richer,
add ¼ cup cream. Just when ready to serve, add the remaining
¼ cup of chopped cress so it looks a brighter green. The more
you bruise and chop the cress the more pungent the flavor.
Serves 8 to 9.

MAIN DISHES

Chicken Mandarin

¼ pound butter
⅔ cup flour
4 cups rich chicken stock
1 tablespoon concentrated
  chicken broth
1 teaspoon salt
¼ teaspoon pepper (to taste)
2 cups cooked white meat of
  chicken cut in bite-size
  pieces

½ cup julienne ham
2 ounces sliced chestnuts
¼ cup peas
½ cup cooked sliced
  mushrooms
4-ounce can mandarin oranges

Melt butter, add flour, and stir until smooth. Add chicken stock, chicken broth, salt, and pepper. Cook, stirring constantly, until thickened. Add chicken, ham, chestnuts, peas, and mushrooms. Heat in top of double boiler, uncovered, until piping hot. Just before serving, sprinkle the mandarin orange sections on the top.

This can be served over fluffy rice, noodles, or chow mein noodles.

Serves 8.

Ham Cornucopias with Saffron Rice (PLATE VI)

Pinch saffron
2 cups cooked rice
1 teaspoon salt

1 teaspoon chopped onion
2 tablespoons cream sauce
12 slices ham

Add saffron to cooked rice and mix. Add salt, onion, and cream sauce to bind the mixture.

Put 1 tablespoon of rice on each slice of ham and roll into the shape of a cornucopia. Serve with Red Eye Country Gravy*.

Serves 6 people (2 to a serving).

Hungarian Gulyás

½ cup chopped onions
3 tablespoons butter
2 pounds beef for stew cut
    into 1-inch pieces
1 tablespoon paprika
2 teaspoons salt

Dash black pepper
1 tablespoon tomato paste
2 cups canned tomatoes
½ green pepper, chopped fine
½ cup water
2 tablespoons flour

Sauté onions in butter. Add beef and brown well. Add seasonings, tomato paste, tomatoes, and green pepper. Let mixture simmer slowly until tender—about 2 hours. Add water and thicken with flour.
Serves 6.

Veal with Fig Sauce

8 4-ounce slices veal
6 tablespoons flour
½ cup butter
3 cups chicken stock
¾ cup sherry
1 cup raw chopped
    mushrooms

¼ cup chopped parsley
1 tablespoon tomato paste
1 tablespoon lemon juice
½ cup sour cream
1 small can Kadota figs

Dip veal in flour and fry in butter until golden brown. Remove veal but save drippings and make a sauce with the chicken stock and remaining flour, then slowly add all remaining ingredients except the figs.
Place the veal in a casserole. Pour gravy over the meat and bake at 350° F. for 1 hour. Just before serving, drain figs and rinse under cold water to wash off syrup. Arrange the figs on top of the casserole; use them whole or quartered, as desired.
Serves 4 to 6.

Arabian Nights Eggplant (PLATE IV)
or
Mediterranean Eggplant

3 pounds tender lamb, cut into 2-inch cubes
½ cup red wine
6 medium-sized eggplants, "short and squat"
Small amount of vegetable oil or butter
¼ medium onion, diced
½ cup cooked brown rice
1 cup fluffy cooked rice
1 cup cooked fresh mushrooms
1 cup frozen hearts of artichoke, briefly cooked
1 cup canned tomatoes
1 teaspoon chopped fresh or dried dill
1 teaspoon chopped fresh mint
¼ teaspoon nutmeg
½ teaspoon curry powder
1 teaspoon salt

Marinate the lamb cubes several hours in the red wine. (You may use julienne beef—similar to Stroganoff beef—in place of lamb.)

Cut off tops of eggplants, and scoop out the contents. Cut off bottoms evenly so eggplants won't rock. Wrap them in Saran Wrap so the inside does not discolor, and set aside.

Sauté lamb briefly in a little vegetable oil or butter, then simmer until tender (about 30 minutes). Meanwhile, fry the extra eggplant, about 1½ cups, and the onion in oil or butter.

Mix all ingredients together except eggplant shells and "lids" and heat in double boiler, or in casserole in oven, for approximately 1 hour at 320° F.

Soak eggplant shells in piping hot water for 15 to 20 minutes. Then fill with the heated mixture and put on eggplant "lids." Serve these on grape leaves or large ivy leaves.

Serves 6.

VEGETABLES

Artichoke Bottoms with Spinach

6 large-size canned artichoke
   bottoms
¼ cup Italian or French
   dressing
½ cup cooked spinach
¼ cup cream sauce

1 teaspoon salt
1 teaspoon grated onion
Pinch sage
3 tablespoons mustard bread
   crumbs

Marinate the artichoke bottoms 3 to 4 hours in the dressing and discard dressing. Place in buttered pan. Mix spinach, cream sauce, salt, onion, and sage and put a heaping tablespoonful on top of each artichoke. Generously sprinkle with the bread crumbs (we add wet mustard to the dry crumbs).

Bake 15 minutes at 300° F.—just until they're piping hot.

Broccoli or pea purée may be substituted for the spinach.

Serves 4 to 5.

Cherry Horseradish Beets
(Good with Roast Beef)

1 cup vinegar
1 cup sugar
1 cup juice from beets
1 teaspoon salt
Dash white pepper

1 teaspoon chopped onion
   (optional)
1 teaspoon grated lemon or
   orange rind
1 tablespoon horseradish
2 cups small cherry-size beets

Blend vinegar, sugar, beet juice, salt, pepper, onion, grated rind, and horseradish and pour over beets. Heat in saucepan or casserole until they are piping hot.

Makes 1 quart.

Serves 8 to 10.

"Hunting Valley" Beets and Apples

½ cup light brown sugar
1 tablespoon flour
1 teaspoon salt
1 tablespoon vinegar
3 tablespoons butter
½ cup beet juice

1 pound fresh cooked beets or
No. 2 can beets, sliced and
drained
2 medium apples, peeled,
cored, and sliced *sideways*

Make sauce of sugar, flour, salt, vinegar, butter, and beet juice. Alternate beets and apples in layers in baking dish.

Pour sauce over to cover and bake at 350° F. for 20 minutes (until the apples are tender).

Turn top layer of beets over before serving so they won't look dried out.

Serves 8 to 10.

Broccoli Croquettes

2 cups broccoli
½ teaspoon salt
1 tablespoon sautéed onion
Dash white pepper
¾ cup thick cream sauce

1 egg
¼ cup cream or milk
½ cup flour
1 cup Rice Krispies or
cornflakes

Let broccoli come to a boil, boil 7 minutes, add salt to water. Drain broccoli. Chop and squeeze all water out. Add onion, pepper, and cream sauce. Roll into balls or croquettes. Beat egg with cream or milk. Roll croquettes in flour, egg mixture, and Rice Krispies or cornflakes.

Fry in deep fat at 375° F. for 3 to 5 minutes.

These can be made ahead of time and reheated in oven or they can be frozen.

Serves 3 or 4.

New Orleans Carrots

3½ cups fresh carrots (cooked but *not* too soft)
¼ cup brown sugar
3 tablespoons melted butter

¼ teaspoon nutmeg
1 teaspoon cinnamon
1 rounded teaspoon salt
Chopped parsley (optional)

Put carrots through a food chopper—grind quite finely. Stir in brown sugar, butter, spices, and salt.

Heat in saucepan or in casserole until they are piping hot. Sprinkle with fresh chopped parsley.

Serves 8 to 10.

French-fried Carrot Balls

3 cups chopped cooked carrots
2 tablespoons chopped parsley
1 tablespoon granulated sugar
1 tablespoon minced onion
Salt and pepper to taste
⅔ cup thick cream sauce

1 cup flour
2 eggs, beaten with 2 tablespoons cream
1 cup bread crumbs or Rice Krispies

Combine carrots with parsley, sugar, onion, salt, pepper, and the cream sauce. Form into 42 balls, roll in flour, then dip in egg mixture, and roll in crumbs or cereal. Fry in deep fat heated to 375° F. until golden brown. Reheat in oven for 20 to 25 minutes before serving. May be served with a mild cheese sauce.

Serves 12 to 14.

Carrot Soufflé

¼ pound butter
6 tablespoons flour
1½ cups milk
6 beaten egg yolks
2 cups cooked chopped carrots

1 teaspoon salt
1 tablespoon chopped parsley
1 teaspoon finely minced onion (optional)
6 beaten egg whites

Melt butter in saucepan. Add flour—stir until well blended over low flame. Add boiling milk, stir until very thick. Add egg yolks, carrots, salt, parsley, and onion, if desired, to the hot mixture. Let cool—then add egg whites, stiffly beaten. Place in buttered casserole and bake in pan of water at 350° F. for 1 hour.

Yields 2 quarts.

Serves 8 to 10.

Braised Celery Virginia

2 cups diagonally cut celery	1 teaspoon salt
1 cup rich chicken stock	1 teaspoon butter
1¼ cups thick cream sauce	½ cup slivered pecans toasted
½ teaspoon grated onion	to a dark brown

Cook celery in chicken stock 45 minutes and drain, leaving about ½ cup liquid. Fold in cream sauce, onion, salt, and butter. Bake at 300° F. for 25 to 30 minutes. Then top generously with pecans.

Serves 8 to 10.

French-fried Cucumber

1 large cucumber	½ cup bread crumbs
1 egg	Rosemary
¼ cup milk	Salt
½ cup flour	

Peel cucumber, cut in half, and then cut each half *lengthwise* into 6 or 7 pieces. Beat the egg with milk. Dip cucumber in flour, next in egg and milk, and then in bread crumbs.

French fry in hot oil (about 375° F.) for approximately 2 minutes, until golden brown and crisp. Place on a paper towel and sprinkle with rosemary and salt. These can be done an hour or so ahead and then reheated.

Serves 3 or 4.

Mushroom Fritters

1 cup flour	1 tablespoon melted butter
1 teaspoon salt	⅓ cup milk
1½ teaspoons baking powder	2 egg yolks, beaten
2 cups raw thinly sliced mushrooms	2 egg whites, beaten
½ teaspoon sautéed, finely chopped onion	

Mix flour, salt, and baking powder with mushrooms. Add onion, butter and milk. Add beaten egg yolks, then fold in beaten egg whites. Drop by heaping tablespoonfuls or from small ice cream scoop into hot fat (375° F.) and fry for 3 to 5 minutes until golden brown.

Serve with Spinach Sauce*, Watercress Sauce*, or with *thin* creamed dried beef.

Makes 12 fritters.

Mushroom Pie

2 cups sautéed mushrooms	½ teaspoon salt
2 tablespoons butter	Dash white pepper
2 tablespoons flour	1 tablespoon sautéed onion
Liquid from mushrooms and enough milk and cream to make 2 cups	1 8-inch unbaked pie shell and dough for top

Drain mushrooms and save liquid. Make a cream sauce of the butter, flour, liquid, and milk or cream. Add salt, pepper, and onion.

Add mushrooms to cream sauce and put into pie shell. Cover with pie dough. Bake at 350° F. for 45 to 50 minutes.

Serves 6.

French-fried Parsnips

4 medium parsnips   ½ cup flour
1 egg, beaten   ½ cup bread crumbs
¼ cup milk   Salt

Wash and cut parsnips *lengthwise* in long strips. Combine the egg with milk, dip parsnips in this liquid, then in flour, and bread crumbs.

French fry in hot oil (375° F.) for approximately 2 minutes, until golden brown and crisp. Place on a paper towel and sprinkle with salt.

These can be done an hour or so ahead and then reheated. Serves 4.

English Pea Timbales

3 tablespoons butter   3 egg yolks, beaten
4 tablespoons flour   1 cup purée of peas (put
½ teaspoon salt   through a sieve)
1 teaspoon curry powder   ¾ cup whole peas
Dash black pepper   3 egg whites, beaten
1 cup boiled milk

Combine all ingredients, adding the whipped egg whites last. Butter 6 or 7 individual Pyrex custard cups and fill ⅔ full. Place cups in drip pan with water and bake at 350° F. for 35 minutes. If you use a ring pan, bake nearly an hour.

Serves 6 or 7.

Hashed in Cream Potatoes

2½ pounds potatoes, peeled   ½ teaspoon white pepper
1 pint whipping cream   1 tablespoon chopped onion
½ teaspoon salt   sautéed in butter

Grind potatoes coarsely in food chopper. Put in colander and wash off all the starch in cold water. Place in towel and squeeze out all water.

Place potatoes in top of double boiler and add cream, salt, pepper, and sautéed onion. Cover the top of double boiler. Simmer for 3 hours, stirring occasionally.

These can be made ahead of time and stored in the refrigerator or in your freezer.

Serves 6 to 7.

Makes approximately 1 quart.

Pear Potatoes

1 egg yolk, beaten	2 tablespoons cream
2 cups firm mashed potato	½ cup fine bread crumbs
¼ cup flour	4 whole cloves
1 large whole egg	

Beat the egg yolk into the firm mashed potato. Then mold ½ cup of potato with your hands into the shape of a pear. Roll each in flour, then dip into beaten egg mixture (cream and whole egg), then into soft bread crumbs. Fry in deep fat 375° F. about 2 or 3 minutes until golden brown. Stick clove in tops of pears to resemble stems. Reheat in oven just before serving at 325° F. for 15 or 20 minutes. Pretty to arrange around roast beef or turkey.

Serves 4.

Creamed Radishes

3 6-ounce packages raw radishes	½ cup liquid from cooked radishes
4 ounces butter	1 teaspoon salt (scant)
2 ounces flour	½ cup buttered bread crumbs
2½ cups milk	

Peel radishes and cook until tender. Drain, saving ½ cup of the liquid.

Make a cream sauce with butter, flour, milk, and liquid. Add salt. Pour over radishes and sprinkle with bread crumbs.

Heat in oven at 300° F. for 20 minutes.

Serves 6 to 8.

Orange Rice Balls

2 cups cooked rice
Grated rind of 1½ oranges
⅔ cup thick cream sauce
Salt and pepper to taste
1 cup flour

3 eggs, beaten with 2
  tablespoons cream
1 cup bread crumbs or
  cornflakes

Combine rice, orange rind, cream sauce, salt, and pepper. Form into 42 balls, roll in flour, then dip in egg mixture, and roll in crumbs or cereal. Fry in deep fat heated to 375° F. until golden brown.

Reheat at 325° F. in oven for 25 minutes. These can be made ahead and frozen.

Serves 12 to 14.

Spinach Croquettes

2 cups spinach (1 pkg.
  frozen)
½ teaspoon salt
Dash white pepper
1 tablespoon sautéed chopped
  onion

¾ cup thick cream sauce
¼ cup cream or milk
1 egg, beaten
½ cup flour
1 cup Rice Krispies or
  cornflakes

Boil spinach in salted water 7 minutes. Drain, chop, and squeeze out all water. Add pepper, onion, and cream sauce. Roll into balls or croquettes. Add cream or milk to egg. Roll croquettes in flour, egg mixture, and Rice Krispies or cornflakes.

Fry in deep fat at 375° F. for 3 to 5 minutes.

These can be made ahead of time and reheated in oven or they can be frozen.

Serves 3 or 4.

Spinach Pie

2 cups cooked, drained,
chopped spinach
½ teaspoon salt
Dash white pepper
1 tablespoon sautéed chopped
onion
¼ teaspoon poultry seasoning

1½ cups cream sauce
1 8-inch baked pie shell
Mustard buttered bread
crumbs
Bacon (optional)
Grated Cheddar cheese
(optional)

Combine spinach, salt, pepper, onion, poultry seasoning, and cream sauce. Pour mixture into baked pie shell and cover with mustard buttered crumbs. Bake at 350° F. for 30 minutes.

Sprinkle with crisp crumbled bacon as soon as you remove from oven; or you can top with grated Cheddar cheese.

Serves 6.

Tomatoes with Fordhook Lima Bean Purée

1½ pints frozen Fordhook
lima beans
1½ teaspoons salt
1 teaspoon baking powder
½ teaspoon white pepper
1 tablespoon sautéed chopped
onion

4 tablespoons cream sauce
2 drops green vegetable
coloring
10 to 12 medium tomatoes,
skinned and scooped out

Cook lima beans until soft, then drain and put through a food mill. Add salt, baking powder, pepper, onion, cream sauce, and vegetable coloring.

Fill each scooped-out tomato with generous tablespoon of the purée. Bake at 350° F. for 15 minutes. Serve at once.

Serves 10 to 12.

Zucchini Squash Casserole (PLATE II)

6 ounces fresh zucchini (not peeled but sliced)
6 ounces yellow summer squash, diced
¼ cup Wesson Oil
4 to 5 water chestnuts, sliced
8 tiny whole ears Sexton's "Baby Corn" from Costa Rica (*not* pickled)
¼ cup butter, melted
2 teaspoons salt
½ teaspoon black pepper

1½ bunches chopped watercress (finely chopped and bruised)
1 teaspoon chopped parsley
1 tablespoon chopped chives (or 1 teaspoon minced onion)
¼ cup toasted croutons
4 slices crisp chopped bacon
1 large giant whole yellow summer squash

Briefly fry the zucchini and summer squash in Wesson Oil.

Into casserole put squash, chestnuts, and corn (each ear broken in half if long) with melted butter, seasonings, and chopped greens.

Bake at 300° F. for 30 minutes. Remove from oven, toss with croutons, and crisp chopped bacon. Serve in a yellow summer squash shell scooped out to resemble a vegetable dish. Line the shell with foil, pour in boiling water to heat it, then pour out the water and put in the vegetables. Garnish squash with curly parsley on your serving tray.

If no summer squash is available, use twice the amount of zucchini.

Serves 8.

This vegetable can be served in a scalloped pumpkin shell, a large scooped-out honeydew melon, or in a regular vegetable dish.

CASSEROLE AND CHAFING DISHES

Artichoke Rarebit

¼ pound butter
¾ cup flour
2 cups cream
3 cups milk
½ pound very sharp cheese
1 teaspoon salt
Dash black pepper
2 to 3 ounces dried beef,
   chopped

1 cup cooked mushrooms
⅛ cup sliced water chestnuts
½ pound frozen artichoke
   hearts
Dry Melba toast
½ cup grated Parmesan cheese
   (optional)

Make a white sauce with the butter, flour, cream, and milk. Add sharp cheese and stir until melted. Put mixture in top of a double boiler to heat and then add salt, pepper, dried beef, mushrooms, chestnuts, and artichoke hearts. Heat thoroughly and serve in chafing dish with dry Melba toast. If you have no double boiler, put the rarebit in a casserole, top with buttered bread crumbs, and heat in oven at 300° F. for 30 minutes.

Serve the Parmesan cheese in a separate bowl. Julienne ham may be substituted for dried beef.

Yields 2 quarts.
Serves 10.

Lobster Capon Madeira

¼ pound butter
1 scant cup flour
3 quarts chicken stock (strong
   broth)
¼ teaspoon thyme

1 tablespoon tomato paste
½ cup Madeira wine
2 cups cut-up cooked lobster
4 cups cut-up stewed breast
   of capon (or chicken)

Make a sauce from the butter, flour, and chicken stock. Add thyme, tomato paste, and wine. Bring to a boil and then add lobster and capon. Do not overcook, as lobster toughens—but be sure it's piping hot. Serves 10 to 12.

Beef Artichoke Burgundy

2 pounds julienne beef cut into strips ½ inch by 2½ inches
1 cup Burgundy wine
3 tablespoons chopped onion
3 tablespoons butter

2 teaspoons salt
Dash black pepper
½ cup sliced raw mushrooms
1 tablespoon flour
1 12-ounce package pre-cooked artichoke hearts

Marinate the beef in wine for about 2 to 3 hours. Sauté onion in butter. Add meat and let brown. Add salt and black pepper. Simmer until beef is cooked through, adding water as needed.

Add mushrooms, thicken with the flour. Add artichoke hearts. Place in casserole and keep hot in oven until needed.

Serves 6 to 8.

Glazed Ham Balls

2 slices bread, crumbled
½ cup water or milk
3 cups ground ham
1 tablespoon French's mustard

1 teaspoon chopped onion
2 eggs, beaten
¼ cup brown sugar

Soak crumbled bread in water or milk. Add the ground ham, mustard, onion, and eggs. Form into balls. Sprinkle ¼ cup brown sugar over balls and bake until golden brown at 350° F. for 20 to 30 minutes.

Makes 25 ham balls.

Lasagne Ercole

1 12-ounce package green spinach noodles
2½ teaspoons salt
1½ pounds ground beef
½ cup chopped onions
¼ cup butter
1 No. 2 can whole tomatoes

½ cup tomato paste
½ teaspoon oregano
¼ teaspoon basil
2 small cloves garlic
1½ cups cream sauce
2 tablespoons Parmesan cheese

Cook noodles with 1 teaspoon salt for 10 minutes. Sauté ground beef and onions in butter. Add tomatoes, tomato paste, oregano, basil, and garlic and 1½ *scant* teaspoons of salt.

In casserole, alternate layers of cooked noodles with meat sauce. Top with cream sauce and Parmesan cheese.

Bake at 300° F. for 30 minutes.

Serves 6.

Yields 2 quarts.

SALADS AND SALAD DRESSINGS

Bing Cherry Salad Mold

1½ cups juice from cherries
1 No. 2 can Bing cherries

1 3-ounce package cherry gelatin
¼ cup port wine

Heat juice from the can of cherries. Dissolve gelatin in cherry juice, then add wine. Let set partially and add the cherries.

You may add a few cream cheese balls if you wish. Cut in 2-inch squares.

Serves 24.

Christmas Salad

1½ cups hot tomato juice, seasoned to taste
1 3-ounce package strawberry gelatin
1½ cups hot water
1 3-ounce package lemon gelatin

1 3-ounce package cream cheese
1 cup cottage cheese
½ cup chopped celery
1 tablespoon diced pimiento
⅛ cup chopped walnuts or toasted pecans

Pour the hot seasoned tomato juice over the strawberry gelatin and let congeal in the bottom of a mold. This is the first layer of a 2-tone Christmas salad.

Pour hot water over the lemon gelatin and let set partially.

Put the cream cheese and the cottage cheese either through a food mill or a coarse strainer. Add celery, pimiento, and nuts.

When the lemon gelatin has begun to congeal, add to the cheese. Pour into mold on top of congealed tomato-strawberry gelatin.

When you unmold salad, it will be red on top and white on the bottom.

Serves 8 to 10.

Coca-Cola Salad

1 3-ounce package lime gelatin	3 cups ice-cold Coca-Cola
2 3-ounce packages lemon gelatin	1 pint fresh strawberries
	1 pint grapefruit sections
1 cup warm Coca-Cola	1½ cups honeydew melon balls
1 tablespoon Knox gelatin	Whipped cream dressing

Dissolve lime and lemon gelatins in the warm Coca-Cola and then add the Knox gelatin. When mixture cools, add the ice-cold Coca-Cola and stir very gently to blend thoroughly—don't agitate.

Line 12 to 14 individual molds with the hulled strawberries, grapefruit, and melon balls. Pour the gelatin mixture over the fruit and chill.

Serve with your favorite whipped cream dressing.

Alternate fruits: pitted Bing cherries and small canned pineapple chunks instead of melon or strawberries.

Makes 12 to 14 individual salad molds.

Kumquat Orange Molded Salad

3 3-ounce packages orange gelatin	½ cup Sauternes
Juice from fruit and enough water to make 5½ cups liquid	1½ 6-ounce jars preserved kumquats, seeded and sliced
	2 cups mandarin oranges

Dissolve gelatin in 2 cups of the liquid over boiling water. Add remaining liquid and the wine. When partially set, add the kumquats and oranges. Pour into 2-quart mold. Chill until set.

Serves 12.

Green and White Fruit Salad

2 pints creamed cottage
  cheese
2 cups honeydew melon balls
2 fresh pineapples
2 bunches watercress
1 pound leaf lettuce
3 apples, peeled, sliced, and
  dipped in lemon juice
1 can Bartlett pears, drained
  (or 6 fresh pears)

1½ cups Queen Anne cherries,
  drained and pitted
1½ cups seedless grapes with
  stems removed
8 sprigs fresh mint
⅛ cup powdered sugar
Paprika Dressing*

Cottage cheese can be put in center of large round tray in the scooped-out honeydew melon "boat." Save the 4 halves of fresh pineapple shells and arrange some of the fruit in these—a chance to make an artistic creation that will bring "oohs" and "ahs!"

Tuck sprigs of watercress around the melon boat of cottage cheese and around the outside edge use the tufts of dampened fresh mint that have been dipped in powdered sugar. Alternate the green and white fruits to get greater contrast. Serve dressing in separate bowl.

Serves 8 to 10.

Rhubarb Strawberry Mold

1 pound pink rhubarb—cut in
  ½-inch pieces
1 scant cup granulated sugar
½ cup cold water

2 3-ounce packages lemon
  gelatin
1 10-ounce package frozen
  sliced strawberries

Place rhubarb, sugar, and water in saucepan. Bring to boil and let simmer 3 to 5 minutes. While hot add 2 3-ounce packages of lemon gelatin and let cool. When starting to jell, fold in 10-ounce package of thawed sliced strawberries. Place in mold.

If served as dessert—unmold and garnish with whipped cream and giant whole strawberries. If served as a salad—use Paprika Dressing*.

Serves 8 to 10.

Green and White Vegetable Salad

1 pound slender zucchini,
  thinly sliced
2 No. 2 cans braised celery
  hearts
2 No. 2 cans white asparagus
1 medium can hearts of palm
1 pint vinaigrette dressing
1 pound romaine
1 large head cauliflower,
  broken in cauliflowerets and
  partly cooked

1 bunch white radishes
  (optional)
5 bunches watercress
1 pint raw white *fresh*
  button mushrooms
1 pint Ruth Just's Roman
  Dressing*
½ pound Feta (goat's milk)
  cheese

Marinate zucchini, celery, asparagus, and hearts of palm in the vinaigrette dressing for several hours. Arrange the romaine on a large round tray. In sections (like spokes in a wheel) pile the cauliflower, asparagus, and celery (also the thinly sliced radishes if you use them), and the sliced zucchini. Make a "wreath" of watercress around the edge, and inside sprinkle the sliced raw mushrooms.

The hearts of palm should be sliced lengthwise and arranged in between sections of vegetables. Generously sprinkle all with Ruth Just's Roman Dressing* and then shower the top with finely crumbled Feta cheese.

Serves 12.

Mexican Vegetable Salad Aspic

1 3-ounce package lemon
  gelatin
2 cups boiling water
½ teaspoon salt
1 tablespoon cider vinegar
1 cup partially cooked
  cauliflower, diced

1 teaspoon chopped red
  sweet pepper or pimiento
1 teaspoon chopped green
  pepper
¼ cup diced celery (optional)

Dissolve gelatin in water and add salt and vinegar. Let this congeal slightly and add the vegetables. Pour into 5 or 6 individual fancy salad molds. Serves 5 or 6.

Swiss Cheese Salad

1 head iceberg lettuce
1 head Boston lettuce
1 head Bibb lettuce
1 head escarole
1 bunch watercress
½ pound Swiss cheese sliced
  in julienne pieces
1 cup mayonnaise
1 cup sour cream

2 tablespoons prepared
  mustard
2 tablespoons fresh
  horseradish
½ teaspoon salt
Coarse black pepper
6 hard-boiled eggs, peeled and
  chopped

Wash greens and tear all but the watercress. Reserve a few sprigs of watercress for garnish. Add Swiss cheese to the greens and then add mayonnaise, sour cream, mustard, and horseradish. Sprinkle with salt and pepper and toss well. Garnish the top of the salad with coarsely chopped egg and the reserved sprigs of watercress.
Serves 8.

Dill Watercress Remoulade Dressing

1 pint mayonnaise
¼ cup horseradish mayonnaise
  (Richelieu brand)
¼ cup (1 bunch) chopped
  watercress

¼ cup chopped parsley
1 dash black pepper
1 dash Tabasco
1 teaspoon dill weed

These ingredients are all blended together and thoroughly chilled. Excellent with fresh salmon or other fish or poured over a head of pre-cooked cauliflower and served cold as a salad.
Makes 2½ cups.
Serves 10 or 12.

Paprika Dressing

1½ cups sugar
2 teaspoons salt
2 teaspoons dry mustard
1 teaspoon dry tarragon
½ teaspoon celery seeds

1 teaspoon lemon juice
3 tablespoons paprika
¾ cup vinegar
2 cups salad oil

Mix all ingredients in electric blender for about 3 minutes until thick. This dressing clings well to salad greens. We often use this blended 1 part to 2 parts Ruth Just's Roman Dressing*.
Makes 2 cups.

Rose Toth Dressing

1 cup tarragon vinegar
2 cups salad oil
½ cup sugar
2 teaspoons salt

¼ teaspoon dry mustard
½ onion, grated (plus juice)
1 clove garlic

Combine all ingredients. Let garlic clove sit in jar with mixed ingredients for 24 hours, then discard.
Makes approximately 3 cups.

Poppy Seed Dressing

¾ cup sugar
1 teaspoon dry mustard
1 teaspoon salt
¼ teaspoon celery salt

¼ teaspoon paprika
⅓ cup vinegar
1½ tablespoons poppy seeds
1 cup salad oil

Place all ingredients in electric mixer and beat until thick. Store in 1 pint glass jar. Refrigerate.
Serves 16 to 18, especially as a dressing for fruit salad.

Ruth Just's Roman Dressing

2 cups salad oil
¾ cup cider vinegar
1 teaspoon salt
1 tablespoon sugar

1 clove garlic, crushed
¼ teaspoon dry mustard
1 tablespoon onion juice

Place all ingredients in a jar and shake together.
Makes approximately 3 cups.

RELISHES AND GARNISHES

Artichoke Relish Mold

4 whole pickled artichoke
  hearts
Juice from the relish plus
  water to make 2 cups
1 3-ounce package lemon
  gelatin
1 tablespoon vinegar

¼ teaspoon salt
Dash Tabasco
¾ cup Artichoke Mustard
  Relish*
20 thin slices of California
  navel oranges

Into the bottom of 20 tiny crinkled tart pans put ⅕ of a pickled artichoke heart.

Heat juice from the artichoke relish and water. Dissolve the lemon gelatin in this mixture. Add vinegar, seasonings, and relish. Pour into the molds over the sliced artichoke.

Chill. When ready to serve, unmold and place on thin slices of California oranges. Use as a garnish around a beef roast or filet of beef tenderloin.

Serves 20.

Horseradish Mousse

1 6-ounce package lemon gelatin	2 tablespoons vinegar
1 cup boiling water	1½ cups horseradish, drained
½ teaspoon salt	¼ teaspoon Tabasco
	2 cups whipping cream

Dissolve gelatin in boiling water. Add salt and vinegar. Congeal slightly, then whip. Add horseradish and Tabasco, then fold in whipping cream. Pour into 1½-quart mold. Excellent with roast beef.

Serves 12 to 16.

French-fried Parsley

2 bunches curly parsley	½ cup flour
½ cup skim milk or water	Salt

Wash the parsley and remove the long stem part. Sprinkle with milk (or water), then dust with flour. I've seen cooks put the parsley in a brown paper bag and shake. The parsley should not be too wet—but damp enough so flour clings.

Fry in oil at 425° F. for about 1 minute, but not too long, as you should keep parsley green. Place on paper towels and lightly sprinkle with salt.

Use as an edible garnish. Excellent with frogs' legs or any kind of fish.

Serves 8.

Cranberry Orange Relish

4 cups fresh cranberries	1 lemon
2 cups sugar	1 apple
2 oranges	1 cup celery

Grind cranberries and add the sugar. Cut and core the oranges, lemon, and apple. DO NOT peel. Grind the oranges, lemon, and celery in a food chopper (medium grind). Chop apple coarsely. Mix all ingredients together and chill for at least 2 hours.

Yield is 1½ quarts.

Serve with any kind of poultry.

SAUCES

Red Eye Country Gravy
(Revised Version of a Southern Delicacy)

¼ pound salt pork or ham
1 pint tomato juice
½ teaspoon instant coffee
¼ cup vinegar
¼ cup brown sugar

¼ teaspoon dry mustard
½ teaspoon Kitchen Bouquet
3 tablespoons bacon fat
1 tablespoon cornstarch
2 tablespoons melted butter

Fry the finely diced salt pork in a skillet. (If you use ham, fry in 1 tablespoon butter.) Brown thoroughly and then remove the pieces of meat and discard. While pan is still hot, pour in the tomato juice. Stir in remaining ingredients gradually, the melted butter last of all. Serve warm.

Makes 2 cups.

Grape Sauce

1 3-ounce jar currant jelly
1 cup port wine
2 tablespoons vinegar

¾ tablespoon cornstarch
1 cup seedless grapes or Tokay
grapes, seeded

Combine jelly, wine, and vinegar and let come to a boil. Thicken with cornstarch. Add the grapes. Serve warm.

Makes approximately 2½ cups sauce.

Serves 12.

Apricot Glacé Sauce

1 No. 2 can peeled apricots
and juice
2 tablespoons lemon juice

1 teaspoon grated lemon rind
1 tablespoon butter
1 tablespoon cornstarch

Put juice from apricots in saucepan, and add lemon juice, lemon rind, and butter. Bring to a boil and thicken slightly with cornstarch.

Cut apricots in ½-inch pieces and add to the sauce. Serve hot or cold.

Makes 2½ cups.

Serves 10.

Watercress Sauce

2 tablespoons butter
2 tablespoons flour
Salt and pepper to taste
1 teaspoon sautéed chopped
onion

1 quart chicken stock
½ cup chopped watercress
¼ cup cream (optional)

Melt butter, add flour, and let simmer 1 minute. Add salt and pepper. Add onion and chicken stock and stir until mixture boils. Add watercress and, if you want sauce a little richer, add cream.

Serves 4 to 6.

Spinach Sauce

Substitute ½ cup spinach for the ½ cup watercress in recipe for Watercress Sauce*.

Currant Wine Sauce

1 cup currant jelly
¼ cup port wine
½ cup finely ground fresh whole orange

Combine all ingredients and heat over low flame. Don't overheat or sauce gets too thin. If you wish this sauce to be thicker, slowly add 1 tablespoon cornstarch blended with small amount of water to the jelly.

Excellent to serve with chicken breasts or Rock Cornish game hens.

Makes 1¾ cups.

Serves 8 to 10.

Mr. Arthur's Butterscotch Sauce

¼ pound butter
2 cups light brown sugar
1 cup whipping cream

Heat butter and brown sugar to a real bubbling point. Slowly add the heavy cream, stirring constantly.

Makes 2½ cups sauce, enough to top 20 to 24 ice cream desserts.

Lemon Sauce

2 tablespoons lemon juice
½ cup sugar
1 tablespoon cornstarch
1 cup cold water
½ teaspoon grated lemon rind
⅛ teaspoon salt
1 drop yellow food coloring
2 tablespoons butter

Combine all ingredients and stir over low flame until thickened.
Makes 1¼ cups.
Serves 7 to 8.

Mandarin Orange Sauce

½ teaspoon grated orange rind
1 cup orange juice
2 tablespoons butter
½ cup sugar
1 tablespoon lemon juice
1 tablespoon cornstarch
⅛ teaspoon salt
1 cup mandarin orange sections

Combine all ingredients except orange sections and stir over low flame until thickened. Add orange sections and let simmer 1 minute.
Makes 2 cups.
Serves 12.

Tart Red Raspberry Sauce

2 16-ounce packages frozen
   red raspberries
½ cup sugar

1 cup water
1 level tablespoon cornstarch

Stir raspberries, sugar, and water over medium heat until they come to a boil. Then strain through cheesecloth. Again let mixture come to a boil and thicken with the cornstarch. Increase cornstarch by 1 teaspoon if you want sauce thicker.
Makes 2 cups.
Serves about 10.

DESSERTS

Coffee Baked Alaska

6 angel food Mary Ann
   shells or 6 rounds sponge
   cake or 1 7-inch sponge
   layer
6 scoops coffee ice cream
6 scoops vanilla or chocolate
   ice cream

6 egg whites
1½ cups granulated sugar
4 teaspoons instant coffee
Powdered sugar

Place cake on cardboard. Fill each cake shell with a scoop of coffee and a scoop of vanilla or chocolate ice cream. Place in freezer 1 hour.

Beat egg whites until stiff. Gradually add sugar and coffee. Beat until stiff peaks form.

Spread meringue generously over ice cream and cake shells. Sift a little powdered sugar over the top of meringue.

Bake at 500° F. for 3 to 4 minutes until brown. These can be made a day or two ahead of your party and kept in freezer (even after browning). I recommend putting under broiler or in hot oven

just before serving so meringue has that nice, warm smell! Serve Mr. Arthur's Butterscotch Sauce* with this dessert.
Serves 6.

Caramelized Cornflake Ring

1½ cups brown sugar	¼ cup butter
2 tablespoons corn syrup	6 cups cornflakes
½ cup milk	

Combine brown sugar, corn syrup, milk, and butter and boil 20 minutes (or to the soft ball stage).

Grease a 1-quart ring mold—the larger the hole, the better. Pour boiled syrup over whole cornflakes. Gently press into the greased mold. Set aside at room temperature for 10 to 12 hours, then unmold. Fill center of ring with balls of sherbet and ice cream or with balls of coffee ice cream. If the latter, serve with crème de cacao.

This cornflake ring should be eaten the day it is made. Double the recipe for filling a 12-inch ring mold to serve 16.
Serves 8.

Frozen Grapes

50 Tokay grapes, each sliced down far enough to remove seeds	⅛ teaspoon cinnamon
	½ cup heavy cream
	1 pint French vanilla ice
1 tablespoon Knox gelatin	cream
2½ cups Catawba juice	1 teaspoon brandy (optional)

Remove seeds from grapes and put in freezer for 24 hours.

Dissolve gelatin in about ½ cup warmed Catawba juice, then stir in the balance of cold Catawba. Add the cinnamon.

Pour into individual ring molds and chill. To be at its best, Catawba jelly should be barely firm—enough to hold its shape, but not rubbery.

Beat cream until stiff and fold into semi-soft ice cream. Add brandy if desired. When ready to serve, spoon this mixture into the center of each ring of jelly, then arrange 6 grapes around the outside and perhaps 1 in the middle. Serve at once while the grapes are still "frosty."

If available, medium-sized grape leaves or ivy leaves (washed and dried) can be used to garnish each dessert plate.

Serves 7.

Orange Blossom Trees (PLATE V)

2 driftwood trees—sand-blasted manzanita or branches from a tree in your yard, 16 to 18 inches tall

2 papier-mâché pots or small jardinieres

1 package of plaster of Paris from hardware store

24 waxed orange blossoms

1 bunch Springerii fern or any kind of waxy green foliage

20 to 22 ¼-inch wide satin ribbons each 15 inches long

20 to 22 3-ounce balls lemon or orange sherbet

6 to 7 pieces dry ice

Several days before the party, "plant" trees in your flower pots or containers—place a little loose gravel around them and then fill with plaster of Paris. Let these harden. Entwine the waxed or paper orange blossoms at the tips of the branches and then wire some green foliage onto the branches. Sometimes we use the feathery Springerii fern, but often we use larger shiny leaves.

Tie 2 or 3 big loose knots in the center of the ribbons and insert deeply into the balls of sherbet. Then let them harden. It is better to place these right on dry ice (with wax paper or foil underneath balls) so the sherbet is really hard.

Just before serving, tie the orange or lemon "fruit" on the branches as you would Christmas tree ornaments. Hand the guest a pair of scissors and let each person snip off his own fruit. Quite dramatic and lots of fun. Be sure to have several extra desserts for each tree just in case one rolls onto the floor—and so no one has to be the "old maid."

May be served with macaroons or individual iced cakes or a Mandarin Orange Sauce*, Lemon Sauce*, or Tart Red Raspberry Sauce* may be passed.

Serves 16 to 18.

Hough's Swedish Crêpes Suzette

3 whole eggs, beaten slightly
1 pint milk
½ teaspoon salt

4 tablespoons sugar
1 cup bread flour
⅛ pound melted butter

Combine all ingredients and beat together about 1 minute. Put a little butter in the frying pan for the first pancake and then no more. Fry over a medium flame.

Serve with Mandarin Orange Sauce* with or without a little brandy, or with your favorite fruit sauce.

Makes 25 5-inch crêpes or 60 3-inch crêpes.

French Twirls

8 ounces finely ground
  toasted almonds
8 ounces granulated sugar
2 ounces cake flour
4 egg whites

4 ounces butter, melted
Mocha buttercream filling
  (optional)
Semi-sweet chocolate or
  chocolate sprinkles

The nuts are best when heated. Blend almonds, sugar, and flour. Add unbeaten egg whites, blend until smooth, then fold in the butter. This mixture is very soft. Put into pastry bag and squeeze out cookies on heavily greased cookie sheets about 4 inches apart.

Bake at 350° F. until edges are brown. Remove from pan immediately with a pancake turner. While still warm, press the cookies between the cups of an inverted cupcake tin. This will cause the edges to curl.

Serve plain or fill with a mocha buttercream filling. Dust the tops with shaved semi-sweet chocolate or chocolate sprinkles. Cocoa or cinnamon whipped cream may be used instead of buttercream but in this case the twirls must be served at once or they will soften.

Makes 84.

Swedish Gaufrettes

1¾ cups bread flour
½ cup sugar
1 cup water

½ cup heavy cream
¾ cup melted butter

Blend flour and sugar in an electric mixer. Gradually add water, cream, and, lastly, butter.

Heat a Swedish Rohn Iron, obtainable at Swedish Style Gift Shop, 5309 N. Clark Street, Chicago, Illinois 60640.

Pour 1 teaspoon of batter on the hot *dry* iron. Bake on one side over a low flame about 1 minute. (If you have a control burner, keep at 275° F.) Turn and bake on the other side until brown—about 25 to 30 seconds.

You can roll these while they're warm to look like diplomas or cornucopias. Cornucopias can be filled with your favorite whipped cream fillings: mocha-rum, sherry, strawberry, or red raspberry. Sometimes we garnish the end with shaved curls of chocolate or with a small, fresh strawberry, red raspberry, or candied cherry.

The flat gaufrettes are often used two at a time for ice cream desserts. It's fun to experiment! Place 1 on a dessert plate, add a thin slice of coffee ice cream, another gaufrette, and then vanilla or chocolate ice cream. Crème de cacao or chocolate sauce may be passed.

Makes 60 to 64 gaufrettes.

Grapefruit Cake

1½ cups cake flour
¾ cup sugar
1½ teaspoons baking powder
½ teaspoon salt
¼ cup vegetable oil
3 egg yolks

¼ cup water
3 tablespoons grapefruit juice
½ teaspoon grated lemon rind
3 egg whites
¼ teaspoon cream of tartar

Sift together flour, sugar, baking powder, and salt. Add oil, egg yolks, water, grapefruit juice, and lemon rind. Beat until smooth. Beat egg whites with cream of tartar until they form and hold very stiff peaks. Pour egg yolk mixture over egg whites and fold gently until blended. Bake in 2 ungreased 9-inch layer pans at 350° F. for 35 minutes.

Serves 8 to 10.

Frosting

6 ounces cream cheese
1 teaspoon grated lemon rind
2 teaspoons instant lemon crystals
1½ cups confectioners' sugar
2 tablespoons crushed grapefruit

A little yellow food coloring (optional)
2 cups frozen grapefruit sections, thawed, or sections from 4 fresh grapefruit
2 cups fresh strawberries or cherries

Combine cheese, lemon rind and crystals, sugar, crushed grapefruit, and food coloring and beat until fluffy. Chill thoroughly. Frost sides and top of cake and garnish with grapefruit sections, fresh strawberries or cherries. The cake should be lavishly garnished both on top and on the sides.

Makes 2 9-inch layers.

Angel Food Crème Brûlée

1 quart light cream
2 tablespoons sugar
1 teaspoon vanilla
8 egg yolks, beaten

8 individual angel food Mary Ann cake shells or 1 10-inch square angel food cake about 1 inch thick
1½ cups light brown sugar

Heat the cream to scalding point. Remove from heat and add sugar and vanilla. Pour the mixture over the beaten egg yolks, beating constantly at low speed.

Butter a shallow Pyrex baking dish, pour in custard, and bake at 300° F. for 1 hour. Chill thoroughly. Then spoon custard into cake shells or spread thickly on the sheet cake. *Sift* the light brown sugar over top at least ⅛-inch thick or *more*. Put under the broiler to caramelize.

This can be served plain or with Tart Red Raspberry Sauce*.

Serves 8.

Chocolate Bourbon Mousse

1 cup semi-sweet chocolate bits (or ¾ cup semi-sweet chocolate bits and ¼ cup unsweetened chocolate)	4 egg yolks
	2 tablespoons bourbon (or brandy)
	4 egg whites
4½ tablespoons boiling water	Whipped cream

Melt chocolate over boiling water. Remove from fire and add the 4½ tablespoons boiling water, slightly beaten egg yolks, and bourbon. Blend until smooth.

Beat egg whites until stiff. Carefully fold chocolate mixture into egg whites. Spoon into sherbet or champagne glasses and chill at least 1 hour. Top with whipped cream.

Serves 6.

Maple Syrup Velvet Mousse

1 tablespoon Knox gelatin	¼ teaspoon maple flavoring concentrate or 1 teaspoon maple extract
2 tablespoons water	
4 whole eggs	
1 cup plus 2 tablespoons maple syrup	2 cups heavy cream

Dissolve gelatin in the water. Slightly beat the whole eggs. Heat the syrup and slowly add to the eggs, blending thoroughly. Cook in double boiler, stirring slowly, over simmering water until slightly thickened. Remove from fire, add the gelatin and maple flavoring or extract. Cool.

Whip the cream and fold in the maple syrup mixture.

Pour into 1½-quart ring mold and let set until firm. Unmold and garnish the ring with halves of walnuts or serve plain. Pass extra maple syrup as a sauce.

Serves 10.

Sherry Almond Mousse

2 teaspoons gelatin
½ cup sherry wine
1 pint heavy cream

½ cup confectioners' sugar
1 cup coarse macaroon crumbs

Dissolve gelatin in wine over hot water; cool to tepid. Whip cream and add the powdered sugar and crumbs. Fold in gelatin mixture. Pour into individual molds.

This dessert is enhanced by topping with a thin, soft custard sauce. Use 2 or 3 cups for 10 people.

Serves 10.

Peppermint Stick Mousse

2 teaspoons gelatin
½ cup water
1 pint whipping cream

½ cup confectioners' sugar
1 cup *finely* chopped
   peppermint stick candy

Dissolve gelatin in the water in a saucepan over hot water. Cool to tepid.

Whip cream to a soft consistency and add sugar. Add the peppermint candy, then fold in the gelatin mixture. Pour into 1½-quart mold or individual molds.

A thick, dark chocolate fudge sauce (either warm or cold) should be passed.

Serves 9 to 10.

Index

NOTE TO USERS OF THIS INDEX: we have tried to include all definitions of foods and prepared dishes, as well as preparation methods and recipes, wherever they occur throughout the text. Many serving suggestions and garnishes, etc., have had to be omitted; the reader should check specific occasions and menus for this information.